To Charles & Jean,
God bless you!
III John 2,

Steve Gaines

10-16-07

WHEN
GOD
COMES TO
CHURCH

STEVE GAINES

WITH DEAN MERRILL

WHEN
GOD
COMES TO
CHURCH

EXPERIENCING THE FULLNESS
OF HIS PRESENCE

B&H
PUBLISHING GROUP
Nashville, Tennessee

ISBN: 978-0-8054-4398-1

Published by B&H Publishing Group, Nashville, Tennessee

Dewey Decimal Classification: 264
Subject Heading: WORSHIP \ WORSHIP PROGRAMS \ GOD

All Scripture quotations, unless otherwise noted, are reproduced
with permission from the New American Standard Bible (NASB)
(Updated Edition). ©1960, 1962, 1963, 1968, 1971, 1972, 1973, 1975,
1977, 1995 The Lockman Foundation.

Other Scripture versions include: New International Version (NIV),
copyright © 1973, 1978, 1984 by International Bible Society and
The King James Version (KJV).

In various Scripture quotations throughout this book, the authors
have chosen to emphasize certain words or phrases by the use of
italics. These italics do not appear in the original texts.

1 2 3 4 5 6 7 8 9 10   11 10 09 08 07

I dedicate this work to my four precious children,
Grant, Lindsey, Allison, and Bethany.
May each of you live long enough to
experience a genuine spiritual awakening
during which the glory of God once
again fills the house of God.
May God grant it for His glory.
—Psalm 85:6

Your daddy loves you.

Contents

Introduction

"Daddy's home!" How I loved to hear those words when our children were younger. I'd enter the front door exhausted from a full day of work. But the moment I heard the excited voices and felt the hugs and kisses of my little ones, the day's frustrations and hardships dissipated. Their mom was working in the kitchen, and now their dad was home too! Our presence brought order, peace, and comfort to their little worlds.

The presence of a parent gives joy and pleasure to the heart of a child. The same is true for a child of God. When a believer in Jesus Christ draws near to God in worship—individually or corporately—and senses His manifest presence, all is well regardless of circumstances. That's why the psalmist said, "In Your presence is fullness of joy; in Your right hand there are pleasures forever" (Ps. 16:11). Whether it's a house church in China or a cathedral in London, all is as it should be when God is among His people.

This book is about God's presence in the midst of His family. In the Old Testament, the glory of God filled the temple of God. In the New Testament, the Spirit of God filled the children of God. The need of the hour today is for our houses of worship to be filled once again with His presence. We must jettison our performance mentality, understanding that everything we do—every song we sing, every prayer we pray, and every sermon we preach—is primarily for the Lord and His pleasure.

By God's grace and blessing, each of the churches I have served has grown. But I can honestly say that church growth has never been my focus. Instead, I have sought the Lord's presence. When He shows up, the people He wants to be present will be drawn to Him. I'm more concerned about God being present in a worship service than I am about how many people are in the pews. Worship services are primarily for God, not for us.

That's what this book is about—God's presence filling His house. Indeed, we need God back in our schools and governments. But more than that, we need God back in our churches! When He comes, He will bring genuine revival and spiritual awakening, which is our nation's greatest need. When God shows up, man will be eclipsed, and God's power will be revealed. Souls will be saved, and lives will be eternally changed.

That's what I live for. That's what I pray for. That's what I long for. I want to be present and accounted for *When God Comes to Church*.

—Steve Gaines
Memphis, Tennessee
August 2006

PART ONE

What Church
Was Meant to Be

CHAPTER 1

Who's in the House?

It was a warm spring Wednesday night in West Tennessee, with lawns turning green and azalea bushes starting to bloom. Fifty or so of us faithful Southern Baptists were in church for the midweek prayer meeting, while our neighbors were out buying groceries at Piggly Wiggly or home watching *M*A*S*H* or *Sanford and Son* on television. I was the twenty-year-old college intern sitting on the back row; it was part of my job, as youth leader, to show up for these kinds of things. After the meeting ended, I'd be driving back to my campus to hit the books again and get ready for classes the next day.

"Our spring revival starts in just a week and a half," the senior pastor was saying up front. He named the evangelist who would be coming to preach and told some of his credentials. "We sure want people to come to Christ during this series of meetings. In fact, before we start the prayer time, let's make a list of people here on the chalkboard. Who of your relatives and friends and neighbors do you want to mention?"

A middle-aged woman with dark hair near the front raised her hand. "I'm going to invite my neighbor in the next apartment. She's having lots of trouble in her life, I know. She really needs the Lord."

The pastor turned to write *Lorene's neighbor* on the board.

A man in a denim shirt spoke up next. "We could pray for my brother-in-law to come. He's got a drinking problem. I don't know if he'd ever show up or not. I sure wish he would."

Roy's brother-in-law was added to the list.

5

"Who else?" the pastor then asked.

At that moment, an unusual thought crossed my brain. I raised my hand.

"Yes, Steve?" the pastor said. "Who would you like us to pray for?"

With all seriousness I replied, "Let's pray that God will show up at our revival." I was totally sincere; I wasn't trying to be a smart aleck. I meant it with all my heart.

An awkward silence came over the room. Heads swiveled partway toward me, then faced the front again. "Well, yes, we know the Lord will be here," a deacon declared, setting the record straight. Right away I could tell I had committed a major boo-boo. People were no doubt thinking, *What's the matter with him? Why's he trying to be so clever?*

Though I had been a Christian only two years, I had grown up in the church and had heard enough sermons to know that God, of course, is everywhere. Along with most people in the pews that Wednesday night, I even knew the big fifty-cent theological term for this: *omnipresence.* We could quote Jesus' famous words verbatim: "Where two or three have gathered together in My name, I am there in their midst" (Matt. 18:20). There is no place on earth where Almighty God is *not.*

But I also knew I had been in at least some meetings where God's presence was undeniably real. It was obvious, manifest, almost palpable enough to reach out and touch with your hand, or so it seemed. Not that anything weird took place, but you *just knew* you were in close range with the Lord.

Some of these occasions were at Christian student gatherings at the University of Tennessee-Martin, where I had gone my first two years on a football scholarship. I met young adults my age who were excited about Jesus and loved to worship Him as well as tell others about Him. During those days (February 1976, to be exact) a roommate invited me to a revival meeting at a small Baptist church. There a pastor named Bill Coleman guided me to give my whole heart to the Lord. I also went to several concerts of well-known Christian groups at the time, where the Holy Spirit seemed to settle down on the arena. In those special, holy times in His presence, you almost didn't want to move or cough for fear of breaking the moment. The leaders or singers on stage were eclipsed by the presence of one greater than they. It was not exaggerating to say that "God was in the house."

In light of those vivid memories, I yearned to have this happen at our spring revival meeting. I knew that if God truly showed up, sinners would be touched and Christians would be stirred. Unfortunately, the week came and went, the evangelist preached solid messages, we sang "Just as I Am," but not much happened. It turned out to be just another set of meetings.

The next Wednesday night, one of the dear saints was blunt enough to ask out loud, "So why didn't we have a better revival this year?"

I wanted to raise my hand and say, "Because God didn't show up!" But I knew I'd already said too much for a rookie youth intern. I held back. The thought did cross my mind, however, that if I ever served as pastor of a church, I hoped to lead people to hunger for the presence of God more than anything else.

Defining a Great Sunday

Here I am now more than twenty-five years later, a fully credentialed, seminary-trained veteran of pastoral ministry. The various diplomas hang in nice frames on my office wall. I've been appointed to denominational boards and committees. Convention organizers have called me to come speak in plenary sessions . . . and still, in one sense I haven't changed a bit from that springtime night long ago. The cry of my heart is still for God to show up.

I'm simply not impressed with religious rituals and routines where dignitaries in dark suits come out onto the platform; the choir sings a call to worship from Habakkuk 2:20 ("The LORD is in his holy temple: let all the earth keep silence before him" KJV); then we sing three hymns, followed by the Doxology; then come the announcements and the offering, followed by a sermon, an invitation, a benediction; and then we go home. Don't get me wrong; there's nothing wrong with these things. But sometimes I'm not sure whether the Lord was indeed in His holy temple—at least not in a way any of us human beings could notice.

I once heard an old-time preacher speaking about God sending fire from heaven onto Mount Carmel during the prophet Elijah's day (1 Kings 18). He said that the manifest presence of God is "when God shows up, and He shows off!" He comes in not to take sides but to take over. When He arrives in splendor and glory, it is obvious to everyone that *He* is present and *He* is in charge. The human agendas fade away in the overwhelmingly awesome presence of the King of kings.

For years now this has been my primary prayer for every worship service in the churches I have served. The longer I live, the less interested I am in how many people we have in the sanctuary. What is far more important to me is *how much of God we have in the place*. If He comes, we will have a wonderful service, no matter if there's only a handful. I know some preachers who think if a thousand people come to their morning services, or fifteen hundred, or two thousand, they've had a great Sunday. Not necessarily. I say to them, *"You haven't had a great Sunday unless God shows up!"*

I am not suggesting that God's people engage in fleshly emotionalism. God gets blamed for a lot that takes place in today's churches when in reality He had nothing to do with it. The Bible does not support Christians barking like dogs, rolling on the floor, laughing uncontrollably, or jerking and contorting wildly. Nor does it mention angel feathers appearing at the church altar, gold dust appearing on the minister's hands, or images of Mary appearing on the side of a building or out in a field. Human emotionalism is behind those bizarre, extrabiblical happenings. God should not be held responsible.

But when God is in the house, it's not fleshly emotionalism. It's more than a whimsical feeling. It's far beyond some talented soprano nailing a high B-flat at the pinnacle of her solo. It's not just a speaker revving up the audience to get happy and clap. All of these things are fairly easy to manufacture by someone who has secular stage presence.

I'm talking instead about something that is *real*. I'm referring to what I read about in the Old Testament, on the day of dedication at the new temple, when "the priests could not stand to minister because of the cloud, for the glory of the LORD filled the house of God" (2 Chron. 5:14). That's one of the best definitions of revival I can think of: *the glory of God filling the house of God*. The Lord invaded the ceremony and basically took over, so that men and women fell to their knees and faces in reverent worship.

The New Testament tells about a prayer meeting where, as the early disciples poured out their hearts to God, "the place where they had gathered together was shaken, and they were all filled with the Holy Spirit and began to speak the word of God with boldness" (Acts 4:31). Those people didn't have an impressive church building. They weren't on weekly television. They lacked all kinds of things we enjoy today in church life, but they had the manifest presence of God in their meeting.

Some of our churches here in the twenty-first century could use some shaking. It would be a good idea for the Holy Spirit to come shake out the sin, the apathy, the pride, the self-centeredness, the satisfaction with church as usual. We don't need a bigger facility or a larger budget nearly as much as we need the presence and power of a holy God.

Through the years I have seen glimpses of what I'm trying to describe. I remember one morning in Jackson, Tennessee. We had enjoyed a wonderful time of worshipping the Lord through congregational singing. When the choir began its song, I don't know how to explain it except to say that God walked in the room. You could literally sense His presence. People, without any human prompting, began to stand with their eyes closed, worshipping the Lord. Some slipped quietly to the front of the church, knelt at the altar, and prayed. At the end of the service, several lost people gave their hearts to Christ and became believers. It was like a little touch of heaven on earth, and we all left wanting more.

I also experienced these "heavenly invasions" on many occasions during a fourteen-year pastorate in Gardendale, Alabama, from 1991 to 2005. In the mid-1990s, many people in that church began to fast, pray, and seek the Lord's presence in their individual lives. People started getting right with the Lord and with one another. God began to bless our worship services with His presence.

During the last several years we saw the Lord do mighty things for His glory. Our church was on the opposite side of Birmingham's booming growth. Yet we led our state convention (more than thirty-one hundred churches) in the number of people who were saved and baptized for seven out of the last ten years I was there. We were second in that category the other three years. God was present and He was moving. It was nothing manufactured by the preacher, the choir, or anyone else. It was simply the work of God.

The Lord knew He was welcome at any time to do anything He wanted among His people. After all, it is *His* church, isn't it? He graciously enthroned Himself on our praises (Ps. 22:3) and met with His people who were hungry for *Him*.

Again, I want to be clear that I'm not talking about anything unbiblical or weird. What I'm speaking about is the real deal found in Scripture—the manifest presence of God. When *He* shows up, no true believer in Jesus has to ask, "Is this really God?" The Holy Spirit within us confirms the obvious: *Jesus is here.*

The Real Quest

I am convinced that one of the reasons so many people are turned off from the idea of church these days is that *it is all so explainable.* Too many churches are growing simply because they are well-oiled machines. Church programs, in and of themselves, will not change one person's life for eternity. Rather, what causes a thief to quit stealing from his employer, what causes divorced people to soften their hearts and remarry each other, what causes a man to stop using pornography, what causes a homosexual to turn away from his lifestyle, what causes grown men to reconcile after not speaking to each other in years is the touch of God. If the Lord is truly our focal point, needy people can come into the house of God and feel His convicting power even during the time of singing, before the preacher ever starts.

James 4:8 says, "Draw near to God and He will draw near to you." We have to focus on Him first of all. It does no good to reach out to human beings ahead of reaching out to God. That's backwards. When we get close to God, He moves close to us—and people come running to get in on the action.

A lot of churches in America have become like the Wal-Mart Supercenter Store down the street. They desire to be efficient, offer a dizzying array of products, and be smooth at the checkout lanes; but there's little if anything that transcends the ordinary. There's no awareness or focus on the presence of God in the place. It's as though the motto of some churches is "Come as you are; leave as you came." Too often people walk out the same as they entered except for a bag of stuff under their arm. They haven't been touched in their soul by Jesus Christ.

It makes me wonder if God can find anybody who wants to pay attention to *Him.* One day Jesus spoke with a Samaritan woman at the well who was seeking to engage Him in a debate about the proper protocols of worship. He said, "An hour is coming, and now is, when the true worshipers will worship the Father in spirit and truth; for *such people the Father seeks to be His worshipers*" (John 4:23). That paints a stark picture in my mind. I envision my city of Memphis with God hovering in a celestial cloud of His glory above us, moving back and forth from the wide Mississippi River to the eastern suburbs, from Millington in the north to down past the airport and on to the state line into Southaven, asking, "Who wants to worship Me? I'm seeking those of My people who possess humble, hungry, holy hearts, regardless of the size of their congregation. Will they rise up from their daily busyness and reach out toward Me in sincere, celebrative adoration and praise?"

The more this kind of seeking takes place, the more Jesus will build His church, and the gates of hell will not overpower it (see Matt. 16:18). It doesn't have to be a Southern Baptist church like mine or a Methodist or any other label; it just has to be a church that loves Jesus, loves the Bible, loves lost people, and is willing to go after God. I don't want to lead or even be part of a church that is built on my personality. I don't want a church merely built on a set of programs. My priority is not to defend the great, historic reputation of my denomination—as wonderful as that is. What I want is to be part of a church that is characterized by God's presence and power and exists for God's glory!

> *It does no good to reach out to human beings ahead of reaching out to God. That's backwards. When we get close to God, He moves close to us, and people come running to get in on the action.*

I want a church where at least *some* things can be explained only by the presence of God. I want a church so dependent upon the Holy Spirit that if He moved out, the whole thing would collapse. But if He stayed in the center of our life and worship, while a tornado wiped out the whole complex, we'd still be the church of the living God. Mind you, I'm definitely not asking for a tornado. But the real church is far more than a brick building. The true church of the Lord Jesus Christ is made up of redeemed humanity—those people who have been washed in Christ's blood and filled with His Spirit.

In this book we will talk about what welcomes the manifest presence of God. Genuine worship is something God uses to till the soil of people's hearts, to break up the hard places, so that the seed planted during the preaching does not fall on stony soil. It softens us to the point that the Holy Spirit can convict us "concerning sin and righteousness and judgment" (John 16:8). I believe the reason we are often seeing such a meager harvest of souls and a lukewarm response from believers is because we are scattering the seed of God's Word on hardened hearts. God uses the time of musical worship and praise in a service to help "break up your fallow ground" (Hos. 10:12) of people's stony hearts so the Holy Spirit can penetrate them with the Word of God that is preached.

Imagine a crusty, hard-living husband who finally decides to humor his Christian wife and go with her, however reluctantly, to a Sunday morning service. If all he sees is glitz and glamour, slick music, and a silver-tongued preacher, he'll say to himself (if not to his wife) on the way home, "Well, I could have watched that on television." But if he finds himself in a church that is prayed up, if he is seated alongside people who are literally going after God, and the worship time somehow makes God's presence so real he can't deny it, and the pastor isn't nervous about that but knows how to shepherd the flow of worship, the man is going to say, like Paul desired for visitors to the Corinthian church to say, "God is certainly among you" (1 Cor. 14:25). He may well end up giving his heart to Christ before the morning is over.

Time for Another Awakening

I know some readers may be saying: "Just what are you talking about? I don't get it. Are you telling us to embrace some sort of weird, unbiblical theology?" Absolutely not! In fact, I'm as solidly Southern Baptist as I've ever been. What I'm advocating is what I read about in the book of Acts, where people got saved by the thousands and whole cities were shaken by the power of God. I want to experience awakening like I studied in seminary: the time of Jonathan Edwards in the early 1700s, the Prayer Meeting Revival of the 1800s, the stirrings in Wales and elsewhere in the early 1900s, even the Jesus Movement of the late 1960s and early 1970s. I've examined these revivals and awakenings since I was in college, but I'm weary of just reading about such things. I want them to happen in *our* time. I want to minister in an atmosphere of spiritual renewal where the body of Christ in America is experiencing genuine "times of refreshing . . . from the presence of the Lord" (Acts 3:19).

Jesus told a somewhat stuffy scribe who had tried to stump Him with a question about which was the greatest commandment, "You shall love the Lord your God with all your heart, and with all your soul, and with all your mind, and with all your strength" (Mark 12:30, quoting Deut. 6:5). I'm all in favor of the *mind* part; that's why I spent ten years in post-college education. But let's not leave out the *heart* and *soul* parts. If we do, our theology will be as straight as a gun barrel—and just as empty.

Worshipping God with all our *strength* is valid as well. It's fine to be busy in the work of God, doing, doing, doing. Seeking God's manifest presence is not a substitute for true commitment and sacrifice. Nor is it a license for laziness. But I'm persuaded that too many believers have gone overboard with assignments and committees and task forces and all kinds of activity. These things need the quickening influence of heart-and-soul worship, or else they become religious drudgery.

> *I want a church where at least some things can be explained only by the presence of God.*

Maybe that's what Isaiah had in mind when he prophesied that the coming Messiah would arrive with a solution for "the spirit of heaviness" (61:3 KJV). Any of us who have sat through long-winded church debates or budget meetings knows what that feels like! We get weighed down with the bureaucracy of it all. Some church services can leave us with the same discouragement. What was God's cure for this? "The garment of praise" (Isa. 61:3 KJV). That's the way out of our religious exhaustion.

One lesson any individual Christian or local church will learn in going after God is this: The devil is allergic to us praising God, while God is attracted to it. When we worship the Lord, He comes with His fresh energy and hope, lifting our spirits in His direction. I'm talking about more than just music. I'm convinced that while it is not possible for Christians truly to worship without ever singing, it is certainly possible to sing without worshipping. Singing per se is not worship. I pray constantly for God to transform my singing *into* worship.

Back in the 1500s we had a reformation of the Word, thanks to Luther, Calvin, Zwingli, Knox, and the others who brought us out of the spiritual and theological bondage of the Dark Ages. Perhaps what we need now is a *reformation of worship*, a whole new understanding based on Scripture of what it means to draw close to God. We need to grasp that when we give our heart to God, He in turn shares His heart with us. When we have genuinely worshipped Him, we leave the service having made a wondrous exchange. He has our heart, and we have His!

I certainly do not claim to have it all together when it comes to awakening or revival or experiencing God's presence in private or corporate worship. But I do have a sincere hunger and thirst for the Lord. I guess I have always longed to be some sort of a catalyst for spiritual awakening here in America. I love this nation. It was founded for the glory of God.

> *Singing per se is not worship. I pray constantly for God to transform my singing into worship.*

It is my personal conviction that God is not ready to throw up His hands and give America over to her sin and His wrath—at least not yet. If God sent a nationwide revival to our country, the evangelistic harvest of souls would be mind-boggling, and the worldwide evangelistic and social effects would last for a hundred years or more. That's why I pray diligently for my country, because we desperately need to turn back to Jesus Christ.

Some Christians talk urgently about getting God back into government. Others talk about the need to get God back in the public schools. What I'm most concerned about is to get God back *into our churches*. When Jesus stood knocking in Revelation 3:20, He was seeking entrance at the door of the *church* of Laodicea, not the door of an individual human heart. When the God of the church is welcomed back to the center of the church of God, I'm convinced that everyone—the world and Christians alike—will see a huge difference.

How many churches across this land *did not see one new person come to Christ* during all of last year? I would be embarrassed to know the figure. I do know the figure for my denomination, and I'm not going to tell you. We're supposed to be famous for our evangelism and missions emphases. When I was attending seminary in Texas and serving as the pastor of a small church there, I knew of one Southern Baptist church nearby that hadn't needed their baptistery for so long, they had begun to use it as a storage bin. A new pastor came and led an eleven-year-old boy to the Lord. Before they could baptize him, they had to clean out all the accumulated junk in the baptistery. When they did, lo and behold, they had a hard time finding the drain plug in order to fill it up with water!

If you're smiling right now at that story, what's the situation in your denomination? Is it any better? We need God to do a fresh work in all our churches. The apostle Paul warned that "in the last days" there would be church folk "holding to a form of godliness, although they have denied its power" (2 Tim. 3:1, 5). The power of God in the house of God is the crying need of our day.

Who's in the House?

Perhaps I can illustrate my passion by telling you something about the city where I live. We have a number of claims to fame. For one thing, Memphis is the center for rhythm and blues. B. B. King's music echoes up and down Beale Street, along with the sounds of everyone from W. C. Handy to Sleepy John Estes to Memphis Minnie McCoy. What Nashville is to country music and New Orleans is to jazz, Memphis is to R&B.

We also have great food, especially barbecue! Every spring the "Memphis in May" festival hosts dozens of the finest barbecue vendors from across the country. The eastern bank of the Mississippi River adjacent to the downtown skyscrapers is literally covered with the rising smoke of tantalizing pork, beef, chicken, and turkey on the grill.

Our name will also be forever linked to Dr. Martin Luther King Jr., who preached what turned out to be his last sermon at Mason Temple Church of God in Christ. The next day on the balcony of the Lorraine Motel, he met his untimely death. You can still visit the site today, along with the National Civil Rights Museum across the street.

If you've ever sent an overnight package by Federal Express, chances are high that it passed through Memphis International Airport in the wee hours of the morning. The FedEx hub has made us the number one cargo airport in the world.

We're also proud of our NBA basketball team, the Memphis Grizzlies. They play in a striking new downtown facility called (what else?) the FedEx Forum.

But our number one tourist attraction by far is the Elvis Presley legacy. Fans come by the busloads looking for "the King." They take tours of his Graceland Mansion (more than 600,000 visitors a year), and they may stay in the Heartbreak Hotel across the street. They spend lots of money in our restaurants and tourist shops.

As a result, our city is plastered with billboards and other promotional signs declaring "Elvis Lives!" If some people want to think he didn't really die back in the summer of 1977, Memphians are willing to smile and keep accepting their charge cards, even though we know better. (The office nurse of my personal physician happened to be present that August day long ago, and she has commented to me, "Make no mistake—the man is *dead!*") The oft-quoted punch line "Elvis has entered the building!" is of course a mythology and nothing more.

What I crave instead for every Christ-honoring, Bible-believing church in this city is that we might be able to say with all truthfulness and humility, "The King of kings is in the house. God has come in His awesome reality to be with us. He's alive; and He is the same yesterday, today, and forever. In His presence we are finding joy, hope, and new life. In His presence the lost are being drawn to the foot of the cross. In His presence relationships are being healed and restored, the confused are being set on a clear path, and the kingdom of God is expanding. Church life is exciting instead of burdensome."

In the spring of my ninth-grade year, I tried out for the high school football team in my small hometown of Dyersburg, Tennessee. Our school hadn't had a winning team in years. A tough, no-nonsense coach had now been brought in to make us winners. It was a daunting assignment.

We practiced hard week after week. But when the season finally opened the next fall, it looked as if we were going to repeat history. We lost two of our first three games.

Then our coach had a talk with us that I'll never forget. Standing by the goalpost, he said something to this effect: "Men, no one around here thinks we can win. Most of *you* don't think we can win. Well, the fact is, we *can* win. But we're going to have to pull together, become a team, work harder, and start seeing ourselves as *winners!*"

Something happened under that goalpost. We won seven of our next eight games, finishing the season with eight wins and three losses. The next season during my junior year, we won ten games and lost only one.

The crowds grew larger. During my senior year we racked up another ten victories and went to the state play-offs in Nashville, eventually losing to the team that won the title. When the dust settled, our team was ranked third in the state! We were the talk of West Tennessee.

Our team and our town had a "football revival." I had heard about the great high school teams of the past. But more than that, I now personally had the joy and privilege of playing on a winning team. I saw a small town come together and beam with pride. It was a wonderful, fulfilling experience.

But it all started under that goalpost. A few "believers" latched hold of a dream that was fragile and nearly elusive. We hungered to be winners, and we were willing to do whatever it took to see our dream become a reality.

Can you picture the Lord right now, talking to His children? In many ways in America, for the past five decades our denominations and churches have been losing. The culture has kicked God out of our public schools. We've legalized abortion on demand, which has stained America's soil with the blood of millions of unborn babies. While sinners have come out of the closet, Christians have seemingly entered the closet, giving in to a spirit of fear. Sexually transmitted diseases, teenage pregnancies, and suicides are all at all-time highs. We can't build prisons fast enough or large enough to house all the criminals. State governments are propped up by the gambling industries. The problems that plague this country go on and on and on.

> *How many churches across this land did not see one new person come to Christ during all of last year? I would be embarrassed to know the figure.*

What's the answer? Revival among God's people! God's Word says: "If . . . My people who are called by My name humble themselves and pray and seek My face and turn from their wicked ways, then I will hear from heaven, will forgive their sin and will heal their land" (2 Chron. 7:13–14). That was *not* just a promise for ancient Israel. The Old Testament Scriptures were written to encourage and instruct Christians of all ages (cp. Rom. 15:4; 1 Cor. 10:11). God said, "If *My* people. . . ." Christians *are* the people of God today.

God's people, not unbelievers, are the ones holding back revival. God wants to return to His people and to His houses of worship in great power and glory. He is graciously knocking at the door of our churches. Are we willing to let Him inside?

CHAPTER 2

Church Is Not a Performance

A pastors' magazine once ran a cartoon that showed a somewhat nervous preacher in the pulpit getting ready to deliver his sermon. To his right on the platform was a table with three seated church members holding three mallets, ready to strike the huge gong overhead. Out on the second row of the congregation, a man says to a young woman, "They say it's a tough church to preach at!"[1]

To be honest with you, that's how it feels sometimes for us preachers. Indeed, some people seem to come into a sanctuary, sit down in the nicely padded pew, fold their arms, and say to themselves, "OK, let's see what you've got up your sleeve today. I dare you to try to impress me!" They're just waiting for the speaker to mess up so they can silently "gong" him.

The same goes for other parts of the worship service. If the musicians happen to falter in any small way, if the sound system isn't adjusted exactly right, if the bulletin has a misspelled word, or if the temperature isn't perfect, today's churchgoers are oftentimes quick to point out the deficiency. Some even go so far as to spend lunch afterward with their friends picking their way through a menu of "hashed preacher." Those people should not wonder why their children, who were forced to hear their criticisms and complaints, have little desire to be part of the church when they grow up.

I sometimes wonder what folks would do if they had to listen to the apostle Peter, who obviously never had a day of college in his life.

When the early Christians met for worship in the Roman catacombs, I'm pretty sure there was no sound technician to control the echo factor. But now in our time, we've grown sophisticated; our expectations have mushroomed for well-produced, high-quality performances in the house of God. We've become a bit like Goldilocks: church must be neither too hot nor too cold, too loud nor too soft, too long nor too short. It has to be just right, or else we "can't worship".

I'm not making a case for sloppiness at all. I appreciate good lighting in a church, quality sound, pleasant temperature control, and all the other creature comforts. In recent years, our churches have rubbed rub off a lot of our rough edges, which is fine. We've become more efficient than we ever were before. But at what cost? Church staffs now talk in their weekly planning meetings about "sets" and "packages" that will comprise the Sunday services. The language of stage production has in too many cases become the language of the family of God.

> *We've become a bit like Goldilocks: church must be neither too hot nor too cold, too loud nor too soft, too long nor too short. It has to be just right, or else we "can't worship."*

If a church is not focused on the Lord, the performance mind-set can really kick into high gear when that congregation decides to air its services on television. Now it's not just the live audience that has to be pleased; it's a whole second tier of viewers sitting at home on their comfortable couches expecting to be entertained. If they're not impressed by what they see and hear on the screen, they can easily click to a different channel. The church service is just one option among hundreds, and the competition is stiff.

Even churches that have television ministries must constantly remind themselves that they are not involved in a performance. To be sure, television outreach has value; I've used it myself for years. But the great danger for pastors, music ministers, and congregations is that the TV tail can end up wagging the whole dog.

Is this what God intended worship to be?

Us, Them, or Him?

The worship of the people of God was never meant to be showtime. Too much of what the contemporary church calls worship is on a horizontal level. We are performing for one another instead of reaching out to God. We aren't vertical enough.

When the things we do in God's house are basically all about us, God surely notices. Oh, we say we're worshipping the Lord, but running through our minds the whole time is: *How is this coming across? Is everybody happy with this music, this sermon? Does this sound good? Does this look right? Are we sticking to the schedule so we won't get out late?* If we're not careful, it can all degenerate and become human centered.

Churches also can err by viewing the proceedings in the worship time as primarily evangelistic in purpose. When that happens, then the focus shifts to "them." *How are the visitors perceiving this? Are we impressing them? Do they think we're cool? Is our service exciting enough that they'll want to come back another time?* Everything being said and sung is put through the grid of outsider perception.

I'm not saying I don't believe in special outreach events. Throughout my ministry the churches I have led have done some of the finest. In Gardendale, Alabama, we put on a patriotic fireworks display on July 4 that drew thousands. We also held a wild-game dinner that attracted more than three thousand every year. Likewise, here in Memphis, our church's Singing Christmas Tree every December is legendary, running for eight performances and drawing thirty to thirty-five thousand people. I think every congregation ought to find creative ways to connect with unbelievers in their community.

But on a Sunday-to-Sunday basis, the agenda is different. Here is what I believe with all my heart: *Worship services should not be designed primarily to attract people. Rather, worship services should be designed to attract the manifest presence of God, and He in turn will attract the people.*

The purpose is to reach out to the Lord. He is the true audience—not the congregation. To put it another way: *Don't seek results! Seek Jesus, and He'll give you the results.* Isn't that what Matthew 6:33 is all about? "But seek first His kingdom and His righteousness, and all these things will be added to you." Go after God, and all the good stuff will come trailing along.

To be honest, it's easier to go after people than it is to go after God. We know how to trigger applause and compliments. Reaching out to God is a different, less familiar endeavor.

But Jesus had good reason for pointing out to the Pharisee questioner (see Matt. 22:34–40) that the first and greatest commandment was to love the Lord our God. The second commandment was to reach out to our neighbor. God comes first. Nowhere should this be more true than in our times of corporate worship. God's people are told to obey the Great Commandment (love God) *before* we obey the Great Commission (make disciples; see Matt. 28:19–20). That means worship must come before witnessing.

This requires a mental shift, I know. It's not the way we're accustomed to thinking. We naturally seek the approval of our peers. We gravitate in the direction of *what will people think?* We have to work hard to make ourselves ask, *"What is God thinking?"*

One of the reasons I encourage churches to use the nontraditional praise music along with the great hymns of the faith is because so many of the modern choruses and praise songs tend to speak *to* God, not *about* Him. "I love You, Lord, and I lift my voice." "Lord, You are good, and Your mercy endures forever!" "Draw me close to You, never let me go. . . . You're all I want, You're all I've ever needed." Yes, songs of testimony *about* the attributes of God have their place. But addressing God directly is more intimate. These songs bring us near to our heavenly Father.

I once heard a famous Christian speaker actually say that any Christian song in a minor key ought not to be used. I beg to disagree. Such a mentality would eliminate such great prayer songs as "Jesus, Lover of My Soul" (Joseph Parry tune), "O the Deep, Deep Love of Jesus," or the moving "O Sacred Head, Now Wounded." I really don't believe that the style of the music is the primary consideration in selecting songs to be used in corporate worship. Church ought not to be about style, which is fundamentally a human issue. Far too much time and energy are being consumed these days in style wars. The point is to get close to God, whose style

> *Far too much time and energy are being consumed these days in style wars. The point is to get close to God, whose style preferences we don't actually know, do we?*

preferences we don't actually know, do we? He hasn't told us whether He's into baroque, big-band, or any other musical format. What He wants more than anything else is genuine contact with us.

The preaching as well needs to focus on God and what He wants to communicate to this particular congregation at this moment in time. The point is not to deliver a masterpiece of oratory, something that would win a prize in an elocution contest. The point is to hear what the Spirit is saying to the church.

Searching for More

A great deal of my passion for the presence of God goes back to the mid-1990s when I was coasting along comfortably as the pastor of an excellent church, First Baptist in Gardendale. I had no complaints about our services. Things were going well in this pleasant town of twelve thousand about ten miles north of Birmingham.

My unrest was rather a private thing: I just wasn't as full of the Lord as I personally wanted to be. Bill Bright, founder and president of Campus Crusade for Christ, was writing at that time about the spiritual discipline of fasting, including the account of his own forty-day fast. He claimed it had made a remarkable difference in his life. A fellow pastor, Ronnie Floyd in Springdale, Arkansas, had done the same thing.

I decided to follow their lead. I would drink juices only as I sought the Lord. After about ten days, I found I didn't care about food anymore. My interaction with God, however, seemed to go into warp speed. I felt like I was on a special retreat with Him, even when in a group of people. The written Word of God began to jump up in front of me as I read. I couldn't get enough Scripture. I couldn't praise the Lord enough.

I didn't boast about this from the pulpit, of course. Jesus clearly taught against that in the Sermon on the Mount. But people could tell I was losing weight and began asking what was going on. Was I sick or what? I told them no, I was simply giving more attention to seeking the Lord these days, and fasting was an aid to that.

Soon members of the church staff began joining me in this, of their own free choice. Some opted for twenty-one days; others, ten days, three days, or even just twenty-four hours. People in the congregation started fasting, too, by the score.

We began to notice a change in our Sunday services. We weren't just going through the same old motions. It seemed as if God sort of settled down upon us when we came together. We sensed His nearness.

One Sunday morning in the fall of 1996, the music was so wonderful and the worship so genuine that we all knew that God was in the house. His presence was so real, you felt you could reach out and touch Him. People were not merely praying and singing. Rather, like Hannah in the Old Testament, they were pouring out their souls "before the LORD" (1 Sam. 1:15). Just as I was about to start the sermon, the Lord strongly impressed me to give an invitation for people to accept Christ—right then. That certainly wasn't on the printed order of service. It was *not* the customary way of doing things in a Baptist church. The normal pattern is to sing, preach, and *then* extend the invitation. But that Sunday was different—very different. I just couldn't resist.

"Folks, before I begin preaching today," I said, "I believe I should offer you a chance to make a decision for Christ." I went on to explain what this entailed, invited people to come forward for prayer and counseling—and seven individuals got saved! God wanted to do something special right at that point in time. I then went ahead to preach the sermon I had prepared, gave another invitation at the end—and *more* people got saved. It was incredible.

Our attendance began to swell. Newcomers began showing up from all over, even though we weren't on the growing edge of Birmingham. The south side of the city was the developing edge, and we were due north. Still, our numbers went from fifteen hundred up to an average of well over three thousand over the next few years. We had to start a third worship service; we had to build new buildings and new parking lots. Offerings increased; missions interest and involvement went up; baptisms soared.

We honestly had no program, no master strategy, no church-growth plan. Fellow pastors would ask me, "What's causing all this?" I would reply, "It's not a *what* but a *who*. God is doing this. Other than His presence and power, I have no idea! We don't know exactly how to do everything we're doing. We're just going after God."

We were out of control in a good sense. God was in control, and we were not. There was no fanaticism or anything unbiblical. There was simply a fresh movement of the presence of Holy God in our midst.

We all knew we were in over our heads, but it was all right because God was present and in charge.

The mayor told me on several occasions that we were the best public relations for Gardendale, better than the chamber of commerce could ever afford to buy. Our television broadcast became a Sunday morning favorite for viewers throughout the central Alabama region. We were even being watched by folks in eastern Mississippi and western Georgia. People would see us on television, sense that God was moving in our midst, and drive to our church to be part of what the Lord was doing. Many of them actually moved to Gardendale just so they could join the church.

Now the Lord has led me to a wonderful place in Memphis with a wonderful heritage. Bellevue Baptist Church has been led by great men of God such as Dr. R. G. Lee, Dr. Ramsey Pollard, and, of course, Dr. Adrian Rogers. For decades it has been a praying, evangelistic, Bible-preaching, Christ-honoring, mission-minded fellowship. Now we are experiencing the privilege of building upon that great heritage and watching God do wonderful things.

The Lord is blessing us with many people being converted to Christ. A host of people are attending our worship services, even on Sunday nights. Church growth gurus (many of whom have never even been pastors, much less led a church to grow) often say that few people in our day will come to church on Sunday nights. Well, they need to visit Bellevue! We are also receiving a host of people into our fellowship as new members. We are planting and watering, and the Lord Jesus is faithfully giving the increase (see 1 Cor. 3:6).

But the greatest part of it all is an increasing awareness of the manifest presence of God. I receive letter after letter and e-mail after e-mail commenting on the obvious anointing of His presence during both the musical praise and the preaching. Just before we depart on Sunday night, we join hands and sing the Doris Akers classic "There's a sweet, sweet Spirit in this place." When we are finished, people spontaneously break out into applause because what we are singing is true. God's Spirit *is* in that place, just as surely as He was in the upper room on the day of Pentecost (Acts 2).

The apostle Paul wrote in 1 Thessalonians 1:5 that "our gospel did not come to you in word only, but also in power and in the Holy Spirit and with full conviction." He said something similar to the Corinthians after planting the church there: "My message and my preaching were not in persuasive words of wisdom, but in demonstration of the Spirit and of power, so that your faith would not rest on the wisdom of men, but on the power of God" (1 Cor. 2:4–5). In other words, human eloquence and programming doesn't get the job done. The supernatural element is absolutely essential.

> ☞ *The world will nearly always be able to outsing, outspeak, and outperform us. The only thing it can't do is "out-God" us.* ☜

Some of us veterans in the church need to notice that younger people today—under age thirty-five—don't really come to church to be entertained anyway. They are a multimedia generation, and they know the outside world can entertain them better than the most polished church. Through television, DVDs, movies, and the Internet, they've been exposed to the highest levels of artistry. The home video market is now twice as big in America as the theater box office.

When young adults come to church, they are looking for something Hollywood cannot give them. That something is the presence and power of God. The world will nearly always be able to outsing, outspeak, and outperform us. The only thing it can't do is "out-God" us. We just have to give Him center stage.

A Different Mind-Set

It's hard for both clergy and laity to shift gears, I admit. We've put on religious programs for so long that we can feel off balance and awkward about change. Nevertheless, I'm convinced that a serious reeducation regarding worship is needed in our denominations and churches.

Music leaders are understandably torn. They've been schooled for years to produce excellence worthy of a concert hall. They naturally want every note right. And we who listen to their choirs and orchestras appreciate the quality they have labored so diligently to perfect.

Concert mode is, however, not the same as worship mode. Musicians at all levels need to comprehend that in church their job is to facilitate the worship of the people. In *Worship Leader* magazine a few years ago, Sally Morgenthaler wrote an intriguing article entitled "Leading vs. Performance." She told about attending a national worship conference that supposedly offered the best of the best. Yet "halfway through the first worship service, I wondered if I'd registered at the wrong conference. Here I was in an ostensibly interactive, God-focused environment, but I had no sense whatsoever of being authentically engaged. It was as if someone had plugged in a pre-fab worship video. . . . There was something hauntingly synthetic about it."[2]

She then went on to draw up a chart with two columns: "Worship Performer" on the left, "Worship Leader" on the right. Some of the contrasts:

Left: Consumed with presenting a glittering image

Right: Consumed with a passion for God

Left: Personal goal: maximum visibility

Right: Personal goal: invisibility

Left: Tries to "work the crowd," to manipulate an
experience

Right: Fosters an atmosphere of worship, then steps back
and lets God meet people where they are

Left: Disallows or interrupts silence

Right: Lets go of control, allows God to speak in the quiet,
to deal with people's brokenness

But it is not just the worship leaders who struggle at this point. Choirs and soloists have to undergo the same paradigm shift. Their service is not to be offered in order to gain the applause of a human audience but to welcome the arrival of the true star, the Lord Almighty. Music is not an end in itself; it is only a means.

Staff members outside the music department must grasp the same purpose. Even ushers need to get the concept. A friend told me about walking into one large church in the Los Angeles area where an upbeat usher reached out to shake his hand at the sanctuary door, gave him a big smile, offered a bulletin, and said enthusiastically, "Good morning, good morning! Welcome to the show!"

My friend said he wanted to snap back, "Excuse me, but I thought Disneyland was down the freeway another few exits." He barely managed to hold his tongue. The usher's assumption that church was just another theatrical venue would have to be corrected by someone else.

When we enter the house of God, there should be only one focus—on Him. We are here to pay full attention to Him. He is what it's all about. He deserves all the spotlight.

My collaborator on this book, Dean Merrill, was traveling a few years ago in a poverty-stricken nation and noticed a unique sign while being driven around the city. Various homeowners had stenciled in large black letters on their perimeter walls or homes, THIS HOUSE IS NOT FOR SALE.

"What's that all about?" Dean asked his host after about the fifth sign. "In my country, we put signs in our yard if our house *is* for sale. Why are these people taking time to say the opposite?"

"Well," the host explained, "we have a little problem here with unethical people posing as realtors when they're really not. They will pretend to offer real estate to customers, saying, 'Here is a lovely property that I'm sure you would like. I'm sorry I can't show you the inside today, but there is a lot of interest in the market for this one. If you want to go ahead and put in a bid for it, we could write up the paperwork, you could put down a deposit, and we could get ahead of any other competition.' Once the guy gets the earnest money, then he disappears overnight. The customer finds out later that the homeowner wasn't interested in selling at all, the money has vanished, and now there's a big legal mess. So these signs let everyone know that this property is *not* on the market."

Maybe in some of our churches we need signs that say, "THIS IS NOT A SHOW." We're not trying to put on a razzle-dazzle performance for the next hour or ninety minutes. If you came looking for a concert, a variety show, or a brilliant speech, you came to the wrong place. We've got something much different in mind here: to have an up-close and personal visit with the Lord. Getting in touch with Him is the only thing we're trying to do.

Dead or Alive?

The price for not making such a shift in thinking is that we are left to our own devices in keeping a church alive. The whole burden for momentum falls heavily upon our human shoulders. We put ourselves in the position of having to think up new brainstorms every month, indeed every week. Our creativity is the only asset we can lean on as the population gets harder and harder to impress with every passing season.

I once preached a sermon series on the seven churches of Revelation. When I got to the church at Sardis, I zeroed in on Jesus' rather blunt summary: "You have a name that you are alive, but you are dead. Wake up, and strengthen the things that remain, which were about to die; for I have not found your deeds completed in the sight of My God" (Rev. 3:1–2).

I told about a seminary professor friend of mine who went fishing one day for bass. He was happily enjoying the warm sunshine by the lake when he suddenly felt a strong pull on the line. He thought he had a whopper for sure. He began eagerly reeling in his catch. But when he got the creature up to the water's surface, he found he had pulled in a snapping turtle instead.

It was nasty and biting, of course. My friend gingerly dragged the turtle up on the bank and thumped it on the head. But of course it wouldn't let go of the hook. He then found a stick and beat the turtle on the back. Still no luck.

Now the next part of the story is not exactly pleasant, but it has to be included. The only way to put the turtle out of its misery, the professor realized, was to decapitate it. So he pulled a knife out of his tackle box and did the job.

He then threw the shell up behind him on the bank. He proceeded to cut his fishing line, forfeiting the hook, and started over again.

A couple of minutes later, when the man had gone back to fishing for bass, he heard some rustling in the grass. Nobody else was fishing in this location. What could the noise be? He turned around, and to his amazement here was the headless turtle shell trying to crawl by instinct back toward the water! It was dead and didn't even know it!

It is sad to say but true: Some churches and churchgoers are just like that. They're spiritually dead but still going through a few religious motions on their own. The lights are on, but there's no life of the Spirit inside. It is only a matter of time before the body stops functioning altogether.

The church at Sardis, according to Jesus, was running on autopilot. But it would soon crumple into a heap if it did not heed the warning to "wake up" (v. 2).

What that church needed was the same thing we desperately need today: a passion for the energizing presence of God in our midst. Our programs and performances will not keep us alive. We need the Lord more than we know.

In Asheville, North Carolina, is a church called Biltmore Baptist Church. In the early 1990s it was about to fold. People were leaving the church left and right. Morale was at an all-time low. But a few faithful members began to pray for the Lord's intervention. They were desperate for God to move in their midst again.

The Lord answered their prayers by sending a pastor named James Walker. He led the congregation to be a praying, reaching, equipping, giving, worshipping church that focused on going after the manifest presence of God. The result? That church has grown in less than fifteen years from under two hundred in attendance to well over four thousand! People are being saved and set free from every type of sin imaginable. They are even witnessing the conversions of many people who have been enslaved to New Age worship, Wicca, and various other forms of the occult. The church is literally covered by the fervent prayers of God's people. And God's presence, in turn, is saturating their entire ministry.

I don't know about you, but that is what I want to see happen in every Bible-believing, Christ-honoring church in the United States of America. Our country needs more than sermons and songs. We've had plenty of those for years, but all too often they have been void of the anointing of the Holy Spirit. What America needs, what the church needs, what we all need is the presence and power of God back in our churches once again.

CHAPTER 3

An Audience of One

People in our church weren't quite sure what to think the Sunday I stood up and said: "Let's run a little experiment here this morning. As soon as I count to three, everybody say your name out loud, all at once. Are you ready? One—two—three—"

The result was a cacophony across the sanctuary as the sounds of "Bill Jones," "Lisa Miller," "Michael Washington," "Susan Kapinski," and several thousand other names all piled on top of one another. You couldn't make out anything distinctly.

Then I said: "OK, now let's do it again, only this time, everybody speak the name *Jesus.* Here we go: one—two—three—"

"*Jesus!*" The unified sound was magnificent.

"My point is this," I then explained. "When we all come together around Jesus, a beautiful thing happens. He brings us into harmony as we focus not on ourselves but on Him. We stop fussing about our individual differences. We're caught up in the glow of His presence. He truly is present right here in this room, you know. Right now, on this date in time, He's moving among these pews, up and down these aisles, from the back wall to the choir loft—He's here! Let's reach out to worship Him today."

One of the most serious things I tell myself every time I stand up to preach is this: *Jesus is here listening to what you're going to say, Steve. He's not five thousand miles away tending to some other business. He's right here. Make sure you handle His Word faithfully. You're speaking on His behalf.*

In other words, instead of merely having a church that's *seeker-friendly*, I desperately want us to be *Savior-focused*. Everything of consequence in a service needs to be aimed His way. We call out to Him in prayer, we sing directly to Him in praise and adoration, we explain His offer of love and forgiveness as clearly as we can, and we invite people to come meet Him at the end. This is His church! He bought it with His blood, and He owns it (Acts 20:28). Jesus is "the head of the body, the church" (Col. 1:18). He is what church is all about.

I recently saw a church's promotional flyer (nicely designed, by the way) that carried this prominent tagline: "[Name] Church: *Built Around You.*" It sounded as if whatever you want for yourself, for your kids, for your particular schedule or preference—hey, we'll try to do it. You're the king around here, and we aim to please you.

I'm sorry, but that's not the mentality that builds the kingdom of God. Only one Lord is to be accommodated, and that's Jesus. He takes center stage. To Him belongs all the glory and attention.

> *Instead of merely having a church that's seeker-friendly, I desperately want us to be Savior-focused. Everything of consequence in a service needs to be aimed His way.*

When we get this truth solidly in place in our minds, it has the wonderful side benefit of keeping us in unity. When we all focus on Jesus, we automatically align ourselves with one another. Imagine a large showroom of pianos that need to be tuned. Does the tuner work on the first instrument, then tune the second piano to match the first, then the third to match the second, then the fourth to match to the third, and so on? Not at all. If he did, he would wind up with an ear-jarring dissonance.

Instead, he makes them *all* align to one tuning fork. The standard is constant, and each piano is brought into compliance with that one pitch. As a result, you could have a concert in that room with any number of virtuosos playing the same piece of music, and the sound would be harmonious.

How much discord and bickering and infighting in the body of Christ could be eliminated by all of us focusing on Jesus? His priorities would become our priorities. Petty issues that don't really matter to Him would be dropped in the dust. Pleasing Him in all things would be central. When it comes to worship services, as well as the Christian life in general, every believer should constantly remind himself, "It is not about *me*; it's about *Jesus*."

More Than Just Showing Up

Reaching out to Jesus with all our mind, heart, soul, and strength means active engagement on the part of every church member. It's not enough just to show up, warm the pew, and put money in the offering plate. I say to congregations, "When you walk in the door, you are just as involved in worshipping Jesus as anyone in the choir or at the pulpit. You have a mission here today: to go after God."

More than one highly ranked sports team with loads of talent has gotten knocked out of the playoffs because they simply "showed up." They assumed the trophy was already theirs. They went out on the floor or field and took their positions, but that wasn't good enough. By the time the clock wound down to 00:00, they had been eliminated.

> *Some of us spend more minutes getting our bodies ready for church than our hearts! What if we gave equal time to preparing our spirits as we do to fixing our outfits and hair?*

It is a danger when any of us church folks just "show up" to sing in the choir, to teach a class, to preach a sermon, or to fill some other role. We have to come instead with a fervent intent to worship Jesus through our actions. In fact, we need to pray consciously about that ahead of time. Some of us spend more minutes getting our *bodies* ready for church than our hearts! What if we gave equal time to preparing our spirits as we do to fixing our outfits and hair? We'd have revival! None other than the Lord Himself would be our concentration.

More than 160 years ago, a Danish philosopher named Søren Kierkegäard compared the church of his day (with which he was fairly unhappy) to attendance at the theater for a play. I'm certainly no fan of Kierkegäard's theology; he was the forerunner of existentialism. However, he offered a devastating critique of church hypocrisy and misdirection. He pointed out that there are three roles at any production:

(1) the audience that watches and listens, (2) the actors who perform, and
(3) the coaches or "prompters" who train the actors to do their job well
and, if needed, remind them of their lines: "It is so on the stage, as you
know well enough, that someone sits and prompts by whispers; he is the
inconspicuous one, he is, and wishes to be overlooked. But then there is
another, he strides out prominently, he draws every eye to himself. For
that reason he has been given his name, that is: 'actor.'"

If we were to diagram what Kierkegäard is describing, it would look
like this:

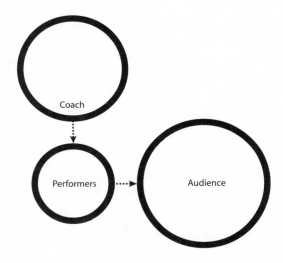

If you transfer this to a church service, God becomes the invisible
coach, telling the pastors and musicians what to do and say, so the audience will be pleased. We can easily understand this model.

No, no, no, says Kierkegäard. You've got it all wrong. Church is not
supposed to be like the theater at all. The assignments are different. In a
worship service the leaders (pastors and musicians) are the *coaches*. They
give guidance to the congregation on what to say and do as the *perform-*
ers, the true worshippers. And who then is the *audience?* God Himself!
He is the one for whom the whole event exists. Human beings seek to
bring Him joy.

> Alas, in regard to things spiritual, the foolishness of many
> is this, that they in the secular sense look upon the speaker
> [clergyman] as an actor, and the listeners as theatergoers who

are to pass judgment upon the artist. But the speaker is not the actor—not in the remotest sense. No, the speaker is the prompter. There are no mere theatergoers present, for each listener will be looking into his own heart. The stage is eternity, and the listener . . . stands before God during the talk [sermon]. The prompter whispers to the actor what he is to say, but the actor's repetition of it is the main concern—is the solemn charm of the art. . . .

The address is not given for the speaker's sake, in order that men may praise or blame him. The listener's repetition of it is what is aimed at. . . . In the theater, the play is staged before an audience who are called theatergoers; but at the devotional address, God himself is present. In the most earnest sense, God is the critical theatergoer, who looks on to see how the lines are spoken. . . .

Oh, let us never forget this, let us not reduce the spiritual to the worldly. . . . As soon as the spiritual is looked upon in worldly fashion . . . then the speaker becomes an actor and the listeners become critical theatergoers. . . . God's presence is the decisive thing that changes all.[4]

Kierkegaard is calling us radically to turn the diagram on its end so that the divine Audience is at the top, and we coaches and performers face Him alone (see diagram on next page). Everything we do is for His benefit. The question from one human to another as we are leaving the building is not, "So did you enjoy church today? What did you think of it?" Instead, the question is, "Do you think God enjoyed our worship today? Was He pleased with what we offered Him?"

Think about what Sunday mornings must be like for God! Imagine Him sitting on His throne looking at His people. Since He is God, He can watch every worship service taking place all at once. My church, your church, everybody's church; His capacity is unlimited (obviously).

Is He captivated by what He sees? Does He lean forward in eagerness to hear more? Is He pleased with our singing and speaking? Does He say to Himself, "Those folks really want to know Me; they want to be close to Me"?

Or is He disappointed with what is before Him? Does He get frustrated with us? Does He think about just turning His head away and refusing to watch anymore? Does He repeat what He once said to Isaiah, "This people draw near with their words and honor me with their lip service, but they remove their hearts far from me, and their reverence for me consists of tradition learned by rote" (29:13)?

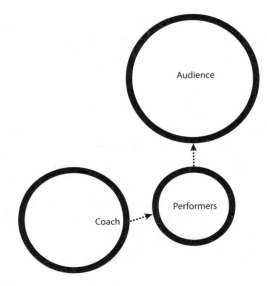

The longing of my heart is to bring God joy through worship. Psalm 104:31 says, "Let the glory of the LORD endure forever; *let the LORD be glad in His works.*" We, His people, are part of "His works" as much as the Rocky Mountains or the nighttime sky full of stars and planets. May we be a source of gladness to Him.

The Trap of "Whatever Works"

What we are talking about here is intimate and relational; it goes much deeper than programs. I'm not against church programs. Our church has a full-blown Sunday school (actually, we call it "Bible Fellowship") and sports leagues and men's conferences and women's groups and ski retreats and an Evangelism Explosion visitation program and all the rest. I value each one of these and the leaders who make them happen.

But at a deeper level, "unless the LORD builds the house, they labor in vain who build it" (Ps. 127:1). God does not need my "arm of flesh" (2 Chron. 32:8). If church life is nothing but a collection of busy programs, we all get tired after a while. Far too many churches and pastors are anxiously looking for a new program every two years or so to jazz up the landscape again. It becomes wearisome. The number one effort must be to seek the manifest presence of God.

If life revolves around programs, then the premier question quickly becomes, does it work? Is this or that program producing the expected results, or should it be scrapped? Such pragmatism can be a curse on a church because it all too easily can lead us away from biblical priorities. What the Word of God highlights is drawing close to God, receiving His life and power as we wait before Him. If we put first and foremost what the Bible urges us to do, the results will take care of themselves.

> *If church life is nothing but a collection of busy programs, we all get tired after a while.*

The work of God is meant to be done with the power of God. And the power of God comes only from the presence of God. If we lack *Him*, we will see little that can be described as having eternal value in the end. God's work is always accomplished "not by [our] might, nor by [our] power, but by [God's] Spirit" (Zech. 4:6).

Many people know the song written back in 1999 by gifted young British musician and worship leader Matt Redman entitled "The Heart of Worship," but not everyone knows what triggered it. The pastor of his church near Brighton, where Matt and his band led each week and were in fact achieving a lot of notice on the British "praise and worship" scene, took a radical step regarding their program. Here's how Matt explains it in his book, *The Unquenchable Worshipper:*

> Some of the things we thought were helping us in our worship were actually hindering us. They were throwing us off the scent of what it means to really worship. We had always set aside lots of time in our meetings for worshipping God through music. But it began to dawn on us that we'd lost something. The fire that used to characterise our worship had somehow grown cold. In some ways, everything looked great. We had some wonderful musicians, and a good quality sound system. There were lots of new songs coming through, too. But somehow we'd started to rely on these things a little too

much, and they'd become distractions. Where once people
would enter in [to worshipping God] no matter what, we'd
now wait to see what the band was like first, how good the
sound was, or whether we were "into" the songs chosen.

Mike, the pastor, decided on a pretty drastic course of
action: we'd strip everything away for a season, just to see
where our hearts were. So the very next Sunday when we
turned up for church, there was no sound system to be seen,
and no band to lead us. The new approach was simple—we
weren't going to lean so hard on those outward things anymore. Mike would say, "When you come through the doors of
the church on Sunday, what are you bringing as your offering
to God? What are you going to sacrifice today?"

If I'm honest, at first I was pretty offended by the whole
thing. The worship was my job! But as God softened my heart,
I started to see His wisdom all over these actions. At first the
meetings were a bit awkward: there were long periods of silence,
and there wasn't too much singing going on. But we soon began
to learn how to bring heart offerings to God without any exter-
nal trappings we'd grown used to. Stripping everything away,
we slowly started to rediscover the heart of worship.

After a while, the worship band and the sound system
re-appeared, but now it was different. The songs of our heart
had caught up with the songs of our lips.

Out of this season, I reflected on where we had come as a
church, and wrote this song:

> *When the music fades,*
> *All is stripped away,*
> *And I simply come;*
> *Longing just to bring something that's of worth*
> *That will bless Your heart.*
>
> *I'll bring You more than a song,*
> *For a song in itself*
> *Is not what You have required.*
> *You search much deeper within*
> *Through the way things appear;*
> *You're looking into my heart.*

I'm coming back to the heart of worship,
And it's all about You,
All about You, Jesus.
I'm sorry, Lord, for the thing I've made it,
When it's all about You,
All about You, Jesus.[5]

Yes, indeed, our worship can become simply "the thing I've made it." What the Audience of One is looking for, however, is a lot more than a thing, an act, a performance, a nice tune, a set of clever lyrics, a chord chart. He's looking for a relationship of love, adoration, and submission. He welcomes us into His arms when we finally get it through our thick heads that church is "all about You, all about You, Jesus."

When we extract ourselves out of program mode and put ourselves at His feet, He welcomes us and blesses us with more fulfillment than we've ever known. He is lifted up, and that is what enables Him to draw all people to Himself (see John 12:32). Christians and non-Christians alike are pulled, as with a magnet, in His direction.

Letting Jesus Call the Shots

Sometimes Jesus pulls us in directions we would never have gone by ourselves. He has a way of surprising us. People have asked me over the years, "What's it like to pastor a church in revival?"

I've answered, "It's sort of like riding a Brahma bull in a rodeo. You're on top, but you're not in charge!"

If Jesus is indeed the Lord of the church, He has the right to steer us any way He chooses. We just have to be flexible and responsive to His leading. One time in Alabama, I received a letter from a tiny, struggling church on the other side of Birmingham, heading out into the countryside, Mount Signal Baptist Church. They were down to just thirteen people attending and thought they might have to close the doors. Their pastor, however, was trying to get them to lift their eyes from their decline and focus outward. In an almost desperate move, he had said one Sunday, "Let's take our whole offering today and give it away to somebody else. Let's bless another part of God's kingdom and see what happens."

They knew from watching television that our church in Gardendale was in a building program. (We were *always* building something, it seemed; we joked that while other churches launched campaigns called "Together We Build," ours was a case of "Forever We Build.") Now here in this envelope with the letter was a check for their entire weekly collection: $662.

What a sacrifice on their part. This was, of course, hardly a drop in the bucket of our current building budget. But I knew it was a big deal to the folks who gave it. I was deeply touched.

I said to our deacons, "Look at what Mount Signal did for us! Isn't this amazing? Do you suppose the Lord would have us turn around and take up an offering for them?"

We agreed to do so during our stewardship month, which was January. We sent our video team to interview the pastor and show a little of their church's ministry, without telling anything about what we planned to do. Then on the last Sunday of the month, I preached on finances, as was my custom. We showed the video, told our congregation about the offering Mount Signal had sent us and then said, "Now today, we're going to take an offering to give back to them!"

We passed the plates. The total came to just under $29,000.

I can't tell you how much fun it was to give that money to that struggling, little congregation that night. We were *both* blessed. We had a sense that we were doing something Jesus cared about. And our needs continued to be met, even without the $29,000.

Not long before this time, something had gone wrong in my life that money could not fix: a serious disease called myasthenia gravis. I started noticing that I was getting weaker. I'd be walking through an airport to go preach somewhere, and I'd have to switch my briefcase from one hand to the other. My normal pattern was to swim a mile a day, but I started wimping out at about two-thirds of a mile, and then even half a mile. I couldn't seem to get enough rest.

Then while on vacation with my family in Southern California, I began having double vision, and my left eye drooped noticeably. Back home in a week or so, a neurologist diagnosed the problem. I'd never heard the name before; it means "grave weakness." What a shock for a former football player. I also had a tumor in my thymus gland that was pushing the disease along. The surgeons opened up my chest and took the tumor out.

All I knew to do was to take the medication prescribed (something that continues to this day) and call on the name of Jesus for help. I talked openly with the Gardendale church about what was going on and said, "Obviously, I need God to touch my body. I'm going to ask you to anoint me with oil like the Bible says and ask Jesus, the Great Physician, to heal me. It is biblical to do this; you can read about it in James 5."

For years I had believed that if we intentionally pray for God to heal, He will heal at least some of us. Now I was acting on that belief. Yes, God uses doctors and medicine. But Christians should also ask the Lord to go beyond all that humans can do to bring healing. We must avoid the mistake of Asa, king of Judah, who although "his disease was severe, yet even in his disease he did not seek the LORD, but the physicians" (2 Chron. 16:12). While God does not promise His children perfect health in this life, God does command us to "pray for one another so that [we] may be healed" (James 5:16). We should pray for healing and then accept the results, whatever they may be, as God's will.

> ☞ *What the Audience of One is looking for, however, is a lot more than a thing, an act, a performance, a nice tune, a set of clever lyrics, a chord chart.* ☜

I believe it's like salvation: more people will get saved in churches that openly preach the gospel and give invitations than in churches that don't. Likewise, I'm convinced that more people will be healed in churches that pray for them than in those that don't. My myasthenia gravis, while not completely stopped, was controlled enough for me to continue the work of a busy pastor. Meanwhile, one woman was immediately healed of an aggressive type of cancer. God began answering our church's prayers.

God also answered our prayers in another key area. Because our church was growing and running out of land, we asked God to give us just a few more acres for the purpose of expansion. His answer was overwhelming! We were soon able to buy a whole new site: 140 acres on the interstate with high visibility, so we could begin a relocation process. Needless to say, all of us were aware that the manifest presence of God was making a real difference in our congregation.

But the greatest miracle had nothing to do with physical healings, the purchasing of land, or constructing new buildings. It was instead that 250 to 300 people were getting saved every year. Probably a dozen couples came to the altar while living together, gave their hearts to Christ, promptly moved out to separate quarters, then got officially married, moved back under one roof again, and joined our church. Others were able to break the bondage of serious addictions. Every week our baptistery was busy. Church was fun!

We didn't make a big deal out of any of this. We didn't go seeking publicity for what Jesus was doing. We just kept following the true Leader of the church.

We never had any weird manifestations. Nothing got out of control. I've heard people worry that if you don't have a preset program, something will get out of hand or into the devil's hand. Actually, some things *need* to get out of our hands and into God's hand. He really can take care of us. As long as our eyes are fixed on Him, we don't need to be afraid.

No Other Name

I'm such a believer in being Savior-focused that I try to say the actual name *Jesus* as often as possible. I recognize that *God* and *Lord* and *Christ* are all good biblical terms. But there's something especially powerful about the name *Jesus*. People in our culture who are faintly religious can easily nod their heads toward God. Pollsters report that as high as 90 percent of Americans say they believe in God. But they need to be brought to the junction that Pontius Pilate eventually ran into: "Then what shall I do with Jesus?" (Matt. 27:22).

The name *Jesus* literally means "Jehovah is salvation." Peter told a hostile panel of religious leaders, "There is salvation is no one else; for there is no other name under heaven that has been given among men by which we must be saved" (Acts 4:12). They weren't thrilled to hear that, just as some people aren't real happy with this message today. Their displeasure, however, does not change the facts of the uniqueness of Jesus Christ.

Perhaps my greatest human hero and role model, Charles Haddon Spurgeon told young preachers in training:

> Let your sermons be full of Christ, from beginning to
> end crammed full of the Gospel. As for myself, brethren,

I cannot preach anything else but Christ and His cross,
for I know nothing else, and long ago, like the apostle Paul,
I determined not to know anything else save Jesus Christ
and Him crucified [a reference to 1 Cor. 2:2]. . . . Preach Jesus
Christ, brethren, always and everywhere; and every time
you preach be sure to have much of Jesus Christ in your
sermon. . . . We preach Jesus Christ to those who want Him,
and we also preach Him to those who do not want Him, and
we keep on preaching Christ until we make them feel that
they do want Him, and cannot do without Him.[6]

No wonder six thousand people came to London's Metropolitan
Tabernacle every Sunday to hear Spurgeon preach! The man didn't
even have a microphone; such things had
not yet been invented in the late 1800s. Yet
the crowds came and sat quietly to catch
his every word. People on the third level
of the tabernacle had to stand throughout
the service.

> *It will be a watershed day when any church realizes that Jesus Himself is the only person in "the audience." The rest of us are worshippers.*

Thousands were saved. Orphanages
were begun and a Bible college as well.
Important dignitaries from Parliament
came and sat in the same place as the poor
and illiterate. The Communists wrote
at one point that their revolution had failed to take hold in England
because Spurgeon reached the masses of poor people before they could
reach them with the teachings of socialism.

When this Prince of Preachers died in 1892, the number of people
who lined the streets of London to watch his horse-drawn cortege pass
by was estimated at 350,000.

All because a preacher and a church specialized in lifting up Jesus.

The apostle Paul wrote, "For to me, to live is Christ" (Phil. 1:21).
Might we also extend his thought in this vein: To worship is Christ. To
do church is Christ. It all revolves around Him.

When people leave our churches today, we have failed if they say to
one another on the way to their cars, "Wow, what a sermon!"

"Wow, what a choir!"

"What a preacher!"

"What a classy building!"

"Wow, did you see that cool thing they projected on the big screen?"

But if they leave saying, "Hallelujah, what a Savior!" we will have succeeded. We will have steered their attention to the only thing—actually, the only One—worth remembering.

It will be a watershed day when any church realizes that Jesus Himself is the only person in "the audience." The rest of us are worshippers. We are not ticket holders attending a performance. We are participants actively revering and worshipping Him. *That* is biblical worship!

A worship service without the awareness of Jesus' obvious presence is a waste of time. He is the One who deserves all the spotlight. He is the focus for every part of genuine worship.

CHAPTER 4

Welcoming God's Glory

Once upon a time God's manifest presence came to earth on a daily basis. I'm not spinning some fairy tale here; it actually happened. Every twenty-four hours the folks in Eden got a Visitor. He came "walking in the garden in the cool of the day" (Gen. 3:8) to talk with them, give them instructions on how to manage the estate, and bless them. It must have been wonderful.

And then, as you know, Adam and Eve messed everything up. They disobeyed the word of their God, sin entered the world like an insidious virus, the couple got kicked out of the garden, and paradise was lost. The intimacy between God and His created beings suffered a devastating hit.

As time went on, the people of Israel seemed prone to commit vile acts that angered the Lord. The most offensive was idolatry, which is any time people devise their own methods of worshipping instead of sticking to God's way. The Israelites worshipped other gods besides Jehovah, a practice strictly forbidden by the first of the Ten Commandments (Exod. 20:1–3). Whether it was the Egyptian calf-idol of Mnevis that Aaron built (Exod. 32:4), the shrine of Solomon for the Moabite idol Chemosh (1 Kings 11:7), the altars erected to the Canaanite fertility gods of Baal and Asherah by wicked kings such as Ahab (1 Kings 16:32–33), or the detestable Ammonite idol of Molech, which demanded that worshippers toss their children into a burning fire as living sacrifices (2 Kings 23:10), the Israelites struggled with pagan idolatry.

You might think God would respond, "That's it. I'm not talking to you anymore. You people are disgusting. Just forget the whole covenant thing. I want nothing to do with you. You're never going to hear My voice or sense My presence again. I'll start over with a new race of people on Jupiter or Saturn. Meanwhile, Earth goes in the trash can like a paperwad."

That's not what happened.

Amazingly, despite the Israelites' spiritual infidelity (which is exactly what idolatry is), whenever they returned to the Lord in sincere, heartfelt repentance, obedience, and worship, He graciously forgave them. He would "revive" them, repairing their spiritual brokenness, renewing and replenishing their strength and fervor. He hadn't written them off after all.

That is why the psalmist pled, "Will You not Yourself *revive* us again, that Your people may rejoice in You?" (Ps. 85:6). The word translated "revive" is the Hebrew *chayah*, which means "to live" or "to make alive." It can also be translated "to quicken" or "to bring back to life."

Chayah also appears in the writing of the prophet Hosea, who preached to God's people in the northern tribes of Israel. He said, "Come, let us return to the LORD for He has torn us, but He will heal us; He has wounded us, but He will bandage us. He will *revive* us after two days; He will raise us up on the third day, that we may live before Him" (Hos. 6:1–2). This man knew God would spiritually resurrect His wayward people if they would only repent of their sins and return to Him in humility and spiritual brokenness.

Likewise, the Hebrew prophet Habakkuk, who ministered to God's people in Judah, used the word *chayah* when he prayed for God to send spiritual awakening. "Lord, I have heard the report about You and I fear. O LORD, *revive* Your work in the midst of the years, in the midst of the years make it known; in wrath remember mercy" (Hab. 3:2). Habakkuk possessed a healthy fear (reverence) for the Lord. He wanted God to come down and interrupt the day-to-day activities of the people ("in the midst of the years") and send them the refreshing vitality of revival.

A second important Hebrew word that connects with revival and awakening is *chadash*. After King David had been confronted by the prophet Nathan about his adultery, David confessed and repented. One part of his prayer says, "Create in me a clean heart, O God, and *renew* a steadfast spirit within me" (Ps. 51:10). The word "renew" is *chadash*; it means to "repair" or "make new." David's life was broken. He needed the Lord to repair his wounded soul. His broken heart needed mending. God forgave David and blessed him in the years following. He and Bathsheba actually had a subsequent son named Solomon, who succeeded David as king of Israel.

David used this word again in Psalm 103:5 to indicate that the Lord is the one "who satisfies [our] years with good things, so that [our] youth is *renewed* like the eagle."

A third word from Hebrew is *chalap*. Like *chadash*, it means "to renew." *Chalap* appears in the well-known verse in Isaiah: "Yet those who wait for the LORD will *gain new [chalap]* strength; they will mount up with wings like eagles, they will run and not get tired, they will walk and not become weary" (Isa. 40:31). This concept of renewing the spiritual strength of God's people is at the heart of revival and spiritual awakening.

Isaiah stressed that this blessing was reserved exclusively for those of God's people who were willing to "wait for/upon" Him. In order to experience it, they would have to submit humbly to Him, diligently seeking Him and His will by means of genuine worship and absolute obedience.

> ☞ *The God of the Old Testament put up with a lot from His wayward people.* ☜

When God's sinful people were willing to repent and return to Him, offering acceptable worship and praise, the Lord would "make alive, repair, and renew" His people by coming upon them in awesome displays of His glory. No wonder the psalmist referred to the Lord as the one "enthroned upon the praises of Israel" (Ps. 22:3). These fresh visitations of God brought spiritual restoration to individual worshippers as well as the entire nation of Israel.

People today commonly accuse the God of the Old Testament of being harsh, remote, austere, and unfriendly. They say they like the Jesus of the New Testament much better because He's "nicer" and "more loving." Such a simplistic conclusion isn't valid at all. The God of the Old Testament put up with a lot from His wayward people. He reached out eagerly to *chayah, chadash,* and *chalap* His people whenever they turned back to His open arms.

Corporate Visitations of God's Glory

When God showed up, God's people prospered, and enemies backed away. God's visitation, in fact, altered the course of Israel's history. Here are three examples:

IN MOSES' TIME

Moses was born during the period of cruel slavery in Egypt. God eventually called him to lead the people to the promised land of Canaan. The Lord delivered them with a series of miraculous plagues upon Pharaoh and the Egyptians. God even parted the Red Sea and allowed the Israelites to pass through it on dry land. When the Egyptians followed after them, the Lord closed the waters and destroyed their armies.

These dramatic actions of God were further reinforced when the people arrived at Mount Sinai. There Moses went up to meet with God and to receive the Ten Commandments. He was gone forty days, but the people were not left out of the interaction. Down on the plain they watched in awe as "the cloud covered the mountain. The glory of the LORD rested on Mount Sinai, and the cloud covered it for six days; and on the seventh day He called to Moses from the midst of the cloud. And to the eyes of the sons of Israel the appearance of the glory of the LORD was like a consuming fire on the mountain top" (Exod. 24:15–17).

This incredible sight held them faithful to the Lord for a while. Later on, however, they strayed terribly from the worship of God. They lobbied Aaron for an idol they could see with their natural eyes, which resulted in the golden calf. A horrible confrontation erupted when Moses came back down from his meeting with God. Swift judgment was dealt out.

When the dust had settled, it was time to break camp and move onward toward Canaan once again. At this moment the Lord said something that sent chills down Moses' spine. "Go up from here, you and the people whom you have brought up from the land of Egypt. . . . [But] I will not go up in your midst, because you are an obstinate people, and I might destroy you on the way" (Exod. 33:1, 3).

Oh no! Moses instantly knew this would be a recipe for disaster. To strike out on the desert trail without the Lord's presence among them—no way! "When the people heard this sad word, they went into mourning" (v. 4). They were not about to take this risk. Everything came to a screeching halt. Moses interceded with the Lord so passionately that He relented and agreed that His presence would indeed continue to go with them. He also promised to give them rest (see v. 14).

How many of us today are that sensitive to the presence of God? Do we panic at the thought of taking on a project or heading into a church service without His closeness? Do we think we're smart enough to run religious rituals and programs on our own? If so, we are in fact less intelligent than the Israelites in the desert, who discovered they needed God.

A few chapters later, the book of Exodus tells about the completion of the tabernacle. It goes into huge detail about scarlet curtains and acacia crossbars and golden loops and silver hooks. We read pages and pages of specifications. It sounds as complicated as any church building program you've ever endured. But when everything was assembled and all the punch lists had been checked off, what happened? Something occurred that all the carpenters and metalworkers and seamstresses could never have engineered. "Then the cloud covered the tent of meeting, and the glory of the LORD filled the tabernacle. Moses was not able to enter the tent of meeting because the cloud had settled on it, and the glory of the LORD filled the tabernacle" (Exod. 40:34–35). God was once again dwelling among His people!

That, in fact, would not be a one-time novelty. Later on, when Aaron and his sons were set apart as priests, "Moses and Aaron went into the tent of meeting. When they came out and blessed the people, the glory of the LORD appeared to all the people. Then fire came out from before the LORD and consumed the burnt offering and the portions of fat on the altar; and when all the people saw it, they shouted and fell on their faces" (Lev. 9:23–24). Once again God was up-close and personal. An overwhelming grandeur accompanied such demonstrations of the glory of God coming down from heaven.

I am not calling for exact replications of what happened there in the desert. But I can't help praying, "O God, may our houses of worship today be ever marked by Your supernatural presence. Come and visit us once again."

I refuse to give in to the despair that characterized Israel in the days of Eli the priest, when corruption had invaded the clergy, and the Philistines were mauling the armies of Israel. It got so bad one day that a newborn baby boy was given the name "Ichabod," which means "no glory." His mother, dying in the throes of a difficult childbirth, said as she breathed her last, "The glory has departed from Israel, for the ark of God was taken" (1 Sam. 4:22).

> ☙ *For every denomination, church, and individual Christian today who seems to have "Ichabod" stamped across their forehead, I believe God has not given up.* ☙

But even then God was already preparing young Samuel to lead the nation back to God. For every denomination, church, and individual Christian today who seems to have "Ichabod" stamped across their forehead, I believe God has not given up. He stands waiting and ready to pour out His blessing in fresh ways if we will turn our faces in His direction.

In Solomon's Time

The tabernacle was eventually replaced by a more permanent place of worship in Jerusalem known as the temple. It was an even more complicated architectural wonder. The Bible again gives lengthy descriptions of all the materials that went into its construction over a seven-year period.

When the temple was finally ready, a great dedication ceremony was planned. The pageantry was elaborate.

> The priests came forth from the holy place (for all the priests who were present had sanctified themselves, without regard to divisions), and all the Levitical singers, Asaph, Heman, Jeduthun, and their sons and kinsmen, clothed in fine linen, with cymbals, harps and lyres, standing east of the altar, and with them one hundred and twenty priests blowing trumpets in unison when the trumpeters and the singers were to make themselves heard with one voice to praise and to glorify the LORD. (2 Chron. 5:11–13a)

But then something unusual happened that was not on the printed program.

> When they lifted up their voice accompanied by trumpets and cymbals and instruments of music, and when they praised the LORD saying, "He indeed is good for His lovingkindness is everlasting," then the house, the house of the LORD, was filled with a cloud, so that the priests could not stand to minister because of the cloud, for *the glory of the LORD filled the house of God.* (vv. 13b–14)

What an awesome experience! Human beings lifted their praise to God, and soon the Lord swept in with an overpowering cloud of His glory. In fact, this phenomenon was repeated before long. King Solomon went on to pray a fervent prayer dedicating the temple to the Lord. When he finished, God answered his prayer with another spectacular display of His glory.

> Now when Solomon had finished praying, fire came down from heaven and consumed the burnt offering and the sacrifices, and *the glory of the LORD filled the house.* The priests could not enter into the house of the LORD because *the glory of the LORD filled the LORD's house.* All the sons of Israel, seeing the fire come down and *the glory of the LORD upon the house,* bowed down on the pavement with their faces to the ground, and they worshiped and gave praise to the LORD, saying, "Truly He is good, truly His lovingkindness is everlasting." (2 Chron. 7:1–3)

From that day on, Israel viewed that temple as the place where the glory of God was supposed to dwell. It was a place of magnificence, splendor, and wonder.

IN ELIJAH'S TIME

Sometimes God's corporate demonstrations of His presence even moved outside the established place of worship. Who can forget what happened when the prophet Elijah confronted the wicked King Ahab and his false prophets on Mount Carmel? More than three years of drought had afflicted the land in payment for its idolatry. Finally, a showdown was arranged.

Elijah allowed the prophets of Baal to go first. They prepared their sacrifice, prayed, shouted, and danced for hours in a frenzied effort to get Baal's attention. But "there was no voice, no one answered, and no one paid attention" (1 Kings 18:29).

Elijah mocked the false prophets, then called the people of God to himself. They repaired the altar to Jehovah and prepared their sacrifice. Elijah had them soak the sacrifice and the altar with water so everyone would know for certain that the coming fire was from God, not humans. Elijah prayed to the Lord, "O LORD, the God of Abraham, Isaac and Israel, today let it be known that You are God in Israel and that I am Your servant and I have done all these things at Your word. Answer me, O LORD, answer me, that this people may know that You, O LORD, are God, and that You have turned their heart back again" (vv. 36b–37).

What happened next was truly amazing. "Then *the fire of the LORD fell* and consumed the burnt offering and the wood and the stones and the dust, and licked up the water that was in the trench. When all the people saw it, they fell on their faces; and they said, 'The LORD, He is God; the LORD, He is God!'" (vv. 18:38–39). Right there on a mountainside, the fire of God's glory devoured the sacrifice, the altar, the dirt all around, and it even evaporated the water in the trench surrounding the altar.

Personal Visitations of God's Glory

But the presence of God in the Old Testament was not reserved solely for large crowds. Individual men and women felt His touch as well. Wherever God sovereignly and graciously meets with a person, that place becomes a hallowed spot. It matters not if it is a beautiful cathedral or a simple setting in nature. For example:

JACOB

Jacob was a deceiver, at least until God got hold of him. He defrauded his twin brother, Esau, of both his birthright and the blessing that was due him since he was the elder of the two boys. This was not a negligible amount of money; Isaac, their father, was a rich man thanks to the inheritance he had received from their grandfather Abraham. Also, Isaac had been successful in his farming business, experiencing an amazing hundredfold harvest on his planting one year (see Gen. 26:12).

Esau was understandably furious at his younger brother's trickery. Jacob quickly hit the road for Paddan-aram to live with his uncle, Laban. On his way Jacob stopped to camp overnight. He was not expecting anything unusual; he just needed a place to sleep until the sun came up again.

But God had something special in mind. After Jacob settled down for the nighttime hours, "he had a dream, and behold, a ladder was set on the earth with its top reaching to heaven; and behold, the angels of God were ascending and descending on it" (Gen. 28:12). In that dream the Lord appeared to Jacob and promised to bless and protect him while he was in Paddan-aram. He also promised to bring him back to his father's house. More than that, he promised to give all of that land (the promised land) to Jacob's descendants as a permanent possession.

What a shock. When Jacob woke up, he exclaimed, "Surely the LORD is in this place, and I did not know it. . . . How awesome is this place! This is none other than the house of God, and this is the gate of heaven" (Gen. 28:16–17). He named that spot Bethel, which is a Hebrew word meaning "house of God."

C. S. Lewis, the brilliant British professor and author, wrote in 1940 about how it feels to discover that God is near. He raised three hypothetical situations:

> Suppose you were told that there was a tiger in the next room: you would know that you were in danger and would probably feel fear. But if you were told "There is a ghost in the next room," and believed it, you would feel, indeed, what is often called fear, but of a different kind. . . . It is "uncanny" rather than dangerous, and the special kind of fear it excites may be called Dread. . . . Now suppose that you were told simply "There is a mighty spirit in the room," and believed it. . . . You would feel wonder and a certain shrinking—a sense of inadequacy to cope with such a visitant and of prostration before it—an emotion which might be expressed in Shakespeare's words "Under it my genius is rebuked." This feeling may be described as awe.[7]

That's how Jacob felt that morning. He wasn't so much afraid or in dread as he was awestruck. *God was right here, alongside my sleeping bag! I can't believe it!*

I long for that reaction to occur across our churches today. People come in half asleep on Sunday morning, expecting to do the typical routine: they'll skim through the bulletin, sing some songs, bow their heads for prayer, put a dollar in the offering, listen to the sermon, wave hello to their friends in the lobby afterward, then head for the restaurant . . . but what if the Lord showed up? What if they got more than they bargained for? What if their little religious ritual was interrupted by the manifest presence of God? They'd go out saying, "Wow, I thought I was just stopping by church for another service, but it turned out the Lord was there! This was the gate that leads to heaven because people can find out about Jesus there!"

That would raise the church routine to a whole new level.

This incident at the roadside camp was not Jacob's only encounter with the presence of God. After he had worked for his uncle, Laban, for twenty years, married his two daughters, and gotten several tastes of the tricky medicine he had dished out to Esau, he decided at last to head back home. It wasn't long before he realized he was facing serious trouble again. His angry brother was apparently coming to avenge himself of the damages Jacob had caused him long ago. Esau had an army of four hundred men ready to help him kill his deceitful brother.

> ☙ *People come in half asleep on Sunday morning, expecting to do the typical routine . . . but what if the Lord showed up? What if they got more than they bargained for?* ☙

Jacob feared for the sake of his family and himself. That night he had an encounter that would alter his life forever. He wrestled with a mysterious Man who showed up out of nowhere. Jacob struggled for some time until the Man touched and dislocated the socket of his thigh. He broke Jacob like a trainer breaks a wild horse. He emptied Jacob of all his self-reliance. He tamed him.

The Man then made Jacob tell Him his name. That was the equivalent of making Jacob say, "Uncle—I give up." All his life Jacob had used his street smarts to advance himself by deception and manipulation. But none of that could help him now. He finally surrendered and let the Lord take control. God not only broke Jacob of his self-reliance, but He also bridled him for future service.

The Man then changed Jacob's name to "Israel," which means, "He who struggles with God." I concur with the many theologians who believe this "Man" was none other than the Lord Jesus Christ manifesting Himself in a preincarnate appearance. Jacob wrestled with the Lord Jesus, Jesus won, and Jacob was blessed!

From then on, Jacob walked with a limp, but every painful step reminded him of God's goodness. God also took care of his brother's anger. When Esau finally arrived, he and Jacob fell into each other's arms, wept, and forgave each other. The Bible says, "Jacob named the place Peniel, for he said, 'I have seen God face to face, yet my life has been preserved'" (Gen. 32:30). When God revealed Himself in glory to Jacob, He turned his problem into a blessing.

MOSES

As we noted earlier, Moses was up-close and personal with God on Mount Sinai as the leader of the Hebrew nation, but that was not the first time he had encountered God. Months before, when he was a nobody tending sheep in an isolated desert, he saw a bush on fire, but it was not being consumed. He decided to check it out. The Bible says, "When the LORD saw that he turned aside to look, God called to him from the midst of the bush and said, 'Moses, Moses!' And he said, 'Here I am.' Then He said, 'Do not come near here; remove your sandals from your feet, for the place on which you are standing is holy ground'" (Exod. 3:4–5).

Moses removed his sandals out of reverence for the Lord and received His call to be Israel's deliverer. Forty years earlier he had thought he was ready to deliver the Israelites from their slavery in Egypt. But the Lord used the forty years he tended sheep on the back side of the Midian desert to teach him to rely totally upon His power to accomplish His will. Moses had been highly educated in Egypt, but he needed one more degree, his "BN" degree, which stands for "be nothing." Now when he looked into that burning bush and heard that heavenly voice, Moses knew he was catching a glimpse of the glory of God.

On another occasion, after Moses had received the Ten
Commandments and had solved the golden-calf crisis, he made a bold
request of the Lord: "I pray You, show me Your glory!" (Exod. 33:18).
He had enjoyed a slight taste of God's glory at the burning bush. He
had been in the Lord's presence on Mount Sinai. Yet Moses wanted
more!

That's the way it works. The more the Lord reveals Himself to a
person, the more that person wants to know Him in a richer, fuller
way.

Moses was actually asking to see the face of God Himself. For his
own good, God denied his request. He answered:

> "I Myself will make all My goodness pass before you, and
> will proclaim the name of the LORD before you; and I will be
> gracious to whom I will be gracious, and will show compas-
> sion on whom I will show compassion." But He said, "You
> cannot see My face, for no man can see Me and live!"
>
> Then the LORD said, "Behold, there is a place by Me, and
> you shall stand there on the rock; and it will come about,
> while My glory is passing by, that I will put you in the cleft of
> the rock and cover you with My hand until I have passed by.
> Then I will take My hand away and you shall see My back,
> but My face shall not be seen." (Exod. 33:19–23)

Soon afterward when Moses returned to the top of Mount Sinai to
receive the second copy of the Ten Commandments, the Lord fulfilled
His promise to him.

> The Lord descended in the cloud and stood there with
> him as he called upon the name of the LORD. Then the LORD
> passed by in front of him and proclaimed, "The LORD, the
> LORD God, compassionate and gracious, slow to anger, and
> abounding in lovingkindness and truth; who keeps loving-
> kindness for thousands, who forgives iniquity, transgression
> and sin; yet He will by no means leave the guilty unpunished,
> visiting the iniquity of fathers on the children and on the
> grandchildren to the third and fourth generations." Moses
> made haste to bow low toward the earth and worship.
> (Exod. 34:5–8)

When Moses returned to the bottom of the mountain and met his brother, Aaron, and the other Israelites, they were shocked at his appearance. His face was literally radiating the glory of God. It was so overwhelming that Moses was forced to cover his face with a veil when he was in the presence of his fellow Israelites. When he would appear before the Lord, Moses would remove the veil to bask fully in His glory once again.

This man, who was not perfect by any means, nevertheless had multiple encounters with the presence of God. He yearned to know God in all His fullness. And he was not disappointed.

ISAIAH

Many years later Isaiah had the privilege to live in Judah during the reign of a good king named Uzziah. He led the nation for a long time—fifty years. When he finally died, Isaiah and his countrymen mourned. During this period God revealed Himself dramatically to Isaiah, as recorded in chapter 6 of his book.

It was almost as if God wanted him to know that although Judah's throne was temporarily empty, heaven's throne was eternally occupied.

> *It is high time for the glory of God to fill the house of God again.*

Isaiah saw the Lord in His glory, surrounded by angels (seraphim) who cried out in antiphonal fashion, "Holy, holy, holy, is the LORD of hosts, the whole earth is full of *His glory*" (v. 3). Isaiah gasped, falling on his face in humble, contrite repentance. He confessed that he was a sinful man and that the people who lived around him were wicked as well. God cleansed him and extended a call to become His prophet. When God asked, "Whom shall I send?" Isaiah quickly responded, "Here am I. Send me!" (v. 8).

This appearance of God's glory began a series of revelations that continued throughout Isaiah's life and ministry. In fact, God revealed more messianic prophecies to Isaiah than to any other Old Testament prophet. Isaiah prophesied Jesus' virgin birth (Isa. 7:14). He also spoke of Jesus' deity, calling Him the "Wonderful Counselor, Mighty God, Eternal Father, Prince of Peace" (Isa. 9:6). Isaiah prophesied that Jesus would rule one day as the greatest of all kings (Isa. 9:7). He went on to prophesy concerning Jesus' atoning sacrificial death for the sins of humanity (Isa. 53:1–9). Isaiah even pronounced that after He died, the Messiah (Jesus) would once again "see His offspring . . . [and] prolong His days," a reference to Jesus' resurrection (Isa. 53:10).

God's glory was revealed to Isaiah early in his life. As his life progressed, Isaiah grew to understand that the coming Messiah would be the ultimate revelation of God's glory.

THEN AND NOW

God still desires to reveal His glory to His people, both corporately and individually. Throughout the Old Testament, God was faithful to come down into the midst of His people in a corporate setting, visiting them in power and glory. When they returned to Him, repented of their sin, and sought Him with all their hearts by means of fasting, weeping, and contrite, humble prayer, God blessed them once again with His manifest presence. Likewise, God radically altered the destinies of individuals who personally encountered His glory.

During one of Judah's darkest hours, the prophet Habakkuk nevertheless predicted that "the earth will be filled with the knowledge of the glory of the LORD, as the waters cover the sea" (Hab. 2:14). Notice, it does *not* say "shall be filled with the knowledge of the Lord." That would be wonderful enough, for people all over the world to know (intellectually) about God. But the prophet said they will also know about the *glory* of the Lord. They will have a palpable sense of His grandeur, His power, His majesty.

Don't you think that the God who worked in Old Testament times would be willing to do the same thing for Christians today? He is still God, and He still wants to bless His children with His presence and power. It is high time for the glory of God to fill the house of God again. We need His glory in our churches and in our individual lives. May Moses' passionate prayer be on the hearts and lips of us all, "Lord, show me Your glory."

CHAPTER 5

A Church with Little but God

When I was a kid, I loved to go to the movies. I vividly remember the smell of hot popcorn at the old Frances Theater on East Court Avenue in my hometown. Back then movies were fairly wholesome. My, how things have changed.

Nowadays Hollywood rarely produces a movie I really enjoy. But occasionally they still turn out a winner like *Glory Road*. It's based on the true story of the Texas Western University Miners, a men's basketball team that rose out of nowhere in the fall of 1965 and the spring of 1966 to win the NCAA championship. They actually upset the heavily favored University of Kentucky Wildcats, coached by the legendary Adolph Rupp.

The Miners' head coach, Don Haskins, had no coaching experience at the college level before coming to Texas Western. He had coached only a girls' high school basketball team. He was, however, a man ahead of his time. Along with recruiting locally, he decided to scour several of the largest cities in the United States for players. Consequently, he assembled a team loaded with talent—many of them African-Americans. Haskins didn't have a problem with that, but several teams that competed against Texas Western in the mid-1960s did.

The movie gives a thrilling portrayal of how Coach Haskins and his players overcame racial differences to become a successful team. Their Cinderella season was more than exciting; it was inspirational. The college didn't have great facilities or a lot of money. In the beginning few people believed in the team. Even after an almost perfect regular season, hardly anyone gave them a chance to beat Kentucky. They shocked the entire nation against monumental odds.

That little team from west Texas was, in some ways, like the Christians of the first century. They too were a hodgepodge of nobodies. They consisted of fishermen, tax collectors, political zealots, and other nondescript people. The apostle Paul pointed out in his first letter to the church at Corinth:

> For consider your calling, brethren, that there were not
> many wise according to the flesh, not many mighty, not many
> noble; but God has chosen the foolish things of the world to
> shame the wise, and God has chosen the weak things of the
> world to shame the things which are strong, and the base
> things of the world and the despised God has chosen, the
> things that are not, so that He may nullify the things that are,
> so that no man may boast before God. (1 Cor. 1:26–29)

Christian congregations of that day consisted primarily of people who were not "wise according to the flesh." Apparently the Corinthian church didn't have many PhDs. There were also "not many mighty, not many noble." That is, most of the political and societal movers and shakers had not joined their ranks. Instead, they were, for the most part, made up of people who were "weak," "base" (i.e., lowly), and even "despised" by the world.

But despite their ordinariness, they were valiant, victorious soldiers of Jesus. Even the non-Christians of their day acknowledged their miraculous impact on the culture by admitting that they had "turned the world upside down" for Christ (Acts 17:6 KJV).

They had little but God, yet they changed their world. Today we Christians have vast resources, but the world seems to be changing us. Does anyone truly believe that we are making the impact for Christ in this world that we should? Considering the fact that we have Christian colleges, seminaries, bookstores, television and radio ministries, Web sites, elaborate facilities, vast amounts of wealth, and in many areas, a church building on every corner of town, one has to wonder where the power is that we read about in the book of Acts.

I realize that "it takes no size to criticize." In no way do I desire to pass judgment or condemnation on any individual, church, or denomination. I simply have yearned my entire Christian life to experience a fresh touch from heaven, a genuine and sustained movement of God's Spirit among His people.

I guess if I didn't read about that type of thing happening in the Bible, I might be content with status quo Christianity. But the pages of the New Testament have ruined me in that regard. What happened back then tells me that there has to be more to the Christian life and to the ministry of a local church than most of us are experiencing.

> ☙ *The early Christians had little but God, yet they changed their world. Today we Christians have vast resources, but the world seems to be changing us.* ☙

They didn't have nice carpet. They didn't have hand-polished pews. They didn't have recessed lighting. In fact, they often didn't even have a roof. They obviously didn't have electronic sound equipment or the electricity to run it. What would happen at your church or mine if on some Sunday morning the local power utility was down? Could we even have church? The early Christians could.

Arthur Fretheim, an Evangelical Covenant pastor who during his career planted six new churches in Minnesota, New Mexico, and Illinois (the last one when he was sixty-five years old), said to fellow pastors, "One thing you learn quickly in church planting is this: All you've really got to offer people is Jesus. You don't have a great choir in the beginning days; you don't have a youth group; you usually don't even have a nice building. The only 'draw' you've got is the Savior. And guess what—that's enough."

As I look at the church of the first century, here is what stands out to me:

A Praying Church

Anyone who studies the book of Acts will be taken back by the vitality of the prayer lives of those early believers. They knew how to spend time with the Lord on their knees in praise, thanksgiving, confession, petition, intercession, and spiritual warfare. They had asked the Lord Jesus to teach them to pray (Luke 11:1). Their request was not merely that He would teach them *how* to pray but also that He would teach them to make prayer a priority. Indeed, Jesus answered their request by teaching them both the priority and the pattern of prayer. They marveled as He modeled a fervent prayer life during His earthly ministry. They understood that the effectiveness of His ministry was in some way linked to the time He spent alone with His Father in prayer.

THE PRAYER MEETING THAT CHANGED THE WORLD

It's not surprising, then, that the early church was literally birthed in a prayer meeting. Just before Jesus ascended back to heaven from the top of the Mount of Olives, He gave His followers these instructions: "And behold, I am sending forth the promise of my Father upon you; but you are to stay in the city until you are clothed with power from on high" (Luke 24:49). Jesus realized that the assignment He was giving them to evangelize the entire world was beyond their human abilities. He knew they needed the power of the Holy Spirit, whom He was about to send to them.

After He was gone, those early Christians left that mountaintop and "returned to Jerusalem with great joy, and were continually in the temple praising God" (Luke 24:52–53). When they arrived back at Jerusalem, "they went up to the upper room where they were staying; that is, Peter and John and James and Andrew, Philip and Thomas, Bartholomew and Matthew, James the son of Alphaeus, and Simon the Zealot, and Judas the son of James. These all with one mind were continually devoting themselves to prayer, along with the women, and Mary the mother of Jesus, and with His brothers" (Acts 1:13–14).

That prayer meeting had several characteristics.

First, it was *united*. Each person was of "one mind" with the others. They were experiencing the same kind of harmony the psalmist called both "good" and "pleasant" (Ps. 133:1). Collectively, they were obeying Jesus' commandment to love one another even as He had loved them (see John 13:34–35).

Second, that prayer meeting was *protracted*. It didn't stop after forty-five minutes. They were "continually" praying. The time between Jesus' ascension and the day of Pentecost was ten days, and they prayed that entire time! No wonder God blessed them with His power.

Third, that prayer meeting was *focused*. They were in that upper room for one purpose—to pray and to wait on the Lord. Although they paused momentarily to choose a replacement for Judas among the twelve apostles (see Acts 1:14–26), they "were continually devoting themselves to prayer" (v. 14).

Is there any wonder why God blessed Peter's sermon on the day of Pentecost with such an amazing harvest of souls? They prayed for ten days, the Holy Spirit fell, and soon a large crowd was hearing "the mighty deeds of God" (Acts 2:11). Then Peter preached a sermon that lasted perhaps just thirty minutes, *and three thousand people were saved!*

Today we try to reverse that order. We pray for thirty minutes, preach for ten days, and wonder why so few respond. It isn't God's fault or the gospel's fault. We fall short of the early church's results because we fail to "pray the price."

PRAYING FOR BOLDNESS

Some time later Peter and John were making their way to the Jerusalem temple for a time of (what else?) prayer. On their way they met a beggar who requested money. Peter replied that while he didn't possess either silver or gold, he did have something much better. He took the cripple by the hand and commanded him to rise up and walk.

The man not only walked, but he also started leaping as he worshipped. A crowd quickly gathered, Peter preached, and many believed in Jesus. But the Jewish priests were filled with anger and jealousy. They had the apostles arrested and brought before the Jewish high council. They commanded the apostles not to preach anymore in the name of Jesus.

The disciples told them that was impossible. They could not stop speaking about all they had experienced as followers of Christ.

When they left the council, they gathered for prayer. They asked God not for protection but instead for boldness to continue preaching and ministering to the crowds in Jesus' name. God heard their prayer and answered accordingly. The Bible says, "And when they had prayed, the place where they had gathered together was shaken, and they were all filled with the Holy Spirit and began to speak the word of God with boldness" (Acts 4:31).

They had requested boldness, and that is exactly what they received. But they also received something they hadn't asked for—a fresh filling of the Holy Spirit. The peace, comfort, and other blessings that resulted are noted in the verses immediately following.

> And the congregation of those who believed were of one heart and soul; and not one of them claimed that anything belonging to him was his own, but all things were common property to them. And with great power the apostles were giving testimony to the resurrection of the Lord Jesus, and abundant grace was upon them all. (Acts 4:32–33)

Doesn't it stand to reason that the same God who blessed those early praying Christians will do the same for us if we too devote ourselves to prayer? I will talk more about how to make a church a house of prayer in chapter 12. For now, let me simply encourage every reader to make an honest assessment of your personal prayer life. Do the same regarding the prayer ministry at your local church. Do you think the Lord is pleased?

That early church had little that human eyes could see, but they actually had much because they had prayer.

A Witnessing Church

Not only did those early believers talk *to* God, but they also talked *about* Him to others. Their strategy was simple: tell everybody about Jesus everywhere you go! While not all of them were called to fill the official office of an evangelist (see Eph. 4:11), all of them engaged in evangelism. Each believer brought the gospel of Christ to lost people with the intent of leading them to repent of their sins and put their faith in Jesus as Lord and Savior.

It should be noted that witnessing to lost people was one of the primary reasons Jesus gave them the Holy Spirit in the first place. The last recorded words from Jesus, just before He ascended to heaven, were, "But you will receive power when the Holy Spirit has come upon you; *and you shall be My witnesses* both in Jerusalem, and in all Judea and Samaria, and even to the remotest part of the earth" (Acts 1:8). The Holy Spirit would not only enable them to live Christlike lives, but He would also empower them to win people to Christ.

A LAYMAN NAMED PHILIP

In Acts 8, Philip, a layman who had been named one of the first deacons, was leading a great movement of God among the Samaritans. Philip was preaching Christ to them, casting out evil spirits, and healing the sick. The Bible describes the reaction to his ministry by saying, "There was much rejoicing in that city" (Acts 8:8).

Then, at the height of that spiritual mountaintop, something interesting happened. God told Philip to go down a desert road that led to the remote district of Gaza. It made no sense. This would be like leaving a great revival in Los Angeles to go spend time in southern Utah. However, Philip obeyed.

When he arrived at the place to which God instructed him to go, he came upon a court official of the queen of Ethiopia riding in a chariot. That man had been to Jerusalem to worship the God of the Jews. Now he was returning home. As he traveled along that desert road, he read a text from the book of Isaiah that told about the coming Messiah. He had no idea what the text meant.

At that exact time Philip ran alongside the chariot and engaged him in conversation. When the official asked him to explain what Isaiah had written, "Philip opened his mouth, and beginning from this Scripture he preached Jesus to him" (Acts 8:35).

> *Philip didn't just run alongside the Ethiopian's chariot setting a good example or living a good life. Rather, he "opened his mouth" and shared Christ.*

That one verse describes the essence of effective personal witnessing. First, witnessing must be *verbal*. Philip didn't just run alongside the chariot setting a good example or living a good life. Rather, he "opened his mouth" and shared Christ! We must do the same if we are going to be soul winners.

Second, his witnessing was *scriptural*. Philip shared "from [the] Scripture." Indeed, God's Word, not our opinion, is a powerful two-edged sword that cuts to an individual's heart and brings about conviction of sin (see Heb. 4:12).

Finally, Philip's witnessing was *Christ-centered*. "He preached *Jesus* to him." He didn't talk about peripheral matters. He spoke about Jesus' sinless life, atoning death, and bodily resurrection. No wonder the man was saved and baptized.

Philip later became a vocational evangelist (see Acts 21:8). But long before that he was a soul-winning deacon!

A Layman Named Dempsey

My father-in-law, Dempsey Dodds, reminds me a great deal of Philip. When he was seventy years old, he was trained in a witnessing program called Evangelism Explosion. Before that, he had never personally led anyone to faith in Christ. But since he went through that training, he has led several hundred people to the Lord in one-on-one settings. He's even led several telemarketers to Christ! Once when we lived in Birmingham, I invited him to a college basketball game with me. While I watched the game, he shared the gospel with several people around us.

He does not come across as pushy. In fact, he's so nice about it and so kind in his presentation that people are hardly ever offended. Like those early Christians, he shares Christ everywhere he goes.

When his wife (my mother-in-law) had surgery, he handed a gospel tract to a nurse working the night shift. He asked her to read it and then said if she had any questions, he'd be glad to talk with her. A little while later as he was about to leave the hospital, the nurse stopped him.

"Where are you going?" she asked. "I want to talk about that pamphlet you gave me!"

"Sure, let's talk," he answered. The two of them then went back to his wife's room, where he shared the gospel with the nurse and led her to Christ.

Again, that's the kind of witnessing you see in the early church. Those first-century Christians not only established relationships with non-Christians, but they opened their mouths and shared Scriptures about Jesus, which resulted in many receiving him as Savior and Lord.

My good friend James Merritt, a wonderful pastor and a great personal soul winner himself, is fond of asking two probing questions to believers.

1. "When is the last time you personally led someone to faith in Christ?"
2. "When is the last time you tried?"

Many Christians get a little antsy at those questions and have a hard time answering them. Do you?

If we truly want to be like the church that had little but God, we're going to have to come to grips with the fact that Jesus has commissioned *all* believers to be His witnesses.

A Miraculous Church

Many aspects of the early church can only be explained by admitting that God was mightily working in their midst. What happens at your church that can only be explained by the power of God? Most churches in America are explainable. What goes on can be easily attributed either to the senior pastor's abilities, the staff's hard work, or the laity's diligence. That's not the case when we look at the book of Acts. What took place in those churches was more than human persuasiveness, power, or personality. It was "a God thing."

One verse sums it up this way: "Everyone kept feeling a sense of awe; and many wonders and signs were taking place through the apostles" (Acts 2:43).

Be honest—is everyone "feeling a sense of awe" when they attend your church? Are people being saved? If no one is being saved, then what is happening is not really miraculous because being born again is the greatest miracle of all. Does your church ever pray for sick people to be healed according to James 5:14–16? Likewise, has anyone at your church been set free from strongholds such as alcohol or drug abuse, homosexuality, or pornography? Are families being restored and put back together?

Those are the kinds of miracles that occurred regularly in the early churches. Why don't they happen in ours?

I can hear someone objecting, "Well, that's because the day of miracles has passed." What chapter and verse supports that line of thought? God hasn't changed, nor has He lost His power. Actually, there has never been "a *day* of miracles." The Bible just says there is a *God* of miracles. While it is true that Jesus warned us not to seek signs and miracles (see Matt. 16:4), nowhere does the Bible say that miracles should not accompany Christians who are walking obediently with the Lord. We should seek the Savior and not the signs. But if we follow

Jesus, signs should, at least occasionally, follow us. Jesus said that whoever believes in Him will do the works He did (John 14:12).

Lost people are not saved by the slickness of our programs or the size of our buildings. They can see better performances on TV and hear better music on the radio. But if God's awesome, manifest presence is among us, they will sense Him and take note.

While the church with little but God won't remind us of a slick sideshow, it will, at least every now and then, be characterized by the miraculous. It will be a place where God is doing "abundantly beyond all that we ask or think" (Eph. 3:20). It will be a church known not primarily for its performances and prestige but for the presence and power of God.

A Spirit-Led Church

The early Christians received their daily marching orders from the Lord. That's because they were filled with and led by the Spirit of God. When the Spirit came at Pentecost, He indwelt every believer. They sought to listen to His still, small voice and obey His promptings in all matters.

Look at what happened in Acts 16, when Paul and his team were on a mission trip. They reached a point where they did not know which way to go next. On two different occasions they started to go into a specific region, but God's Spirit said no. "They passed through the Phrygian

> *Actually, there has never been "a day of miracles." The Bible just says there is a God of miracles.*

and Galatian region, having been *forbidden by the Holy Spirit* to speak the word in Asia; and after they came to Mysia, they were trying to go into Bithynia, and *the Spirit of Jesus did not permit them*" (vv. 6–7).

Isn't that interesting? *They* wanted to go one way, but *the Holy Spirit* had other plans. And they wisely chose to follow His leadership.

When you read the text a little farther, it becomes obvious that the Spirit wanted Paul and his fellow missionaries to minister in a province called Macedonia. Apparently, the Lord had someone else in mind to share the gospel with the folks in those other regions.

Is your church led by the Spirit of God? Again, I don't want to sound critical, but one has to wonder if the Spirit is always in control of some churches. I've been in a few that seemed more like the group in Ephesus who, when Paul asked if they had received the Spirit, replied, "We have not even heard whether there is a Holy Spirit" (Acts 19:2b). Does that sound like any Christians you know?

Someone might object to all of this by saying, "God has given us a mind to think for ourselves. The Spirit will lead us automatically through sheer common sense!"

But is that true? Was it common sense that caused Noah to build his ark? Did common sense lead Abraham to offer his son, Isaac, on the altar? Would common sense have prompted Paul and Silas to sing praises to God after they'd been beaten and imprisoned at Philippi?

Christians must be careful to balance common sense and the guidance of the Holy Spirit. The fact is, sometimes God's perfect will for our lives may not make sense to us. That's why God says, "Trust in the LORD with all your heart *and do not lean on your own understanding*" (Prov. 3:5).

God's ways are not always our ways. His thoughts are not always in line with ours. In fact, His ways and thoughts are always superior to ours (Isa. 55:8–9). Sometimes what He tells us to do might not make good sense to us, but if His Spirit is truly leading us to do something or say something, then we should obey, even when we don't understand. Failure to do so will quench the Spirit's power in our lives.

A church with little but God is led by the Holy Spirit. And only those who are led by the Spirit can bear witness to the fact that they are children of God (Rom. 8:14).

A Growing Church

The church that had little but God grew rapidly. As we've already noted, they went from 120 people praying in an upper room (Acts 1:15) to more than three thousand (Acts 2:41) after only one evangelistic sermon. Now *that* is fantastic church growth.

Acts 2:47 reports, "And the Lord was adding to their number day by day those who were being saved." That is, they were growing by means of conversions. There weren't any other churches from which they could draw members by means of transfer, as many so-called "growing" churches do today. Rather, they were growing because people were being saved, and the kingdom of God was expanding.

Church growth, incidentally, was a by-product, not a goal, of this early church. Worshipping and serving Jesus was their priority. Church growth was just the natural result. Jesus had said *He* would build His church (Matt. 16:18). These early Christians were simply living holy lives, loving lost people and one another, and sharing the gospel of Christ in the power of the Holy Spirit. They were planting and watering, and *God* was causing the growth.

Some people today say churches shouldn't be large. Others say churches should never keep track of numbers. The simple fact that Acts mentions the number of believers several times (Acts 2:41; 4:4) shows that the early church did keep up with its statistics. They had lots of people and they counted those people, because people mattered to God.

One of my favorite verses in Acts says, "So the church throughout all Judea and Galilee and Samaria enjoyed peace, being built up; and going on in the fear of the Lord and in the comfort of the Holy Spirit, *it continued to increase*" (Acts 9:31). Not only was there unity, spiritual growth, edification, and reverent worship in that early church, but they also experienced tremendous numerical growth.

I know some Christians believe large churches are a bad thing. I've heard people say, "Large churches are not as friendly as small churches." Do you really think churches grow to be large because they're unfriendly?

Maybe someone in your church has said something like, "I think a church can get too big." I believe many of the people who say things like that are actually insecure. They feel threatened that they might lose their position of influence to some of the newcomers.

Personally, I like the gospel song that says, "There's room at the cross for you. . . . Though millions have come, there's still room for *one*; yes, there's room at the cross for you." A church has room to keep growing as long as there are still lost people who need to be saved. The church with little but God understands that—which is one of the main reasons they keep growing when other churches do not.

WHY ARE WE SO DIFFERENT?

The church with little but God is at the same time both inspiring and convicting. I look at the book of Acts and then say to myself, "Why are we so different from them?" Sometimes I identify with the cry of Elisha the prophet when he asked in anguish, "Where is the LORD, the

God of Elijah?" (2 Kings 2:14). He desperately wanted to see the evidences of God's power and presence that occurred under his predecessor. My version of his question comes out like this: "Where is the God of the book of Acts?"

When Billy Graham went to the old Soviet Union back during the Cold War, he met with all kinds of people, declaring the gospel wherever he was. That was his style, of course; he didn't care whether he was in a Kremlin office, talking to students at Moscow State University, or meeting the patriarch of the Russian Orthodox Church. He'd talk about Jesus anywhere.

> *A church has room to keep growing as long as there are still lost people who need to be saved.*

Some Christians back in America criticized him for hobnobbing with the "oppressors." They said he should have taken a stronger stance against the abuse of human rights and religious liberty. One man accused Graham of setting the Russian evangelical church back fifty years.

"I am deeply ashamed," the evangelist responded, lowering his head. "All my life and ministry I have been trying very hard to set the church back two thousand years."[8]

That is what I want to see as well. The sooner we embrace the power and results of the book of Acts, the faster we will fulfill God's calling in our generation. He is right where He's always been, waiting to show Himself among His people. If we set ourselves to be a church with little but God, we will have more than enough.

CHAPTER 6

On American Shores

If you think the events I have described in the previous two chapters were just for long ago in a land far away, that nothing this remarkable would happen on our side of the world, then I need to take you on a little tour of the great spiritual awakenings that have swept across the United States from time to time. God is always looking for responsive people. He never stops seeking worshippers who will open their hearts and minds to His purposes. He is as eager to touch Americans as He was ancient Jews, Greeks, Romans, and any other nationality.

Let me spotlight just three "times of refreshing" (Acts 3:19) that occurred in the eighteenth and nineteenth centuries. (In the next chapter I will introduce you to three more from the twentieth century.) Along the way you will meet some fascinating people who experienced the manifest presence of God and brought others along with them.

The First Great Awakening

During the early and mid-1700s, the Lord moved mightily among the people of the American colonies. Historian Richard Bushman compares this revival to the impact of "the civil rights demonstrations, the campus disturbances, and the urban riots of the 1960s combined. All together these may approach, though certainly not surpass, the Awakening in their impact on national life."[9]

America had been experiencing tremendous population growth. Within only a century of the arrival of the European settlers, more than half a million people had arrived from England, Scotland, Ireland, Germany, Switzerland, the Netherlands, and other neighboring countries. The slave trade also brought a growing number of native Africans to the southern colonies.

A series of wars on the western frontiers led to a spirit of fear among the settlers. In wilderness areas, drunkenness, sexual immorality, and lack of respect for human life were the order of the day. Many of the churches struggled as well. In 1662, the Puritans of New England had succumbed to what was known as "The Half-Way Covenant." This practice allowed people who had merely been baptized but were not necessarily converted to Christ to join the church for social and economic reasons. Consequently, the congregations took in many unconverted members. Into that setting God called some of the greatest preachers of Christian history to lead in a revival among His people.

In 1720 a young minister from the Netherlands named **Theodore J. Frelinghuysen** (1691–1747) arrived in New York. He longed to see revival in the Dutch Reformed Church. The English evangelist George Whitefield referred to Frelinghuysen as "the beginner of the great work"[10] (i.e., the First Great Awakening). Frelinghuysen stressed that people should not call themselves Christians unless they had first experienced conversion. Baptism and church membership were not enough. He also insisted that Christians should live lives of spiritual enthusiasm and passion.

As he ministered in New Jersey, revival broke out. Many opposed his emphasis on authentic piety. The Dutch Reformed Church eventually split into pro-revival and anti-revival groups. Those who favored the revival founded Queens College, which in time became what we know today as Rutgers University.

William Tennent Sr. (1673–1746) was a Presbyterian minister who built a log cabin next to his home to train his sons in theology. Similar log colleges emerged all across the colonies. They were precursors to modern seminaries. Tennent's log cabin school ultimately evolved into Princeton University.

His son, **Gilbert Tennent** (1703–1764), became a mighty force in the Awakening. In 1740 Gilbert preached a scathing sermon entitled "The Danger of an Unconverted Ministry." He confronted the Presbyterian clergy of his day, saying most were not even Christians. "Is a blind man fit to be a guide in a very dangerous way? Is a dead man fit to bring others to life? A mad man fit to give counsel in matters of life and death? . . . Isn't an unconverted minister like a man who would learn [instruct] others to swim, before he has learned it himself, and so is drowned in the act, and dies like a fool?"[11] Tennent's sermon infuriated many, but the Lord used it to help bring about revival.

The greatest theologian of the First Great Awakening was **Jonathan Edwards** (1703–1758). He graduated from Yale as valedictorian of his class when he was only seventeen. He later succeeded his grand-father, Solomon Stoddard, as pastor of the Congregational Church in Northampton, Massachusetts, in 1729. The congregation grew under the young pastor's preaching, and revival soon broke out in Northampton and the surrounding regions.

His most famous sermon was something you may remember from your high school American literature class: "Sinners in the Hands of an Angry God," preached at Enfield, Connecticut, on July 8, 1741. It was based on Deuteronomy 32:35 (KJV), which says, "Their foot shall slide in due time." Edwards said the only thing that prevents a person from going to hell is the pleasure of God. Man is like a spider that hangs help-lessly over a flame, held back from destruction by only a thin cord of his making.

The audience's response was startling:

> Probably no sermon has ever had the effect of this one. It was interrupted by outcries from the congregation—men and women stood up and rolled on the floor, their cries once drowning out the voice of the preacher. Some are said to have laid hold on the pillars and braces of the church, apparently feeling that at that very moment their feet were sliding, that they were being precipitated into hell. All through the house one could hear the cries of those feeling themselves lost, cry-ing to God for mercy. Through the night Enfield was like a beleaguered city. In almost every house men and women could be heard crying out for God to save them.[12]

Some complained that the Awakening was little more than a display of religious fanaticism. "Throughout New England people declared their opinions of the revival, insomuch that two antagonistic bodies began to form, the one favoring it and the other opposing it. These were later to be termed the *New Lights* and the *Old Lights*."[13] One of the leading opponents of the Awakening was a liberal Boston preacher named **Charles Chauncy** (1705–1787). He paved the way, incidentally, for the Unitarian movement that would later engulf many churches in America.

Eventually, the congregation at Northampton grew uneasy when Edwards insisted that only believers should take Communion, and they forced him to resign. He left graciously, traveling westward to Stockbridge to minister among the Indians for seven years. But then he was elected president of Princeton University. Within a few weeks of taking office, he received something new in the medical field: a smallpox vaccination. Tragically, it gave him smallpox, and he died a month later at the age of just fifty-four.

But by then a young English preacher named **George Whitefield** (1714–1770) had come to America. Whitefield "may have been the best-known Protestant in the whole world during the eighteenth century. Certainly, he was the single best-known religious leader in America of that century, and the most widely recognized figure of any sort in North America before George Washington."[14] He made seven trans-atlantic evangelistic trips from England to the colonies. If Edwards was the greatest theologian of the First Great Awakening, Whitefield was without doubt its greatest preacher.

> ☞ *Through the night Enfield was like a beleaguered city. In almost every house men and women could be heard crying out for God to save them.* ☜

In his thirty-four-year ministry, Whitefield preached eighteen thousand times, primarily in the out-of-doors. He attracted crowds that often numbered from ten to twenty thousand. His voice could be heard clearly a mile away. His extemporaneous style kept his listeners spellbound. One esteemed Englishman said Whitefield could make grown men weep simply by the way he pronounced "Mesopotamia!" Benjamin Franklin was his friend. Although Franklin never retracted his Deism, he supported Whitefield financially and published many of his sermons.

Whitefield's itinerant ministry connected the pockets of revival among various churches and helped escalate the movement into one gigantic spiritual awakening. When he came back to Boston after preaching farther south in various cities, he happened to meet Charles Chauncy on the street one day. The minister scowled as he said sarcastically, "Mr. Whitefield! I'm sorry to see that you have returned."

Replied the evangelist without missing a beat, "So is the devil."

Whitefield preached the night before he died in Newburyport, Massachusetts, and was buried under the pulpit of the local Presbyterian church.

It is estimated that the Awakening resulted in thirty to forty thousand converts in New England alone—some 10 to 13 percent of that region's entire population. The number of new churches established in that region plus New York and the mid-Atlantic colonies came to 150.

Meanwhile in the southern colonies, the primary Christian denominations were Baptists, Presbyterians, and Methodists. Two leading Baptists of the Colonial era were **Isaac Backus** (1724–1806) and **Shubal Stearns** (1706–1771). Backus began as a Congregationalist who came to believe that immersion was the correct mode of baptism. He was baptized and became a Baptist pastor in 1756, serving the same church in Connecticut for fifty years. He traveled extensively by horseback preaching thousands of evangelistic sermons.

Shubal Stearns was another Baptist whom God used mightily in the Awakening. He had been saved listening to a George Whitefield sermon. He and Daniel Marshall traveled to Sandy Creek, North Carolina, and formed the first Separate Baptist Church in the South in 1755. Within just a few years, the church grew to 606 members. Stearns helped spread the fire of revival in the Carolinas and in Virginia.

The Second Great Awakening

In time, the First Great Awakening lost its momentum. Americans were distracted by the campaign for independence from Great Britain. Many preachers in New England left their churches to fight in the Revolutionary War (1775–1783). Those leaderless churches began to decline. Drunkenness, profanity, gambling, robbery, and sexual promiscuity became rampant across the nation. If you study carefully the birth and marriage records of that era, you find that one out of every three firstborn children was conceived out of wedlock. Due to a lot of hurried weddings, of course, only one of every fifteen babies was *born out of wedlock.*[15]

Spiritual decadence also came from the influences of the French Enlightenment. Opponents of Christianity such as Hume, Rousseau, and Voltaire ushered in the anti-Christian views of Deism, skepticism, and atheism. Even Colonial war heroes such as Thomas Paine and Ethan Allen joined the attack against the Christian faith in America. These infidel philosophies caused American colleges to become seed-beds of liberalism.

But then, at the close of the 1700s and the beginning of the 1800s, the Lord sent another revival, commonly called the Second Great Awakening. Ironically, He started on college campuses. The first was possibly **Hampden-Sydney College** in Virginia, where four embattled Christian students—William Hull, Cary Allen, James Blythe, and Clement Reid—decided to meet privately for prayer, Bible study, and theological discussions. When the other students discovered their gatherings, the campus nearly experienced a riot.

The president of the college, however, was a man named John Blair Smith, who had been converted during the First Great Awakening. He immediately stopped the persecution against the young believers, opened his own parlor to them, and began to meet with them. Others soon joined in. As they met, prayed, studied the Scriptures, and discussed theology, revival occurred. "Soon half of the students were deeply impressed and under conviction, and the revival spread rapidly through the neighborhood."[16] It crossed over into several surrounding counties.

When **Timothy Dwight** (1752–1817), grandson of the late Jonathan Edwards, became the new president of **Yale University** in 1795, he could find only ten Christian students on the entire campus. He boldly confronted their opponents. Because of his personal character, persuasive preaching, and apologetic reasoning, the student body began to listen to what Dwight had to say. In time many were converted to Christ. "The salvation of the soul was the great subject of thought, of conversation, of absorbing interest; the convictions of many were pungent and overwhelming; and the 'peace of believing' which succeeded, was not less strongly marked."[17] By 1802 Yale was experiencing genuine awakening. "A third of the 225 students were converted, and many of these became agents for revival and reform in New England, upstate New York, and the West."[18]

At **Williams College** in Massachusetts, revival broke out among several students, including Samuel Mills. One day in 1806, as the young men gathered for prayer, a torrential rainstorm drove them to seek shelter under a haystack. There Mills sensed a divine call to become a missionary. Two years later he and several others requested that the General Association of Massachusetts send them to minister in India. On June 28, 1810, the association founded the first foreign mission agency in America, the American Board of Commissioners for Foreign Missions. By 1812, Adoniram Judson, Samuel Nott, Luther Rice, Gordon Hall, and Samuel Newell were commissioned as missionaries at the Tabernacle Congregational Church in Salem, Massachusetts. Mills didn't go to India after all, selflessly giving up his spot to Gordon Hall, who was the better linguist of the two.

> *As the young men gathered for prayer, a torrential rainstorm drove them to seek shelter under a haystack. There Mills sensed a divine call to become a missionary.*

Meanwhile, the fires of the Second Great Awakening were also burning in the **Frontier Camp Meetings**. Back in 1797, Presbyterian pastor **James McGready** led his church members in Logan County, Kentucky, to pray every Saturday evening, Sunday morning, and the third Saturday of each month for one year for an outpouring of the Holy Spirit on their county and the world. McGready instigated the first "camp meeting"—a four-day event to which people came from miles around by horseback, wagon, and on foot. They prayed, sang, listened to preaching, and repented of sin.

Barton Stone (1772–1844) visited McGready's camp meeting and was moved with the deep sense of spirituality among the participants. Stone went back and held a similar camp meeting of his own at Cane Ridge, Kentucky, in 1801. A large assembly of Presbyterian, Baptist, and Methodist pastors and parishioners that numbered between twenty and twenty-five thousand people gathered at Cane Ridge. Although there were a few instances of emotional excess and fanaticism, a great movement of God's Spirit occurred. Numerous non-Christians were converted to Christ, countless Christians experienced a renewed passion and zeal for spiritual matters, and many new churches were established as a result of these meetings.

The renewed interest of the faith touched off at Cane Ridge and similar camp meetings led to a rapid growth of Presbyterian churches in the South. By comparison, however, Presbyterian efforts paled beside the accomplishments of the Methodists and Baptists. Methodist circuit riders and Baptist farmer-preachers fanned out through the South and the open West in unprecedented numbers. By the 1830s these groups had replaced the Congregationalists and Presbyterians as the largest denominations, not only in the South but in the whole United States.[19]

After the Cane Ridge camp meeting, many other successful camp meetings took place. Itinerant Methodist preachers known as circuit riders helped spread revival across the frontiers. They took the gospel to those in isolated places. One of the most famous **Circuit Riders** was a Methodist patriarch named **Francis Asbury** (1745–1816). In 1772, John Wesley, leader of the Methodists in both England and the colonies, had appointed the young Asbury as his chief assistant for the Methodists in America. Asbury rode approximately 300,000 miles and preached 16,500 sermons.

Though a British citizen, he refused to return to England during the Revolutionary War.

I can by no means agree to leave such a field for gathering souls to Christ, as we have in America. It would be an eternal dishonor to the Methodists, that we should all leave three thousand souls, who desire to commit themselves to our care; neither is it the part of a good shepherd to leave his flock in time of danger; therefore, I am determined, by the grace of God, not to leave them, let the consequence be what it may.[20]

When the war ended, Asbury was still alive and preaching.

Asbury was a passionate proponent of the camp meetings. He wrote a letter warmly describing the camp meeting at Cane Ridge, Kentucky. "The work of God is running like fire in Kentucky. It is reported that near fifteen if not twenty thousand were present at one Sacramental occasion of the Presbyterians; and one thousand if not fifteen hundred . . . felt the power of grace."[21]

Asbury was a disciplined man who used his time wisely. He rose no later than five and retired each evening by nine. He studied as he rode his horse, covering up to a hundred pages per day. He also read his Bible regularly. One journal entry notes that on one occasion he read through the entire Bible in only four months. In time Asbury became the symbol of American Methodism.

Another famous Methodist circuit-riding preacher was **Peter Cartwright** (1785–1872). Like Asbury he supported the camp meetings. He took his itinerant ministry across the western areas of America, preaching more than fifteen thousand sermons. He stayed in a community until there was a response. He denounced both slavery and liquor as he went. He even ran for a seat in the U.S. Congress, losing to Abraham Lincoln.

One of the most important figures connected with the Second Great Awakening is **Charles Grandison Finney** (1792–1875). Finney was a twenty-nine-year-old lawyer when he was converted to Christ. He rejected theological training at Princeton. Instead, he used reasoning and logic, which he had learned as a lawyer, to argue the Lord's case from Scripture. His preaching was passionate, polished, and persuasive. He turned from staunch Calvinism to preach a gospel of free salvation. He believed in a general atonement while at the same time maintaining the doctrine of election, insisting that man's free will and God's sovereignty were compatible concepts. He preached for a verdict, offering people the opportunity to make decisions for Christ at the conclusion of his messages.

From 1824 to 1832, Finney experienced the most fruitful years of his ministry. He traveled countless miles and preached numerous revival meetings. His greatest impact was in Rochester, New York, where more than 100,000 were saved in one year and more than forty men surrendered to the gospel ministry, with several becoming missionaries. "The whole community was stirred. Religion was the topic of conversation, in the house, in the shop, in the office, and on the street. . . . Grog [liquor] shops were closed; the Sabbath was honored. . . . There was a wonderful falling off in crime. The courts had little to do, and the jail was nearly empty for years afterward."[22]

In time Finney's health failed due to his relentless preaching schedule. He stopped traveling as much and became the pastor of New York

City's Broadway Tabernacle. During the fall of 1834 and the winter of 1835, Finney gave twenty-two lectures on revival to his congregation. They were transcribed and put into book form under the title *Lectures on Revivals of Religion.*[23] There Finney said revival was not primarily a miracle sent from heaven. Rather, he believed it to be the result of the correct use of biblical methods. He stressed that just as a farmer plants seeds and bears a harvest, God will send revival when we appropriate the God-given means that produce it.

Finney's methods came to be called the "New Measures." One was the "anxious meeting," a service in which people who were concerned about their spiritual condition came together so Finney could lead them to Christ. The "anxious seats" were in the front of church sanctuaries, reserved for those who wanted to come sit there and be led to Christ. This practice was, of course, a precursor to public evangelistic invitations. The "protracted meeting" was a series of revival services held on consecutive nights, not just on weekends, which had previously been the norm.

Until Finney's ministry, revival had been understood primarily as a sovereign work of God. But he stressed that if people would meet God's prerequisites for sending revival, God would do just that. That was a new concept that was especially difficult for hard-core Calvinists to embrace.

One opponent of Charles Finney and his "New Measures" was a Calvinistic evangelist named **Asahel Nettleton** (1783–1844). He was a student at Yale when revival had broken out under Timothy Dwight. He traveled extensively for many years as an itinerant preacher of the gospel. He often led hundreds to faith in Christ in a single evangelistic service. Although he and Finney disagreed sharply concerning election, the Lord used both of them in revival, just as in earlier times He had used both John Wesley, an Arminian, and George Whitefield, a Calvinist.

Some eminent historians believe that the Second Great Awakening's impact was even greater than that of the First. Mark Noll, for example, calls the Second Great Awakening "the most influential revival of Christianity in the history of the United States."[24]

The Prayer Revival of 1858

By the late 1850s, the Second Awakening had lost its power. Once again churches began to decline in membership and attendance. "For several years, from 1843 to 1857, the additions to the churches scarcely equaled the losses sustained by death, removal or discipline, while a widespread indifference to religion became prevalent."[25]

The famous Gold Rush of 1849 was symbolic of the fact that many citizens were more interested in gold than God. America soon experienced financial difficulties. In 1857, the nation's banking industry crashed, and numerous citizens lost everything. The country was also divided over the issue of slavery. Southern states began making plans to break away from their northern neighbors to begin a new nation.

In that setting God chose godly laymen, not preachers, to spark a spiritual awakening. Lay-led prayer meetings began to form. Perhaps the most famous of these took place on Fulton Street in New York City's financial district.

In 1857, the North Reformed Dutch Church called one of its own members, a businessman named **Jeremiah Lanphier,** to serve as a lay minister. The church, like most others, was in a state of decline. People were leaving the downtown district to move to neighboring residential areas. As Lanphier walked the streets of Manhattan, he could not help noticing the discouraged looks on the faces of the businessmen. He was also disturbed by the spiritual decadence of the city as well as the apathy in the churches. One day he offered up a simple prayer: "Lord, what wilt Thou have *me* to do?"

Shortly after that, he decided to host a prayer meeting for businessmen. They would meet once a week at noon for an hour in one of the lecture rooms on the third floor of his church on Fulton Street and pray for spiritual awakening. The businessmen could come and go as they pleased without having to stay the entire hour, since many had busy schedules. Lanphier proceeded to pass out fliers inviting men to attend.

The first prayer meeting was held on September 23, 1857. Roy Fish gives a graphic description of what occurred on that day:

> For thirty minutes, Lanphier prayed alone. At 12:30, a step was heard on the stairs. Soon another came, and another, until finally six men were there to inaugurate the Fulton Street

prayer meetings. It was almost prophetic of a proper spirit of cooperation that, at the first meeting, the six men present represented four different denominations.[26]

The next week twenty men showed up to pray. The week after that, between thirty and forty men came. The format was simple: (1) take requests; (2) pray; (3) share brief testimonies (no preaching!). They decided to start praying every day instead of weekly.

On October 14th, over one hundred men attended the meeting, many of them unconverted. The meetings grew, and before the close of the second month, all three of the lecture rooms of the church were filled. Within six months of the beginning date, as many as fifty thousand were attending this and other union prayer meetings daily in New York alone. Within two years, the fires of revival had swept the entire nation, and some one million people had been added to the churches nationally.[27]

This is an amazing statistic, considering the fact that the nation's population at that time was only thirty million! Approximately one out of every thirty Americans experienced a meaningful encounter with Jesus Christ, either by conversion or rededication.

The revival sent shock waves down the East Coast and into the southern states. It also reached the great cities of the Midwest, such as Chicago, where some two thousand showed up at the Metropolitan Theater for noontime prayer. One of them was a young shoe salesman newly arrived from the East. His name was **Dwight Lyman Moody** (1837–1899). After the prayer meetings he wrote his mother back in Massachusetts that he thought he might try to start a Sunday school class for boys from the street.

> *Within two years, the fires of revival had swept the entire nation, and some one million people had been added to the churches nationally.*

Soon D. L. Moody was working with the Young Men's Christian Association (YMCA) to do evangelistic work in Chicago. Eventually he began preaching to large crowds in crusades. It was with Moody's ministry that "business principles entered the field of mass evangelism."[28] He introduced large-scale preparation for revival meetings with comprehensive organization. His ministry had a worldwide effect as he traveled across America and to England preaching the gospel.

He and his evangelistic musician, Ira D. Sankey, enjoyed success that was similar to Whitefield's ministry in the 1700s. His preaching was theologically conservative, easy to understand, and aimed at the common man. Like Jesus, people heard Moody gladly—some 100 million of them, it is estimated.[29] The impact for the kingdom of God was massive.

More Than Accidental

These revivals were more than just accidental. They came about because men and women, often just a few in the beginning, wanted the presence of God more than anything else. They cried out on their knees for a new touch from heaven. And God did not turn them away. He heard their call, and He sent His Spirit to awaken His church and shed light into the darkest corners of the American society. He came to their aid, and the nation was radically changed.

CHAPTER 7

Crusades and Coffeehouses

D. L. Moody had been in his grave less than a week when the calendar turned momentously to announce the year 1900. What eminent historians would eventually call "the American century" was dawning. In the coming ten decades of brilliant invention, dreadful wars, rising affluence, social upheavals, and stunning space exploration, the nation also experienced at least three surges of spiritual revival.

The Early Years

Actually, credit must be given to what God began to do in Wales, which then quickly spread to this side of the Atlantic. As early as 1902, at a Keswick convention, Christians who had been deeply touched by the Lord's presence formed a circle of prayer for worldwide revival. Many Welsh preachers were deeply touched by God.

In the summer of 1903, **Joseph Jenkins,** pastor in New Quay, Cardiganshire, began to seek the Lord for personal revival. He changed the high-church nature of his worship services, encouraging his members freely to share testimonies, pray, read Scripture, and sing as the Lord prompted them. One Sunday morning Jenkins asked his youth to give testimonies of what God was doing in their lives. A young girl named Florrie Evans rose to declare, "If no one else will, then I must say that I do love the Lord Jesus Christ with all my heart." With that statement the Holy Spirit fell upon those attending the meeting.

That event started an extended revival in New Quay. After six months a young pastor named **Seth Joshua** attended one of the meetings and was deeply touched by God. Later on, his preaching deeply affected a young coal miner named Evan Roberts. At the end of one service, Joshua was heard to pray, "Lord, bend us." **Evan Roberts** knelt at the altar and echoed, "Lord, bend *me*."

From that time on, revival seemed to focus on Roberts, who was still in his mid-twenties. He spoke of a mysterious vision from God assuring him that 100,000 people in Wales would soon come to Christ. In the fall of 1904, Roberts returned to his hometown of Loughor and preached his four tenets of revival: (1) You must put away any unconfessed sin; (2) you must put away any doubtful habit; (3) you must obey the Spirit promptly; and (4) you must confess Christ publicly.

Within six months more than 100,000 people had been saved, just as he had envisioned. All of Wales was aglow with fire from heaven. People came from around the world to experience what the Lord was doing there, then took it home again to the rest of Great Britain, various parts of Europe, India, Africa, Latin America, the Orient, Australia, and North America.

The United States certainly needed revival again. Mary Baker Eddy had founded the Christian Science church in 1879. Five years later Charles Taze Russell had started the Zion's Watch Tower Society, a group we know today as Jehovah's Witnesses. Theological liberals such as Washington Gladden and Walter Rauschenbusch led the Social Gospel movement, applying the principles of Christianity to social problems such as poverty, alcohol and drug abuse, crime, racism, inadequacies in education, and the dangers of war but neglecting people's spiritual need of salvation in Christ.

Against this backdrop, many Christians in America began to call out to God. Prayer meetings began to spring up everywhere. In 1905 several college and seminary campuses reported strong movements of God among their students. Traveling evangelists, following Moody's example, reached great cities for Christ by means of large area-wide crusades.

One of those was a pastor named **Reuben Archer Torrey** (1856–1928). He graduated from Yale with a bachelor of divinity degree in 1878. While there Torrey toyed with liberal theology, but he soon abandoned it. For the next eleven years, he served as pastor of three churches, until in 1889 he became the superintendent of the Chicago Evangelization Society and the Bible institute Moody had founded. From 1902 to 1906, he traveled overseas in evangelistic crusades and led multitudes to Christ in Great Britain, Germany, India, New Zealand, Australia, China, and Japan.

J. Wilbur Chapman (1859–1918) was a Presbyterian evangelist. In 1878, he had attended a revival meeting where D. L. Moody was preaching. Chapman was unsure of his salvation, so he went forward to be counseled. Moody personally spoke with him in the inquiry room, using John 5:24 to give him the assurance he desired. He became a pastor, and at the First Reformed Church of Albany, New York, attendance grew in five years from approximately 150 to just over 1,500. His tenure at Bethany Presbyterian Church in Philadelphia resulted in one of the largest Sunday schools in the world at that time. But that was not all. Some members of his church started a weekly prayer meeting on behalf of their pastor. The prayer meeting grew to more than 1,000 in attendance. Many were saved and the church grew.

Chapman began his itinerant evangelistic ministry in 1904, conducting massive citywide meetings using highly structured organization. That first year he took seventeen evangelists to Pittsburgh, divided the city into nine districts, and they preached simultaneous crusades. Seven thousand people were saved. Chapman is still remembered today for the song he wrote, "Jesus! What a Friend of Sinners."

In 1907 another evangelist, **Charles M. Alexander,** joined Chapman. In 1908 they went to Philadelphia with other evangelists. The combined attendance in the simultaneous crusades averaged 35,000 people for six weeks for a total attendance of 1,470,000, with 8,000 professing faith in Christ.

William Ashley Sunday (1862–1935), known as "Billy," played professional baseball for eight years. He entered the ministry in 1891, working for the YMCA in Chicago. In 1893 he worked briefly for Chapman, who taught him about organizing revival meetings. In 1896 Sunday began preaching, and as he became more well-known, his meetings turned into citywide crusades. His delivery was high-spirited and dramatic, but he made a lasting impact well into the 1920s.

Another unlikely character whom the Lord used in an amazing way was **Sam Jones** (1847–1906). Before his conversion Jones had struggled as an alcoholic. Then at his father's deathbed, he fell on his knees and asked the Lord Jesus to save him. Almost immediately he became a Methodist preacher. In 1880 he began to travel and preach while raising money for an orphanage. While preaching in Nashville, he led riverboat captain Tom Ryman to Christ. Ryman built the Union Gospel Tabernacle for Jones and other preachers to use in evangelizing the citizens of that city. The Tabernacle later became the Ryman Auditorium, the longtime home of the Grand Ole Opry.

The Englishman **Rodney "Gypsy" Smith** (1860–1947) was born in a tent and raised in a Gypsy camp, never attending school. After his conversion as a teenager, General William Booth asked him to do evangelistic work as part of the Salvation Army. Smith traveled as an evangelist to the United States on thirty different occasions. He preached literally around the world, leading multitudes to faith in Jesus.

Charles Parham (1873–1929) was a Holiness preacher who in 1900 started Bible schools in Topeka, Kansas, and later in Houston, Texas. One of his students there was an African-American named **William J. Seymour** (1870–1922) who, in early 1906, was invited to preach in Los Angeles. Things did not go well when he spoke about his belief in speaking in tongues. The local pastor locked him out of the building, saying he was teaching heresy. Undaunted, Seymour found refuge in a home, where a group began to pray for the Pentecostal experience. Crowds flocked to the house; preachers preached from the front porch until it collapsed. Soon a larger building was found at 312 Azusa Street, which, though in poor condition could accommodate some 350 people. For the next three and a half years, meetings went on morning, afternoon, and night seven days a week. Blacks, whites, Hispanics, and Asians worshipped together freely. People began coming from all over the world to see what God was doing. The Pentecostal movement had begun.

Once again it must be noted that not all of these Christians agreed with every point of one another's theology. Yet they all lifted up Jesus and called men and women to surrender to Him. Just as Wesley and Whitefield did not see eye to eye on certain doctrines 150 years previous but were still used by God to extend His kingdom, so the revival voices at the beginning of the twentieth century emphasized the central message of salvation through faith in Christ alone. Vast numbers of people were touched, and they responded.

After World War II

The 1940s was a bittersweet decade in America. During the first half, the Allies fought powerful enemies to the east (Japan) and in Europe (Germany). More than sixteen million Americans wore the uniform during that war, three times as many as had served in World War I. This conflict resulted in well over 400,000 American deaths, while almost 700,000 soldiers were wounded.

When it was finally over, millions of young soldiers returned home to secure jobs and start careers and families. They sought a more prosperous and happy lifestyle that many referred to as "the American dream." But all was not well. The Soviet Union, which had been a United States ally during the war, was now forcing its doctrines of socialism upon many of the nations of Europe. Communism became the new global threat. The ensuing cold war resulted in a nuclear arms race between the two superpowers.

Meanwhile, morality in America began to decline. While people were making more money than ever and the standard of living was increasing, alcoholism and divorce rates were also climbing. A great deal of theological liberalism sprouted in many churches as well as the colleges and seminaries affiliated with them. Conservative Christianity with its emphasis on biblical preaching, personal conversion, evangelism, and missions was all but gone in most of the established, mainline denominations.

In April 1949, four young ministers—Billy Graham, J. Edwin Orr, William Dunlap, and Jack Frank—prayed together specifically for God to send revival to campuses in America. Orr soon went to Bethel College and Seminary, a Baptist institution in Minneapolis, and gave a series of lectures on revival. The president, Dr. Henry C. Wingblade, was willing to cancel classes to allow students to participate in the prolonged chapel services. Dorm rooms were filled with students praying and worshipping God. Students who attended the chapels were also confessing their sins and making restitution with anyone they had wronged. A spirit of holiness pervaded the entire campus.

In *The Standard*, a Baptist newspaper, Dr. Wingblade described the meetings: "We have had a marvelous visitation. The Holy Spirit has wrought a marvelous work indeed on our campus." In a later edition of that paper, he added, "I do not think we have had anything quite like the wonderful meetings of last week in all the history of Bethel."[30]

Similar events soon began to take place at other colleges in the region, such as St. Paul Bible Institute (Christian and Missionary Alliance), Northwestern College (where Billy Graham was president at that time), and various campuses of the University of Minnesota. An awakening also occurred that summer (1949) among five hundred college students at Forest Home Conference Grounds in Southern California as Billy Graham and J. Edwin Orr spoke. Many students were saved while the others were revived. They returned to their various colleges in the fall on fire for God. Northern Baptist Theological Seminary in Chicago experienced a fresh visitation of the Spirit during those years, as did neighboring North Park College (Evangelical Covenant Church). Colleges across the country were being revived.

The student awakening was further fanned by the influence of **Bill Bright** (1921–2003), who in 1951 founded Campus Crusade for Christ, International. This evangelistic organization sought to win college students to Christ, especially on state campuses, using a simple piece of literature called "The Four Spiritual Laws." Its presentation of the gospel led millions to faith in Jesus.

Billy Graham's ministry, of course, had begun attracting notice back during the war under the umbrella of Youth for Christ (its motto: "Geared to the Times, Anchored to the Rock"). The YFC coordinator, **Torrey Johnson,** organized a series of Saturday evening youth rallies in Chicago and asked Graham to be the main speaker. More than twenty-eight hundred attended the first meeting. By the twenty-first meeting, a twenty-thousand-seat stadium was necessary to accommodate the crowds. Graham soon resigned his pastorate at a suburban Baptist church and began traveling across America and Canada; he even made trips to England as YFC's evangelist. With his young musician, Cliff Barrows, the team spent five months in Great Britain in 1946, where they conducted 360 meetings in twenty-seven cities and towns.

The big breakthrough for Billy Graham came in 1949, this time back in Los Angeles. The crusade crowds numbered about six thousand nightly for the first three weeks. God's blessings fell upon the meetings, and they lasted another five weeks, with attendance reaching over nine thousand in the final meeting. Several famous people were converted to Christ during that crusade, including renowned Southern California film and radio star Stuart Hamblen. When Hamblen's friend, actor John Wayne, asked him if he really didn't want to drink beer or whiskey anymore, Hamblen replied, "No, John. It's no secret what God can do." Wayne suggested that Hamblen write a song using those words. He did, and it became a Christian favorite.

The Hearst newspaper chain, national television and radio networks, as well as *Time* and *Newsweek* magazines covered the Los Angeles crusade. Within two months Graham became well-known across America. In 1950 he held a successful crusade in Boston that grew so large it had to be moved to the Boston Garden for the final service. Some sixteen thousand people attended, and another ten thousand were turned away.

In 1957 Graham went to New York City. The crusade lasted sixteen weeks. More than two million people heard him in person at either Madison Square Garden, Yankee Stadium, Central Park, Wall Street, or Brooklyn. One service at Yankee Stadium attracted more than 100,000 people, with 20,000 having to be turned away. More than 55,000 people were converted to Christ during this effort.

> ⇨ *Evangelicals who worked together to help [Billy Graham] learned they could do more for Christ's kingdom when they were united than when they were divided.* ⇦

Graham's meetings in America stirred the flames of revival in churches across the land. Evangelicals who worked together to help him learned they could do more for Christ's kingdom when they were united than when they were divided. Did the revival of the 1950s result in these crusades, or did the crusades result in revival? No one can answer that. They simply go together, regardless of which was the primary cause.

There was also a renewed emphasis on Pentecostalism during the 1950s. Revivalist **Oral Roberts** became widely known for his healing ministry during those years. Roberts would erect an enormous tent filled with thousands of seats and a platform from which he preached and ministered. At the end of his message, he would sit on a chair and invite individuals to come up onto the platform so he could pray for their healing. The services were usually televised and attracted national attention. Roberts later founded a school (Oral Roberts University in Tulsa) and became a voice for awakening in the Methodist Church. This crossing of traditional lines made him one of the premier leaders in the charismatic movement, which was a new branch of Pentecostalism.

While some scholars question whether the revival of the 1950s was a genuine national awakening, it must be said that the churches of America experienced tremendous growth and renewed spiritual zeal during that decade.

The Jesus Movement

The 1960s will always be remembered in America as a time of societal chaos. During that decade, many Americans lost their faith in Western theism, the federal government, and social idealism. There was a fundamental shift in the artistic, moral, and religious attitudes of many Americans, particularly those under thirty.

> *Playboy* publisher Hugh Hefner successfully marketed a philosophy of sexual hedonism in the thin wrappings of intellectual respectability. Episcopalian Joseph Fletcher formulated a New Morality that left God out of decision-making, a system that provided conscience-soothing rationale for an if-you-love-her-why-wait? lifestyle. Courts permitted—and many people supported—a flood of "old immorality" in our theaters and on our newsstand racks.[31]

Americans were crying out in protest over such issues as civil rights, the Vietnam War, students' rights, and ecology. It was a decade of social transition.

Meanwhile, most Christian churches in America during the 1960s were in a state of decline. Most major denominations were losing members. Christians themselves were disgruntled over politics in the churches, a lack of relevance in the preaching, and a lack of genuine fellowship. A few churches were experiencing moderate growth, but as a whole, the young people of this country, along with many adults, began to lose faith in the gospel and the church that proclaimed it.

Antiestablishment demonstrations on college campuses were becoming counterproductive. Four students were killed at Kent State University in Ohio by National Guard troops. Political activism did not bring the rapid changes that many young people desired. A sense of emptiness and lack of direction set in.

Into this context came a big surprise: the Jesus Movement. This spiritual awakening did not begin with one person or in a single place. Instead, it developed gradually up and down the West Coast at first. A Christian coffeehouse opened in the Haight-Ashbury district of San Francisco in 1967, run by a group of young people who had been converted to Christ and had left the hippie culture. The next year Hollywood Presbyterian Church opened a similar coffeehouse in Southern California called the Salt Company. The church's college minister, Don Williams, offered youth-oriented worship services that included upbeat Christian music and a contemporary gospel presentation. Hundreds of students from nearby Hollywood High School as well as other teenagers and people in their early twenties walked in off the street to see what was happening. In 1969 Linda Meissner opened a coffeehouse to minister to the teenagers of Seattle. Jack Sparks started an organization called the Christian World Liberation Front on the campus of the University of California at Berkeley.

These four ministries were the springboard that launched a nationwide revival among youth. By 1970 the Jesus Movement was gaining national recognition. *Time* magazine gave major coverage and pointed out at least three streams of people in the movement:

1. The Jesus People, also called "Jesus Freaks," were the most visible. They dressed like the hippies of that era and linked the movement with the youth counterculture.

2. The Straight People composed the largest group in the movement. They weren't ex-hippies but instead worked primarily through local churches and interdenominational parachurch organizations such as Campus Crusade for Christ, Inter-Varsity Christian Fellowship, Young Life, and Youth for Christ.

3. The Catholic Pentecostals had emerged in 1967. They remained in the Roman Catholic Church but were also actively involved in the neo-Pentecostal/charismatic movement, which grew during the Jesus Movement.[32]

Among the key individuals who led this revival was **Chuck Smith,** pastor of Calvary Chapel in Costa Mesa, California, a suburb of Los Angeles. He opened his church's doors and hosted youth services three nights a week. More than two thousand young people attended on an average night. Kids wore hip fashions—long hair, beards, and blue jeans—and nobody seemed to care. Services began with a Christian band playing contemporary music followed by praise choruses and a simple Bible study led by Smith, who taught while sitting on a stool.

Calvary Chapel ended up supporting five different Christian bands, a Bible school, drug abuse programs in schools, beach evangelism (which culminated in baptisms in the Pacific Ocean), and the Maranatha! publishing organization. Smith explained: "God prepared us, because I preached on *agape* love for two and a half years. . . . When the kids began to come, we accepted them as they were—long hair and all. We don't ask them to change—it is part of the cleansing work of the Holy Spirit to change them and to get rid of things like drugs, hair, cigarettes, and attitudes."[33]

Another strategic leader was **Jack Sparks,** a bearded PhD. His Christian World Liberation Front (CWLF) at Berkeley opposed the left-wing political group on campus called the Berkeley Liberation Movement. He also was the editor of a Christian underground paper called *Right On.* CWLF members passed out Christian tracts at the university and sold Christian books and Bibles from a table.

On Memorial Day, 1967, **Arthur Blessitt,** along with seventeen young people from five churches, had his first major encounter with a group of street people at a hippie love-in at Griffith Park in Los Angeles. Blessitt was permitted to preach about the love of Jesus. Fourteen hippies prayed to receive Christ. News went around the world that the hippies were "getting religion."

Blessitt continued to witness to young people on Sunset Strip as well as to various camps of the Hell's Angels motorcycle gang. He opened a coffeehouse on the Strip called His Place. In two years, more than ten thousand young people accepted Christ as Savior and Lord. Blessitt eventually became famous for carrying a cross on his shoulder everywhere he preached.

Linda Meissner had left her ministry with Teen Challenge in New York after envisioning a massive group of young people marching with Bibles in hand into the city of Seattle. She relocated to Seattle and opened a coffeehouse called The Eleventh Hour, later renamed the Catacombs. It became the largest Christian coffeehouse, reaching hundreds of young people for Christ.

All in all, the Jesus Movement was a genuine spiritual awakening among the youth of America. From California to Maine, groups of teenagers declared themselves to be "pro-Jesus." Christian music festivals attracted tens of thousands of kids. New college campus ministries sprang up. Asbury College in Wilmore, Kentucky, and other schools experienced fresh visitations from heaven that caused classes to be temporarily suspended in favor of all-campus, student-led worship services, which usually featured testimonies, prayer, worship, and repentance. Billy Graham affirmed the Jesus Movement by saying: "By and large it is a genuine movement of the Spirit of God that is affecting nearly every denomination and social and educational stratum, and is causing discussion from the editorial room of the *New York Times* to the dining room of the White House. . . . Nearly all observers agree that a major spiritual phenomenon is taking shape in young America."[34]

Many Christian denominations that had declined numerically in the 1960s began to see marked increases. For instance, Southern Baptists experienced their greatest number of baptisms in a consecutive five-year period from 1971 to 1975. Each of those years, more than 400,000 people joined Southern Baptist churches by way of conversion and baptism—many of them teenagers. The denomination had never seen that many baptisms for that many consecutive years, nor has it happened since.

Again?

Now another three decades have passed. Good things have occurred in churches during these years, to be sure. But we cannot say we have continued to experience the presence of God and the salvation of the lost to the degree we did in 1905, or 1952, or 1970.

I am not satisfied to be simply a *historian* of those things. The same Lord who sent those revivals is still able to send revival to our generation. The cry of my heart is what Isaiah prayed, "Oh, that You would rend the heavens and come down, that the mountains might quake at Your presence" (64:1). Our new century, the twenty-first, stands in great need of a divine visitation that awakens our souls and brings needy human beings close to the heart of God.

He has done it before. I believe with all my heart that He wants to do it again.

PART TWO

Hoisting the Sails

The refreshing, revitalizing wind of God is His alone to send. None of us can manufacture it. Moses and the threatened Israelites at the edge of the Red Sea could do nothing to part the waters, until God blew upon them. Ezekiel stared at a valley of bones, knowing only that the divine breath could make them come to life. So it is in our time; we cannot initiate revival on our own.

But we can hoist certain sails to catch God's wind once it begins to blow. We can prepare our hearts and revise our traditions to be ready for a spiritual resurgence. The next seven chapters of this book are meant to serve as a "rigging guide" to maximize our quest for the manifest presence of God.

CHAPTER 8

The Leader's Heart

We begin with leadership. But not with the usual approach of setting out action steps and tactical maneuvers. Our human habit is to start outlining what leaders must *do* to make the church experience better. After all, they are in charge, aren't they? They should seize the initiative, people say.

Before we leaders—whether ordained ministers or lay folk with a designated responsibility—ever start writing an order of service, we must stop and bring ourselves to the foot of the true Leader, Jesus Christ. Glorifying Him and welcoming Him is what church ministry is all about. Before any talk about *doing*, let's talk about *being*. What kind of people does Jesus see fit to use in His kingdom work? Who we *are* is more central than what we can accomplish.

Some years ago I awoke in the middle of the night with a sense that God wanted to speak to my heart. This doesn't often happen to me. I can assure you that I'm no recipient of dreams or visions the way Joseph or Solomon or Paul heard from God.

But on this occasion I was aroused enough to get out of bed, go to my desk in my study nearby, and pull out a piece of paper. Three words kept coming to my mind so strongly that I wrote them down:

Humility
Hunger
Holiness

I then stared at my paper in the soft light from a nearby lamp. "God, what does this mean?" I asked.

He did not directly answer my question, at least not in any way I could discern. He simply left me to ponder. I was not troubled by this, because I assumed the significance would come clearer in the days to follow. I went back to bed.

A few weeks later it dawned on me that the three words synchronized perfectly with the familiar text of 2 Chronicles 7:14, which says, "[If] My people who are called by My name *humble* themselves and *pray and seek* My face and *turn* from their wicked ways, then I will hear from heaven, will forgive their sin and will heal their land." The three words were the God-given keys to revival. If we meet these conditions, we put ourselves in position for God to open the windows of heaven to hear us, forgive us, and bless us with His goodness.

I can think of no qualities more vital to the heart and life of any Christian leader who yearns for the presence and power of God.

Humility

"If My people . . . humble themselves."

My pastor friend Ronnie Floyd has said more than once, "When pride walks into a church or its pulpit, God walks out." God is not interested in pumping up any man's résumé or reputation. He cares little for what people say about our successes. The only personage to be exalted in a church is Jesus.

That's one reason I try to avoid giving elaborate introductions to guest speakers and musicians who come to our church. If a denominational dignitary comes to preach, I will usually say no more than a generic sentence or two: "We're glad to welcome So-and-so today; he's involved in helping lead the Southern Baptist Convention in Nashville. Please open your hearts and minds to hear the Word of God as he speaks." The printed bulletin may offer a little more detail, if necessary. Not that those things are unimportant, but they can start to pull the attention away from Jesus. I simply don't want to do that.

Look at the bare-bones simplicity of Micah 6:8:

> He has told you, O man, what is good;
> And what does the LORD require of you

But to do justice, to love kindness,
And to walk humbly with your God?

If humility is that important to God, it ought to be that important to us. When we "walk humbly," we find ourselves moving alongside God Almighty; the word here is not to walk *after* your God" or "*following* your God." Instead, we get the high privilege of walking *with* Him.

The apostle Peter wrote: "Therefore humble yourselves under the mighty hand of God, that He may exalt you at the proper time" (1 Pet. 5:6). If leaders humble themselves, God exalts them. On the other hand, if we exalt ourselves, God will humble us. The obvious conclusion is to let God do any exalting. The results come out much better that way.

Paul wrote much the same thing to the Philippian church:

Do nothing from selfishness or empty conceit, but with
humility of mind regard one another as more important than
yourselves; do not merely look out for your own personal
interests, but also for the interests of others. Have this attitude
in yourselves which was also in Christ Jesus, who, although
He existed in the form of God, did not regard equality with
God a thing to be grasped. (2:3–6)

And what was the result of Jesus taking the humble road? "For this reason also, God highly exalted Him, and bestowed on Him the name which is above every name" (v. 9). The Son's eminence and prestige were secured for all time by His willingness to embrace the low position.

Probably the most graphic case of Jesus looking out for the interests of others came in the upper room on the evening before He died. His disciples were still fussing about who was the greatest, the most gifted, the most likely to succeed in their group. Jesus

> ☞ *God is not interested in pumping up any man's résumé or reputation. He cares little for what people say about our successes.* ☜

pulled out a bowl and a towel, saying in essence, "I'll show you who's the greatest." He then proceeded to wash their dirty, stinking feet—a chore that none of them had volunteered to do.

Humbly washing another person's feet is something that would do most of us some good. Don't brush off the suggestion by saying, "Oh, that's what those *Primitive* Baptists do," or Mennonites, or Grace Brethren, or Church of God folk. If the Lord has ever prompted you to wash another believer's feet, you understand why people cry when they do it. So do those whose feet are being washed. It's an act of unavoidable humility.

When Jesus finished washing and drying twenty-four different feet, He then came back to the table and asked His disciples a question: "Do you know what I have done for you?" No doubt the answer, had they voiced it, would have been *"Not really."* The spirit of pride dies hard. Later in the evening Peter was still boasting about his courage to face any challenge—only to prove otherwise within a matter of hours.

On that same evening Jesus gave the group His analogy of the vine and the branches.

> Abide in Me, and I in you. As the branch cannot bear fruit of itself unless it abides in the vine, so neither can you unless you abide in Me.
>
> I am the vine, you are the branches; he who abides in Me and I in him, he bears much fruit, for *apart from Me you can do nothing.* (John 15:4–5)

The Greek word for "abide" is *meno;* it means "to stay, to continue, to remain, to endure, literally to dwell or to live." Abiding in Christ has to do with yielding ourselves to Him, even abandoning ourselves to His purposes. We rest in Him, trusting Him with our future.

People can do all kinds of religious acts week after week and still not *abide* in Christ. They can check things off a list without having their heart engaged. Preachers can deliver sermons without even focusing on the One whose Word they declare. Christians can come to church and sing every word of every praise song, but it's only a recitation. Jesus calls us to *abide* in Him.

Robert Boyd Munger, the beloved author of the little classic "My Heart—Christ's Home," spent his later years teaching at a seminary. He stood one day just a few weeks before graduation and addressed a class of seniors.

> You're all very bright. You've just about completed your seminary training. You've acquired great knowledge and a wide range of skills. I'm impressed with you.

But I'm also worried about something. I'm not sure you really believe John 15:5, "Apart from Me you can do nothing." That doesn't seem to fit with all the competence represented by earning your degree, does it? You think more highly of yourself than that.

I need to remind you, though, that Jesus told the truth that night. Without Him, you will go out of this seminary and fail miserably.

We leaders have to remember that all our degrees, all the books we've read, all the seminars we've attended, and all our accumulated expertise are not what gets the job done. The only hope we have is depending on Jesus. He is the one who began the greatest sermon ever preached with this poignant sentence: "Blessed are the poor in spirit, for theirs is the kingdom of heaven" (Matt. 5:3). That phrase, "poor in spirit," means humbly acknowledging the fact that you can't make it without Jesus. Just as you couldn't get saved without Him, you cannot lead a church without Him. For that matter you can't be a good spouse, a good father, or a good administrator without the Lord.

Over the years I have learned I can't even walk across the floor without Jesus. Paul admitted to one church that "I was with you in weakness and in fear and in much trembling" (1 Cor. 2:3). The leader God uses is the one who is entirely meek before Him and simply resting—*abiding*—in His sustenance.

In the late 1800s Charles Spurgeon told his students who were concerned about getting started in the ministry:

> Formal officials do lack and suffer hunger, but the anointed of the Lord need never be without a charge [pastorate], for there are quick ears which will know them by their speech, and ready hearts to welcome them to their appointed place. Be fit for your work, and you will never be out of it. Do not run about inviting yourselves to preach here and there; be more concerned about your ability than your opportunity, and more earnest about your walk with God than about either.[35]

These are the servants God can use to bring revival in any century. Humility is a key that must not be assumed. It is a trait of character that no leader can afford to skip past.

Hunger

"If My people . . . pray and seek my face."

For too many leaders the life of devotion has become a duty, a routine, something you'd better do because if the congregation found out you were slacking off, it would be embarrassing to your ministerial image. But there's little sense of desire, of "want-to."

If you're physically hungry because you've been running from one appointment to another all day and have skipped lunch, you don't have to be coaxed to come to the dinner table. The smell of food draws you like a magnet. You can't wait to sit down to a warm plateful.

God is looking for church leaders who are *eager* to spend time with Him alone. They don't have to be cajoled or nudged. They run in His direction every chance they get.

Acts 6 tells about a church with a problem in its senior adult department. The Hellenistic widows were unhappy about how the Hebrew widows seemed to get preferential treatment. The apostles knew they had to come up with a solution, so they developed the concept of deacons. Why not do the job themselves? Because, as they explained to the congregation, "We will devote ourselves to prayer and to the ministry of the word" (v. 4).

Most preachers I know are comfortable with the second of these priorities: the ministry of the Word. They give a great deal of time to preparing their Sunday sermons. They know this is the premier slot of the week, when the most eyes are on them. They have to be on top of their game, they tell themselves.

But how many of us give equal attention to the first thing the apostles mentioned: devoting ourselves to prayer? Are we guilty of what the prophet Jeremiah sternly rebuked when he said, "The shepherds have become stupid and have not sought the LORD; therefore they have not prospered, and all their flock is scattered" (Jer. 10:21)?

A pastor or other church leader needs to enjoy spending time in the presence of God. The psalmist wrote: "In the morning, O LORD, You will hear my voice; In the morning I will order my prayer to You and eagerly watch" (5:3).

He didn't feel obligated to drag himself through a prayer ritual each morning. He said he was *eager* to talk with the Lord. Apparently that's how Jesus felt as well. Immediately following what Bible commentators

call "the busy Sabbath" in Capernaum (synagogue teaching in the morning, which included a tense interruption by a demonized man; healing
Peter's mother-in-law in the afternoon; then an all-community outdoor
healing/exorcism marathon in the evening), Jesus might have been excused
for sleeping in the next day. Surely He had pumped a lot of adrenalin
and was exhausted. But what does Mark 1:35 say? "In the early morning,
while it was still dark, Jesus got up, left the house, and went away to a
secluded place, and was praying there."

When His disciples finally rolled out of bed, they were perplexed
about where He was. What had happened to their Master? He was
nowhere to be seen. It took some hunting on their part, say verses 36–37,
before they finally tracked Him down.

These kinds of scenes gave Jesus the credibility to say in the Sermon
on the Mount, "When you pray, go into your inner room [the King
James Version says "closet"], close your door and pray to your Father
who is in secret, and your Father who sees what is done in secret will
reward you" (Matt. 6:6).

Why close the door? Well, think about it this way: Why does a married couple close the door? For intimacy.

That's what we seek with our heavenly Father as well. We reveal
things to Him that we would reveal to no one else. We're completely
open and honest about our lives, our fears, our hopes, ourselves. We
want Him to know us completely.

Some people in America today think revival will come when the sinners get back in the closet. No, it's when *we, the church*, get in the closet
and get honest with God that He will send revival to our land. He wants
to be alone with us. He will change our churches and our nation when
we pray and seek His face. If having the sinners out in the open where
we can plainly see them drives us to greater prayer for their salvation, so
be it. That's what God desires for them, and so should we.

In my own life and ministry, I believe that absorbing God's Word
and responding back to Him about it are absolutely essential. I have
no right to stand up and try to speak *for* God if I haven't spoken *with*
God. So my pattern includes reading the Bible from cover to cover at
least once a year. I need to confront it all—not just my favorite passages
or books—in order to hear everything God has to say. Bible intake
(reading, study, memorization, meditation) is vital for any leader.

I'm sometimes amazed at how many other books pastors are reading these days apart from the Bible. No wonder they struggle to feed their souls. Yes, God can influence us through the writings of human authors. But none of them will ever come close to the power of the inspired Word of God.

Likewise, I believe a daily prayer time is fundamental. I choose to pray while I'm working out on my treadmill. People have asked me, "Why there?" I've answered with a smile, "Because early in the morning, if I just sit still to pray, I fall back to sleep. But on a treadmill, you won't fall asleep but one time! That'll break you real quick."

One day back in 1998, I realized I was anxious and nervous about a number of things in my life and work. Philippians 4:6–7 came into my heart: "Be anxious for nothing, but in everything by prayer and supplication with thanksgiving let your requests be made known to God. And the peace of God, which surpasses all comprehension, will guard your hearts and your minds in Christ Jesus."

> ☞ *Some people in America today think revival will come when the homosexuals get back in the closet. No, it's when we, the church, get in the closet and get honest with God that He will send revival to our land.* ✑

In response I said, "Lord, I'm sick of worrying. I'm going to do what this verse says. In fact, I'm going to write down everything that's bothering me on a stack of little cards, so I can start praying about them and quit stewing."

I got a batch of a thousand blank business cards and began filling them out. I made one for every person in my church who had told me about a need in their life. I made one for every speaking engagement on my calendar in the next nine months. I wrote down any financial concerns, the various committees in my church, each of my children, and assorted other items. Whenever I came across something in my Scripture reading that I wanted to pray about, it went onto a card. I then began praying through the stack. And I found that Philippians 4:7 proved true. The peace of God came over my heart and mind.

Today that card deck is almost two inches thick. I try to pray through it on the treadmill twice a week. I keep shuffling the stack to keep it fresh as I go along. I've seen God do some amazing things because He and I have talked together about them in specific terms.

Talking with God can also branch beyond the discussion of requests and needs. I'm a firm believer in worshipping the Lord in private. Personally, I like to sing to the Lord, sometimes using my guitar. Others who don't have musical ability can just put on a worship CD and begin to seek God's face as they listen. What I'm saying is, this doesn't have to be a large-group thing; we can build intimacy with the Lord one-on-one in the "closet."

One thing that will definitely sabotage this, however, is if the leader's marriage is not right. First Peter 3:7 says clearly, "You husbands in the same way, live with your wives in an understanding way, as with someone weaker, since she is a woman; and show her honor as a fellow heir of the grace of life, *so that your prayers will not be hindered.*" I believe with all my heart that if I'm not treating Donna, my wife, sensitively and respectfully, my prayer life will be snagged. God isn't interested in helping the man who is distant from his wife. Closeness at home has a connection to closeness with God.

As we hunger for God, He reaches out to affect every corner of our lives and ministry, private as well as public. I love what one old country preacher said when asked how he went about his preaching: "I read myself full, pray myself hot, and then turn myself loose!" That just about covers the essentials. If we overemphasize reading and study to the exclusion of fervent prayer, our sermons will have little power. If we pray up a storm but don't read ourselves full, the result will be a lot of froth and emotion. We need both disciplines as part of our overall yearning for God.

Holiness

"If My people . . . turn from their wicked ways."

The third condition for God's outpouring has to do with the cleanness of our hands and hearts. I know a lot of people think this doesn't matter all that much; after all, "Nobody's perfect," as the saying goes, and God uses cracked vessels in the ministry all the time. We've all heard about preachers who kept right on using their oratorical abilities even though their personal lives were a mess. And the crowds kept coming to hear them regardless.

That's not what the Bible endorses. It draws a straight line from personal holiness to public effectiveness. Notice the last two lines of this excerpt from David's prayer of repentance after his moral slip with Bathsheba:

> Create in me a clean heart, O God,
> And renew a steadfast spirit within me.
> Do not cast me away from Your presence
> And do not take Your Holy Spirit from me.
> Restore to me the joy of Your salvation
> And sustain me with a willing spirit.
> Then *I will teach transgressors Your ways,*
> *And sinners will be converted to You.* (Ps. 51:10–14)

David knew he would not see sinners converted until *after* he himself was cleaned up. A spiritual harvest was just not going to happen ahead of his own personal repentance. Says Proverbs 28:13, "He who conceals his transgressions will not prosper, But he who confesses and forsakes them will find compassion."

Preachers who harbor sin in their lives undermine both their prayers and their sermons. They cannot expect God to bless their work without dealing with their own transgressions. I am not saying that we *earn* the blessings of God. I am simply saying that He puts a high value on integrity. He is also gracious, however, and if we repent of our sins, He will cleanse and forgive.

BENEATH THE BUZZ

These matters of the heart do not always receive a great deal of attention in the leader's life. Church boards don't talk about them at the annual evaluation. Our pursuit of results, preferably measurable results that can be shown on a chart, tend to override the things 2 Chronicles 7:14 focuses on.

But underneath, the heart of the leader determines everything else.

It's sad to say: you can get so caught up in "doing the ministry" that you forget the Master. You become perfunctory, going through the motions of your profession. You prepare sermons, go visit people

in the hospital, attend meetings, speak at events—all without being
fully in love with Jesus Christ. You're almost like the sleepy guy in the
Dunkin' Donuts commercial: "Time to make the donuts again." After
all, Sunday is just around the corner, and the customers will be expecting you to produce the goods once more.

If you are halfway skilled at it, you can produce fruit in the sense
of growing statistics for your church without having the fruit of the
Spirit in your life. Hanging around
with Jesus, however, brings the love,
joy, peace, patience, and other traits
listed in Galatians 5. When you
acquire the fruit of the Spirit, the
church numbers have a way of taking care of themselves. The main
thing God is trying to achieve in our
lives, after all, is to see us "become
conformed to the image of His Son"
(Rom. 8:29).

> ☞ *I love what one old*
> *country preacher said*
> *when asked how he went*
> *about his preaching:*
> *"I read myself full, pray*
> *myself hot, and then turn*
> *myself loose!"* ☜

A growing church program creates its own false buzz. A "successful"
pastor, like a successful athlete, would do well not to read his own press
clippings. It's too easy to mistake the temporarily growing numbers for
God's approval of our individual lives.

The ultimate reward is one day to hear the Master say, "Well done."
That will not automatically come by building a "great church." Instead,
His accolade comes to those who, like the most noteworthy apostle of
all time, have made it their passion in life "that I may know Him and the
power of His resurrection and the fellowship of His sufferings, being
conformed to His death" (Phil. 3:10). Of course Paul knew Christ in
salvation. But here, years later in his ministry, writing from a Roman
prison, he was still obsessed with getting to know Christ better.

He wanted to know the reality of resurrection power. Ministry that
could be easily explained by mere human effort was not good enough
for him. He sought the supernatural dimension.

But he also was willing, even eager, to embrace the suffering side.
This, he said, was also part of intimacy with the One who had been
crucified. In fact, he saw what this might mean for his future: "being
conformed to His death." And before long a Roman executioner "conformed" Paul's body with the sharp edge of a hefty sword.

Regardless of how well we think we know the Lord, there is always more to discover. Offices and systems and church growth theories are not what it's all about. At the core it's about loving and seeking the face of Jesus.

> ☞ *A growing church program creates its own false buzz. A "successful" pastor, like a successful athlete, would do well not to read his own press clippings.* ☜

Isn't that where our ministry began in the first place? Long before there were appointments and budgets and staff meetings and sermon outlines and denominational machinery, it was just Jesus and us at an old-fashioned altar. He saved us and called us to preach the gospel. We didn't have much of anything but a Bible. No impressive library, no seminary education, no titles or credentials. All we had was a sense burning inside of "Come, follow Me, and see where I lead you."

We need to get back to that. He's waiting for us, in fact. He wants nothing more than for us to move close to Him with humility, hunger, and holiness. Then He can bless our lives and our ministry more than we could ever imagine.

CHAPTER 9

What Attracts the Presence of God?

Anyone who has heard more than half a dozen Christmas sermons has heard preachers make the point about *where* God placed His Son. The baby Jesus didn't show up initially in Herod's palace or among the educated priests and scribes. He was born to a simple village girl, probably still a teenager, named Mary. And the first public announcement went not to the social elite but to dusty shepherds out in a field.

When God comes to visit our world today in the twenty-first century, where does He land? Of all His available options, from Gothic cathedrals to Chinese house churches hiding in a back room, to denominational conferences filling civic arenas or major hotels, where does He prefer to reveal His manifest presence? After all, none of our venues comes even close to His natural abode in the splendor of heaven. You might say He is "moving out of His comfort zone" whenever He visits this chaotic, messed-up planet. What kind of atmosphere could we put together that would make the God of the universe most comfortable and welcome?

The previous chapter described what is essential for the Christian leader's heart. Actually, the story is much the same for the church at large. What's good for the pulpit is good for the pew as well. In this chapter I want to expand the prior points and apply them to all of us who seek to attract God's nearness, whether we're ordained ministers or not.

Years ago I heard a godly man named Don Miller speak about "living under an open heaven." My heart jumped at that word picture—the idea that God might approach us with no impedance, no barriers in between. *That's what I want!* I whispered to myself.

Miller, who is now in his mid-eighties and still travels from his home in Fort Worth, Texas, to give three- and four-day prayer seminars around the country, pointed out that Luke's account of the baptism of Jesus says, "While He was praying, heaven was opened, and the Holy Spirit descended upon Him in bodily form like a dove" (3:21–22). *While He was praying*, this amazing visitation of God's presence took place.

"I take that as a clue," said Miller, "that prayer is one of the actions on our part that opens the windows of heaven."

I have been thinking about this ever since. Here is my list of things we can do to help attract the presence of God. The first two came from Don Miller; I have added the other four. Some of them will sound obvious to you, but others may catch you by surprise.

Sincere and Passionate Prayer

If ever there was a person on earth who might have been excused from the need to pray, it was Jesus. After all, He was God incarnate! He knew all things. He held all power. His link to the Father had never been in question. Why should He need to pray?

Yet He prayed incessantly. He prayed early in the morning (Mark 1:35). He prayed in the middle of the day; Luke 5:16 says, "But Jesus Himself would often slip away to the wilderness and pray." Before taking the huge step of choosing His twelve disciples, "He went off to the mountain to pray, and He spent the whole night in prayer to God" (Luke 6:12).

No wonder the disciples asked Him for prayer instruction, their only such direct request. We never read of them saying, "Lord, teach us to preach." "Lord, teach us to grow a church." "Lord, teach us how to raise money." No, but they did say, "Lord, teach us to pray" (Luke 11:1). They had watched Him enough to know that without prayer their future ministry didn't stand a chance.

The prayer life of Jesus was so strong that it got Him arrested! Judas knew exactly where to go to find Him that night. The betrayer knew his odds were high of locating Jesus in the garden of Gethsemane, praying as usual. "Just follow me," he told the militia. "He was at a house having Passover when I left a couple of hours ago, but by now He's probably left. I'm almost sure I know where He is, though." And Judas was correct. The Son of God was locked in prayer, surrendering Himself to the Father's ultimate plan.

Three of Jesus' famous "seven last words" on the cross (immortalized in the great music of Bach, Haydn, and others) are prayers:

- The first one: "Father, forgive them; for they do not know what they are doing" (Luke 23:34).
- The fourth: "My God, my God, why have You forsaken Me?" (Mark 15:34).
- The seventh: "Father, into Your hands I commit My spirit" (Luke 23:46).

Thus, Jesus prayed at the beginning of His ordeal, in the middle, and at the end.

He even felt the need to pray in His resurrected state. At the table with the two Emmaus disciples on Easter night, "He took the bread and blessed it" (Luke 24:30). This was perhaps His first earthly morsel to eat

> We never read of [the disciples] saying, "Lord, teach us to preach." "Lord, teach us to grow a church." "Lord, teach us how to raise money." But they did say, "Lord, teach us to pray."

since His resurrection. He wouldn't put it into His mouth without first thanking the Father for it.

Would you believe that Jesus is still praying today? That's what Hebrews 7:24–25 says. "He continues forever. . . . Therefore He is able also to save forever those who draw near to God through Him, since He always lives to make intercession for them."

The disciples certainly got the picture. They returned from the ascension of Jesus and promptly headed to the upper room for an open-ended prayer meeting: "These all with one mind were continually devoting themselves to prayer" (Acts 1:14). Ten days later they were still at it. Then Peter preached for thirty minutes or so, and three thousand people were saved.

Where prayer becomes the focus of a church, God's power falls. Every church needs to be aggressive in prayer. I believe in designated prayer rooms and organized prayer ministries. What could be clearer than Isaiah's directive, "My house will be called a house of prayer for all the peoples" (56:7)—a statement that Jesus quoted when cleansing the temple? *Get the money changers out of here!* He was saying by His action. *Let's get back to praying!*

I will say more about the practical implementing of a church's prayer life later in chapter 12. But before moving on, I want to emphasize that I'm not talking about dead, boring prayer recitations. We are God's children, and it's a good thing if we stay childlike in reaching out to our heavenly Father. Have you ever watched a child ask his mom for his favorite chocolate-covered candy bar in a grocery store? Does he say, "Mom, you know, those Whoop-de-dos are my favorite, and, well, I know you and Dad are a little tight for money right now, but if you could maybe squeeze it into the budget, I would kind of like one of those. If you can't swing it, though, it's OK; I understand"?

That is *not* how it goes!

The child pleads with all his might. He's passionate about getting a Whoop-de-do. "Please, Mom! I really, really want one!" (Sounds like a man begging his wife for a truck. "Honey, just think of all the stuff I could haul back from Home Depot to fix up this place for you!")

I'm not saying we should manipulate God. He wouldn't be persuaded by that, anyway. But I'm saying it's a good thing to pour out our feelings to God in prayer. That, in fact, is another good reason to "close your door" (Matt. 6:6) at least some of the time. It's OK to be passionate.

Even Jesus was. "In the days of His flesh, He offered up both prayers and supplications with loud crying and tears to the One able to save Him from death, and He was heard because of His piety" (Heb. 5:7).

When was the last time you prayed like that?

This does not indicate we need to yell at God. People who get in the habit of hollering every time they pray need to adjust their hearing aid. God isn't deaf.

But He isn't nervous, either. He welcomes the full range of our feelings and passions. He knows we hit roadblocks in life that absolutely devastate us. It's all right to tell Him openly how we're feeling in those moments. Somewhere I heard someone say, "People usually don't believe in miracles until they need one." We don't pray desperately until life turns desperate on us.

At other times our passion turns the opposite direction; we pray with "joy unspeakable and full of glory" (1 Pet. 1:8 KJV). This, too, as long as it's authentic, is a sweet sound to the Father's ears. He responds with a swelling tide of His presence.

Tithing

This was the second key Don Miller highlighted, based on the clear wording of Malachi 3:10. "'Bring the whole tithe into the storehouse, so that there may be food in My house, and test Me now in this,' says the LORD of hosts, 'if I will not *open for you the windows of heaven* and pour out for you a blessing until it overflows.'"

I know some Christians think this is merely an Old Testament concept, and they can ignore it. But since when did the New Testament ever *lower* an Old Testament standard? Jesus scolded the religious hairsplitters of His day by saying, "Woe to you, scribes and Pharisees, hypocrites! For you tithe mint and dill and cummin [in other words, the tiniest herbs from the garden], and have neglected the weightier provisions of the law: justice and mercy and faithfulness; but these are the things you should have done *without neglecting the others*. You blind guides, who strain out a gnat and swallow a camel!" (Matt. 23:23–24). He clearly was upholding the importance of tithing. He just wanted them to remember some additional things at the same time: justice, mercy, faithfulness.

I believe Jesus tithed. If He had not, the Pharisees would have jumped all over Him. They nit-picked Him for everything they could think of or dream up. Yet we never read of them criticizing Him for not tithing.

I have been a tither all my Christian life, and I believe it's one reason God has blessed our family. So have the church members I've been privileged to serve. A group of bankers said to me one time, "We've never seen such per-capita giving in a church. It's through the roof. Or do you have a few rich folks over there?" No, in fact, we did not. This was an ordinary congregation in the economic sense. Yet God blessed us with finances that we put to use in His kingdom work.

Jesus said, "Where your treasure is, there your heart will be also" (Matt. 6:21). He led off His sentence talking about money and said our dedication would follow our spending patterns. That is significant.

Churchgoing people will say to me sometimes, "Well, pastor, you don't know what's in my heart."

I reply, "Actually, yes I do. There are two things that give it away for all of us. One is the way we talk; Jesus said, 'The good man out of the good treasure of his heart brings forth what is good; and the evil man out of the evil treasure brings forth what is evil; for his mouth speaks from that which fills his heart' (Luke 6:45). So if Jesus is in our hearts, we're going to talk about Him.

"The other test is how we spend our money. One look at a person's checkbook tells where their heart is, what is truly important to them.

"Speech and finances—these reveal more about our insides than we want people to know sometimes."

God notices these things. As Malachi said, He responds by pouring out His blessings on us. Our God is a God of abundance. He doesn't depend on what the Dow Jones Industrials Average is doing. He doesn't get stressed about the economy. The world's silver and gold are His; and for those who freely give to Him regardless of the economic times, He gives His best.

If we tithe, and especially if we go beyond the strict Old Testament figure of 10 percent to "freely give" (Matt. 10:8) or sow "bountifully, [we] will also reap bountifully" (2 Cor. 9:6). The result will be "all sufficiency in everything" (v. 8). A church full of tithers doesn't have to mess with things like yard sales and bake sales. Where in the Bible do you find God's people having to sell doughnuts or fertilizer to pay for summer camp? It gets a little embarrassing after a while. Not long ago the nationally aired CBS radio news picked up a story about a church in Pendleton, Oregon, that was selling toilet paper in bulk to help pay its bills. The pastor was quoted as saying, "We've got a great price on a quality product that everybody needs." CBS found that amusing, to say the least.

I'd much rather follow the example of Nehemiah, who records in great detail what he, as the governor, gave to the Lord's work (see Neh. 7:70). The next verse shows how the heads of the families promptly followed his example. And verse 72 records the total given by the rest of the people. There's a cascading effect. Senior leaders gave first, supporting leaders gave next, and soon the whole population got in step.

Then what happened? Revival broke out. Read all about it in the next chapters (8–10).

What does the Bible say about nontithers? "You are robbing Me! . . . You are cursed with a curse, for you are robbing Me, the whole nation of you!" (Mal. 3:8–9).

If you don't tithe, you shouldn't be a minister or a deacon. How can you truly serve God if you can't trust him with your tithe? Nor should you be a committee member, deciding how the church spends its resources. If you don't tithe, you shouldn't be an usher taking up the offering. The same goes for teaching Sunday school or singing solos in the music department.

Pastors and churches that sincerely want the presence of God in their midst can't afford not to tithe. It is part of opening up the heavens so God can pour out His unrestrained blessing upon us.

Fasting

When our hunger for God exceeds our hunger for double mocha chocolate chip ice cream, then we forgo the second in order to satisfy the first. Fasting is not strange or fanatic behavior, as some people think; it is simply another part of developing a heart for God.

I don't totally understand how it works. I just know that fasting puts prayer into a whole new dimension. I may not understand all the dynamics of an automobile engine, either, but I still put it to use by driving my car every day. So it is with fasting. More than my next meal, more than any material blessing, more than my paycheck, more than any spiritual gift, I want to draw close to God.

Psalm 27:4 says:

> One thing I have asked from the LORD, that I shall seek:
> That I may dwell in the house of the LORD all the days of
>   my life,
> To behold the beauty of the LORD
> And to meditate in His temple.

Do you know what one of our major problems is in the current church? We want more than *one thing!* We want outward success and prestige and money and all sorts of items. David said he had only *one thing* on his mind: to gaze upon the beauty of the Lord.

A few verses later, he added:

> When You said, "Seek My face," my heart said to You,
> "Your face, O LORD, I shall seek." (v. 8)

When Martha got swept up with all the demands of food preparation, Jesus told her, "You are worried and bothered about so many things; but only one thing is necessary" (Luke 10:41–42). Food has a way of taking over our lives. We hardly finish one meal before we start imagining the next one, where we'll go out this time, and what we'll order from the menu. Fasting, on the other hand, takes a break from all that obsession to focus on *one thing*.

I appreciate the words of a 2003 song written by Paul Baloche and Don Moen:

> *One thing we ask of You,*
> *One thing that we desire,*
> *That as we worship You,*
> *Lord, come and change our lives.*
> *Arise, arise, arise, arise,*
> *Arise, take Your place,*
> *Be enthroned on our praise.*[36]

If Queen Esther found it important to fast (see Esther 4:15–17), if Daniel fasted in "sackcloth and ashes" (Dan. 9:3), if the Twelve were told by Jesus that some strongholds of the enemy would not be dislodged except by fasting (see Matt. 17:21), who are we to try to bypass this spiritual discipline?

It's a little like starting a new business. In the beginning you're focused. You work long hours. You return phone calls. You're eager to get every sale you can. You're scared you might fail.

Then you start making a little money. You get comfortable. Your edge isn't quite so honed. You can forget about the *one thing*.

> *Fasting is one of the best ways I know to signal to God that we are dead serious about realizing His presence and power.*

Whenever we lose our focus on seeking God, we can forget about experiencing the blessings of revival. Fasting is one of the best ways I know to signal to God that we are dead serious about realizing His presence and power. We want Him more than our daily food.

He takes notice of that, I can assure you.

Repentance

The closer we get to God, the more embarrassed we are likely to become about our sins and shortcomings. The spotlight of His holiness grows brighter and brighter, exposing the dark blotches of our humanity. God says to us, "I love you, but you need to repent."

He already knows, of course, what we are doing and thinking and saying that we shouldn't. There are no secrets with Him. The sooner we decide to get clean and change course, the more intimate we can be with Him. Proverbs 3:32 puts it bluntly: "The devious are an abomination to the Lord; but He is intimate with the upright."

If we think we are exempt from the practice of repentance, we are making the same mistake the Israelites made during the time of the later kingdom of Judah. Prophets kept coming for some 125 years saying repent, repent, repent of your wickedness. The population mainly brushed them off, thinking, *Yes, God judged the folks up north in the other tribes by sending the Assyrian army. But this is Jerusalem! God's got too much invested here to ever discipline us.*

Sounds a lot like the United States of America, doesn't it? Hey, we're the red, white, and blue. We give so much money to missions all over the world. God would never mess up our party.

Let me just say this: I'm an American, but God is not. And if we don't repent in this country, God owes us nothing. America needs God a whole lot more than God needs America. He won't hesitate to strike us with the same punishment He unleashed on Jerusalem in 586 BC if necessary.

The apostle Peter stood up before a tough Jewish audience in the temple courts and said, "Repent and return, so that your sins may be wiped away, in order that times of refreshing may come from the presence of the Lord" (Acts 3:19). Do you see the clear linkage between repentance and revival? If we *walk* to God in repentance, He will *run* to us in revival. If we will reach out to Him with the hand of faith, He will touch us with His hand of grace.

Whenever I read that verse about having our sins wiped away, I can't help remembering the time one of our kids spilled gravy all over our dog's back. Sophie is a long-haired little thing, kind of a dust mop on four legs. Now sweet-milk gravy is good on biscuits, but it doesn't go very well on a teacup Yorkshire terrier.

She needed to be wiped clean. When she finally got a bath on Saturday, she was so happy.

In the sight of God, you and I have more than gravy spilled on us. We have a plague called sin that will eat us alive if we don't repent. We'll stay mad all the time. We'll live feeling condemned. We'll be afraid of a dozen different threats. But when we repent and return, God will change all that in an instant.

My wife, Donna, went on a mission trip with a group to Romania and told me an interesting fact when she returned. During the Communist era, it became common to ridicule the Christians there—specifically the Baptists, the Brethren, and the Pentecostals—as *pocăiți*. The word means "repenters." Police, school officials, and anyone in power snarled the term at those who served God. It carried the connotation of being weak, apologetic, and somewhat dumb in the face of state atheism.

The Christians of that time, however, embraced it as a badge of honor. The word is still in use today.

Here in America we tend to call ourselves "believers," which, when you stop to reflect on it, signifies the act of affirming a set of doctrines. "I believe in God the Father, in Jesus Christ His only Son," etc. It's predominantly mental, rational, propositional. We would rarely think to typify ourselves as *pocăiți*, as "repenters." That just wouldn't cross our minds.

Maybe it should.

Advance Worship

Naturally we all view corporate worship in the house of God as the encounter with Him. In a sense this whole book is about the worship experience. But what I want to emphasize in this chapter is that worship plays an important role (along with prayer, tithing, fasting, and repentance) in laying out the welcome mat *ahead of* the manifest presence of God.

The best illustration of this truth that I know is what happened in 2 Chronicles 20. King Jehoshaphat and his people had been attacked by a huge army coalition of three nations working together. They were about to launch a massacre. The king "was afraid and turned his attention to seek the LORD, and proclaimed a fast throughout all Judah. So Judah gathered together to seek help from the LORD" (vv. 3–4).

He prayed a desperate, emotional prayer in front of everyone, concluding with this ringing confession: "We are powerless before this great multitude who are coming against us; nor do we know what to do, but our eyes are on You" (v. 12). The Holy Spirit responded by inspiring a man named Jahaziel to give a strong word of encouragement. Then, the Bible says: "Jehoshaphat bowed his head with his face to the ground, and all Judah and the inhabitants of Jerusalem fell down before the LORD, worshiping the LORD. The Levites, from the sons of the Kohathites and of the sons of the Korahites, stood up to praise the LORD God of Israel, with a very loud voice" (vv. 18–19).

They were still in big trouble. The advancing armies had not backed off an inch. Jehoshaphat and his people had no earthly reason to think they wouldn't be slaughtered by the next day. Yet they gave themselves to worshipping God.

> *I'm an American, but God is not. And if we don't repent in this country, God owes us nothing.*

I've heard some people say, "Well, I'll thank the Lord when He gets me out of debt." Or, "I'll praise the Lord when He heals my body." Or, "I'll thank the Lord when my rebellious child comes back home." In contrast, the people of Judah gave God praise before anything supernatural occurred.

If you know the rest of the chapter, you know that the worshippers kept on singing and praising the Lord as they moved out toward the battlefield. Suddenly, the attacking coalition began falling apart. One group started arguing with another, and soon their swords were turned on each other. By the time the full Judean army arrived at the top of the ridge, they stood staring at nothing but dead bodies lying across the landscape.

Talk about God showing up and showing off! He knocked out a powerful invasion force all by Himself. All the people of Judah had done was give themselves to openhearted worship in advance. God took care of the rest.

Some of their worship was "with a very loud voice" (2 Chron. 20:19). The apostle Paul wrote once that "the Lord is the Spirit, and where the Spirit of the Lord is, there is liberty" (2 Cor. 3:17). It is entirely appropriate for us today to use biblical expressions in our worship, as long as they're done in reverence and under authority. God wants to sense our passion for Him.

The same Paul, by the way, worshipped in advance when he and Silas were sitting bound in the Philippian jail, their backs bleeding from the torture, rats probably running across their toes. Yet "about midnight [they] were praying and singing hymns of praise to God" (Acts 16:25). Soon an earthquake hit that block and set everybody loose!

When we fail to worship God, we forfeit the power of praise. We forfeit the warfare of worship. But when we open up to Him ahead of time, incredible things happen.

Unity

The final thing that welcomes the presence of God is unity. When we come together in harmony with one another, the Lord is free to move among us, knowing that nobody is going to jam a stick into the spokes. We're going to flow in the same direction with God.

Look at Psalm 133:

> Behold, how good and how pleasant it is
> For brothers to dwell together in unity!
> It is like the precious oil upon the head,
> Coming down upon the beard,
> Even Aaron's beard,
> Coming down upon the edge of his robes.
> It is like the dew of Hermon
> Coming down upon the mountains of Zion;
> For there the LORD commanded the blessing—life forever.

The two word pictures of the psalm are significant. First, David says that unity is like the anointing oil that was used to consecrate the high priest. It started at the top of man's head and gradually traveled downward, by gravity, onto his beard, then his robe, and finally dripped off onto the ground.

The second picture is of the water runoff from Mount Hermon, way up north in Israel, in the territory originally assigned to the tribe of Dan. On a trip to the Holy Land, I got to see this impressive ninety-one-hundred-foot mountain from a distance. Our guide said it is the only snow-capped peak in the whole Middle East. It produces 40 percent of Israel's freshwater supply as its streams run down into the Sea of Galilee and feed the Jordan River. *Jor* in Hebrew means "to descend from." So the river's name is simply "descending from Dan," which is literally where the water originates.

The psalmist made this into a picture of spiritual unity, just like the anointing oil. Both of them start at the top and flow downward. That's how unity works in a church: It has to start with just the senior pastor and Jesus. Next it comes to the pastor and the church staff. From there on it flows to the lay leaders and finally trickles on to the rest of the congregation.

Nothing quenches the Holy Spirit so fast as when staff members or deacons are doing their own thing, resisting the God-ordained leadership of the senior pastor. I'm not saying we pastors are always right or that we are justified in being little dictators. But we have been placed in an office that God created. If there is tension and fighting anywhere along the line, the anointing of God is simply not going to flow.

Instead, you'll have a situation like at the end of the book of Judges. The last verse of the entire book sums it up: "In those days there was no king in Israel; everyone did what was right in his own eyes" (21:25). Things were a mess. It was one of the darkest, most wicked, most brutal periods in Israel's history.

I'm afraid I know some churches today where everybody's doing what's right in their own eyes. A couple of deacons are leading one faction, while the women's organization is pushing a different agenda, the youth department is doing its own thing, and everybody's mad. Some people even say this is normal!

I heard somebody say, "It's the Christian way to fight." No, it's not. That's the devil's way. We don't need to be airing all our dirty laundry in front of everybody, especially new Christians. Far better to do what they did in Acts 15, where the leaders came together behind closed doors and hashed out the question of whether Gentiles had to obey the Old Testament Law or not. Then they were able to make a unified, godly announcement to the whole church.

In the time of Nehemiah, revival was triggered when "all the people *gathered as one man* at the square . . . and they asked Ezra the scribe to bring the book of the law of Moses which the LORD had given to Israel" (8:1). These people were not interested in fighting with one another. They came together to hear what God would say. Within a few hours they were "lifting up their hands; then they bowed low and worshiped the LORD with their faces to the ground" (v. 6). By the second day they were organizing a weeklong Feast of Booths (Tabernacles), which had not been celebrated for decades. Full-scale revival was underway.

When leaders at all levels are united, it filters down to the congregation, and God's people become truly of one mind and heart. In that environment, anything is possible. "Behold, how good and how pleasant" (Ps. 133:1) it is, indeed! Even the Lord smiles on this climate of unity and comes to visit with His awesome presence.

These six keys play a major role in making God welcome in our lives and our churches.

CHAPTER 10

Flow, Not Show

The crowd was buzzing in the Samford University auditorium that
night as the Junior Miss talent competition got underway. Forty
or fifty high school seniors would be taking the stage, one at a time, to
perform—including our oldest daughter, Lindsey. My wife and I were as
excited as the rest of the parents and friends who had come.

The acts ran a gamut from tap dancing to a classical sonatina to a
dramatic monologue to jazz piano to one girl who performed a country
song with her guitar. Lindsey's talent was interpretive dance, portraying
the song "Shackles (Praise You)" by the contemporary Christian singing duo Mary Mary. She began in a drab, brown costume that eventually was transformed into a flowing white dress with gold trim, as the
song spoke about freedom in Christ.

We cheered wildly at the end, while a group of her friends held up
letters spelling L-I-N-D-S-E-Y. We were even happier when the judges
announced her name among the top ten finalists. Outside her dressing
room after the show, we presented her with flowers and hugs. It had
been quite a show.

When the full competition, including categories for physical fitness
as well as poise and appearance, was over, our daughter did not win the
title she had sought. But we were proud of her nonetheless and told her
so repeatedly. She would always be a winner in our eyes.

Such a community program is certainly worthwhile and enjoyable.
But we in the church make a serious mistake if we bring across the same

tactics to our practice of worship. There is a huge difference between a Savior-focused worship experience and a Christian variety show.

If all we are doing when we plan a church service is Scotch-taping together a crowd-pleasing lineup of bits and pieces—a welcome, a couple of fast songs, then a slow song, some announcements, a choir song, perhaps a solo, maybe a video clip, a sermon, maybe a baptism or a Communion observance, with several prayers spliced in here and there, all to fit nicely in sixty or seventy-five minutes—we have badly missed the mark. We have forgotten who our True Audience is. We have slid from the realm of an *encounter* with God down to just an event, and the two are not the same at all.

Staging events is a common human skill. Preachers know how to do it; so do singers, entertainers, and comedians, as well as business leaders, wedding planners, and politicians. Having encounters with the living God is a whole different thing altogether.

> *Many church services today have become far too choppy. Nobody intended for this to happen, but it has become part of our tradition.*

Many church services today have become far too choppy. Nobody intended for this to happen, but it has become part of our tradition. Just when the Spirit really begins to breathe in a congregation, He gets interrupted by a welcome time, a drama skit, or an announcement. We shoot ourselves in the foot. The protocol of *OK, what's next on the list?* takes over. *Gotta keep this moving.*

A Seamless Core

As I have thought about this problem over the years and have sought the Lord for guidance, I have come to see the value of building *one continuous flow* throughout the core of the service with as little disruption as possible. If you were to visit our church on a Sunday morning these days, here is what you'd experience. (I'm not saying we have reached perfection by any means. But I do find that our focus on Jesus is enhanced.)

I start by moving to the side of the pulpit and saying in a normal tone of voice, "Let's begin today by inviting the presence of the Lord to come be with us in this service. Jesus goes wherever He's invited. All of you who'd like to join me here at the altar for a time of prayer, come ahead." Several dozen people immediately begin moving forward to kneel on the steps that go up to the platform.

I continue, "And across the sanctuary, let me ask any men who'd be willing to 'take a knee' in the house of God, go ahead and kneel there in your row. Let's wait upon the Lord." There's a shuffling sound as big, husky men turn around and bow. Even some women who happen to be wearing slacks that day will join them.

By this time I'm down on one knee myself, and the auditorium gets quiet; only a soft worship chorus from the piano is heard. We pray individually for several minutes. Eventually, I say, again in a subdued tone, something along the lines of "Lord, we welcome You today. We gather together in Your name to focus solely on You. Let the words of our mouths and the meditations of all our hearts be acceptable in Your sight. In Your presence, there is fullness of joy. We bless and praise Your holy name."

I usually lead out in singing the chorus the musicians have been playing, such as "My Jesus, my Savior, Lord, there is none like You" or an old hymn such as "Draw me nearer, nearer, blessed Lord, to the cross where Thou hast died." By the time we finish, everyone is back at their seats, usually standing.

After a short welcome to our guests, the minister of music moves to continue the worship and praise. No break, no shift, no interruption. We keep right on going with at least four or five songs to give honor to the Lord. Some are up-tempo; others are slow and meditative. Some were written just last year; others were written a hundred or two hundred years ago. The style or genre is not the issue here; the point is to go after God with all our hearts. We love Him and want to express that love in a sustained, ongoing way.

Yes, we project the words onto three big screens—not because we're trying to be cool but because they aid in maintaining the flow of worship. There's no need to stop and say, "Now turn to page 342." Younger people are of course entirely comfortable with projection technology, and even senior adults appreciate being able to see the words in larger print than what would appear in a hymnal or bulletin insert. The volume of the singing is also greater because people's heads and throats are *up*, not buried in a book.

I know some purists argue that screens lack the musical notes and thus prevent people from reading the score in four-part harmony. That is true. But how many of us never paid attention to the notes in a hymnal anyway? To me this is a modest downside in exchange for the great benefits of getting the steady flow of robust singing that is enabled by screens. And if you want to point note-readers in the right direction, you can always add a small line at the bottom of each slide that reads, "For the musical score of this song, see page 147 in the hymnal."

As the final song comes to an end, the worship leader says something like, "Bow with me in prayer, please. Heavenly Father, thank You for hearing us today. We have offered to You our praise and worship out of sincere hearts because we love You so much. You are the most special Person in all our lives. Now we're going to bring You another gift, the gift of our tithes and offerings. Receive these things from us and use them for Your purposes. We pray today in Jesus' name, amen."

The people sit down as the ushers promptly move into position to pass the offering plates. There's no lurch, no change in the mood of the service. The offering is a continuation of the gift of musical praise that has just been going on. It is another way to worship the Lord. The focused atmosphere is maintained by a soloist, a small ensemble, or the choir that sings while the offering is being collected.

Some pastors will say, "But wait a minute. That doesn't give an opportunity to introduce the offering, spotlight the need, and urge people to give. I want to make a speech before the plates are passed."

My response is to say I have no problem talking to my congregation about money—but not in the middle of a worship encounter. I will preach boldly about tithing during our stewardship month (every January) and elsewhere throughout the year. There is a time and place to exhort Christians to honor God with their finances. It's all part of the larger lordship of Christ. But I am not willing to disrupt the worship for an offering pitch.

By the time the giving is concluded, we move directly into hearing from God through His Word. I am careful not to break the flow at this point through any long-winded introduction of a guest speaker, as mentioned before. If I am preaching myself, I don't waste time with excessive humor or personal tales from the past week; I go straight for the Scripture. These people have not come to hear a pastor's comedy routine; they have come to gain a word from God. I am merely the messenger.

Charles Spurgeon put it vividly when he said to his young preachers, "As long as the guests get the spiritual meat, the waiter at the table may be happy to be forgotten."[37]

Once again screen projection helps engage more of the worshippers' senses. The listeners become seers as well, as the speaker's main points appear in visual form. In addition, if the congregation is asked to read a portion of Scripture aloud, the screen is a useful way to unify everyone on one Bible translation for that reading, even though individuals may have brought varying versions into the service.

The climax of the sermon moves seamlessly into the invitation for response. This is a vital part of our encounter with God. I believe in asking listeners to make a public indication of what they have decided about following Christ. I know some preachers balk at this, claiming that public invitations are awkward and unnecessary. Some have even suggested they are unbiblical. I respectfully disagree. To preach the gospel of Christ without giving listeners an opportunity to receive Christ as Savior and Lord, crossing the line from darkness to light, is unthinkable in my view. It is like telling a thirsty person about water without putting a filled glass within his reach.

This is not a distraction or detour in the worship experience. This is engaging God in the closest, most intimate way possible. (I will say more in a future chapter about how to make this effective.)

But What About . . . ?

Now immediately you will recognize that I have left out some things from the normal church service. What about the announcements, for example?

Yes, there are a number of "people items" to cover. I have tried several strategies over the years, discarding those that didn't really help. I have gradually come to two conclusions:

1. Quite a few of the things preachers think they *must* talk about aren't all that mandatory. They can be handled just as well in the church bulletin. For example, instead of introducing a soloist, our bulletin now simply reads: "Solo today: Charlotte Guffin." If we have a guest

speaker, the bulletin can carry a full paragraph about the person's various exploits, thus saving time in the service.

A congregation quickly figures out whether the church bulletin is worth reading or is a waste of time and paper. By conveying vital information in this format, people learn to pay attention to it.

2. Things that must be done verbally are best if they are grouped at one end of the service or the other. For example, we do our baptisms at the start of the service. We give enough time to make it meaningful, but we don't elongate

> ☞ *Some pastors and worship leaders, I know, get anxious about moving away from the script. They're so concerned about wildfire that they end up missing heavenly fire.* ☜

the process. The focus of attention, naturally, is on the baptismal candidate, which is as it should be. We rejoice together at each person's public declaration of following Christ.

As already mentioned, we also make time at the beginning to welcome visitors to our services. But once these things are taken care of, we head straight into worship. From that moment on, no interruptions are allowed. We are united in going in the direction of God's heart. No "patchwork," no miscellaneous this-and-that. The flow must be preserved. Any announcements that I feel absolutely must be mentioned are usually saved until the end, after the invitation. As Paul said in 1 Thessalonians 2:4, "So we speak, not as pleasing men, but God who examines our hearts."

How Much Control?

So far in this chapter, I have emphasized careful planning that maximizes our encounter with God and reduces distractions. I believe the Spirit of God can guide us in a Thursday morning planning meeting as well as on the spot during a Sunday morning service. We spend at least an hour or two each week designing our upcoming services along the lines I have outlined.

But what if we, in our humanity, forgot something? What if we didn't clearly think through the flow from one part to the next? Or what if the Holy Spirit had a novel idea that He couldn't get us to listen to?

What if He wanted us to go in a different direction, and we were tone-deaf in the planning meeting?

Where worship leaders get in trouble is when they write an order of service and then behave as if it is cast in stone. The only things they can do are what is preprogrammed. If the order says we're going to sing such-and-such a song, then we're definitely going to sing it no matter what. We have to follow the script.

Pastors need to be the leaders of a worship service, but they also need to be careful not to resist or quench the Holy Spirit. Sometimes the Spirit may be a mile or two ahead of us in knowing what's best for the congregation. (That possibility may be hard to imagine, but it's true!) The question is, can the Spirit get our attention to step outside the mold? Isaiah 64:3 describes a wondrous occasion "when You did awesome things which we did not expect, You came down, the mountains quaked at Your presence." Wouldn't you hate to miss such a divine visitation?

When I played football at Dyersburg High School, we had a quarterback named George Guthrie. I was part of the offensive line. We'd get in the huddle, and George would say, "OK, we're going to run Thirty-seven Slant." But we all knew that if we came up to the line of scrimmage, got down in our three-point stance, and then suddenly heard George call out, "Blue Forty-two," that meant things had changed. He had seen something in the defensive lineup that was different, and he was now calling an "audible." The defensive back was playing a good ten yards off our split end, which meant he was wide open for a quick pass with plenty of room to run.

Pastors are like quarterbacks; they need to have the freedom to go up to the mike and say, "I'm just sensing now that we need to go a different direction. I believe the Spirit of God would have us to . . ." This ought not to dismay the minister of music or anyone else on the platform. They need to understand that written plans are always subject to change.

I remember one Sunday morning in Gardendale when the initial prayer time became so sweet that I didn't want to stop it. We sang one worship chorus and then another and another. The musicians followed along beautifully, supporting the tide of worship in the congregation. None of this was written down, but nobody got upset about that.

I let the minister of music take the lead at this point, and he kept going with more songs of praise and adoration. He was improvising on the spot just as I had been. By the time I finally looked at my watch, forty minutes had passed.

I said to the congregation, who were still standing, "If you're tired and would like to sit down at this point, go ahead. But we're going to keep worshipping the Lord through singing." A little while later, when this intimacy with God came to a natural conclusion, I said, "I'm not going to preach the message I had prepared for today. I preached it in the earlier two services, but this one is different. What I want to emphasize to you just now is . . ." and I proceeded to talk about why Jesus is so special and why we all need Him in our lives. I gave a gospel invitation. People came forward to be saved. People came forward to arrange for baptism and for joining the church. God was in the house.

Now don't get worried; that was the only time in fourteen years in Gardendale that a service unfolded to the point of not having a sermon. I don't want to make anyone nervous. Some pastors and worship leaders, I know, get anxious about moving away from the script. They're so concerned about wildfire that they end up missing heavenly fire.

But if God is truly our focus, He will let His leaders know what to allow. There have been times in a service when I have strongly sensed the Lord saying to my heart, *Pray for people who are discouraged today*. Or, *Give a chance for people who are sick to be prayed for*. I've said to the congregation, "If you're hurting in some way today, either in your body or in your spirit, just come to the altar. We will stand beside you and pray for you, like the Bible says." This has turned out to be a precious time of intercession for those in pain.

Each worship service has its own fingerprint. For one thing, the crowd is different from the hour before or the Sunday before, and so their expression to God is unique. The same book of the Bible that says, "Shout joyfully to the rock of our salvation" (Ps. 95:1) also says, "Be still, and know that I am God" (Ps. 46:10 KJV). Part of my job as a pastor is to pray, "Lord, how do You want to be worshipped today? Do You want us to shout to You? Or do You want us to be silent? Do You want us to lift our hands or just bow our heads? Do You want us to sing right now or pray for awhile? What do You have in mind?"

I'm sure that in trying to be led by the Holy Spirit in a service I have missed God's direction more than once. But God allows for human fumbling and misjudgments. He can be flexible, too. I would rather seek His guidance for the congregation and make an error than to say, "I've written my order of service, and that's that. We're going to do it my way, period."

If we're not careful, we pastors can turn into pharaohs. We sit on our thrones and declare how things are going to proceed. We veto certain expressions because "we don't do things like that at this church." Our control is not to be questioned.

Meanwhile, God is trying to say, "Let My people go, that they may worship Me! Quit squelching their sincere and openhearted devotion. They want to pour out their love to Me. Stop blocking their way. Release My people."

If somebody is genuinely worshipping the Lord by lifting hands or saying amen, and it's not overly distracting, I'm not going to be a pharaoh and tell them to stop. I want people to connect with God. Some of them are wired to be more expressive than others, and that's all right.

I also want them to give me grace in return when I feel led to

> *If we're not careful, we pastors can turn into pharaohs. Meanwhile, God is trying to say, "Let My people go, that they may worship Me!"*

step out of the ordinary. I've been known to mention a song in the middle of my sermon and then to say, "Well, instead of quoting the words, let me just sing it for you!" I'll cut loose and sing it a cappella right there.

On one of my early Sundays at Bellevue, I was doing a sermon series called "I Believe." I was covering the basics of theology over about a thirteen-week period. The graphics team had even created an attractive banner that rose up hydraulically out of the floor behind me to set the "I Believe" theme at sermon time.

On this Sunday the sermon was going to be "I Believe in Salvation." Just before I was to preach, the choir did an outstanding rendition of the James Huey song "When I think about the Lord, how He saved me, how He raised me. . . ." It was awesome. The people gave a standing ovation.

Then everybody sat down again, and it was my turn to preach. Up came the banner. I jumped up and said, "Sing it again! Put down the banner. That was incredible, choir! Take a breath and sing it again!"

Soon the crowd began to clap, and the choir launched into an instant rerun. The song was even better the second time around. From that point I preached with extra anointing about the joy of salvation, and a good number of people came to Christ that morning.

Some of our churches are like going to a ballet performance. The actors on stage are all highly trained, dazzlingly dressed, and wonderfully synchronized as they go through their leaps and twirls. But we sit there knowing that everything is canned. Nobody is going to move a muscle that hasn't been rehearsed a hundred times.

Personally speaking, I'd rather go to a good old football game. Yes, there are rules and boundaries that define the field of play, just as at the theater. But within those parameters, you never know what's going to happen. You can guess, based on past games you've watched—but you might be in for a surprise this time. You're on the edge of your seat with anticipation. No wonder football sells a ton more tickets in this country than ballet.

Jesus was just about the most unpredictable person who ever lived. People never knew what He was going to say or do. That's part of what they found fascinating about Him. His ultimate surprise, of course, was the resurrection. All of a sudden, here He was, alive again! What a shock.

> *Jesus was just about the most unpredictable person who ever lived. People never knew what He was going to say or do.*

I find it interesting that, of all the hundreds of new cable TV channels that have tried to get a footing in the market the past few years, one of the most successful has been TLC—The Learning Channel. You wouldn't have predicted that from the name alone. You would have put more hope in others that have faded.

But with shows from *Trading Spaces* to *Overhaulin'* to *What Not to Wear,* The Learning Channel has become a leader in the field. Have you ever noticed their slogan? Right beneath their distinctive TLC lettering is this tagline: "Life Unscripted."

TV viewers who are bored to death with far more expensive dramas and action programs have found this approach refreshingly real. Perhaps there's a lesson for us church folks here.

Beyond Clock-Watching

Does "calling an audible" on Sunday morning mess up the time schedule? Probably. But so what? Relationships that are chained to the clock are inevitably stunted. Have you ever gone to a doctor who was in a hurry? You tried to describe your problem, and within about eight minutes the guy was standing up and already hanging on the doorknob trying to get out of there to go see the next patient. Did you feel heard? Not at all.

When God shows up in a service, He forgets about time, and so should we. Jesus is there, and that's all that matters. So what if the next service has to start ten minutes late? We can adjust for that, can't we?

What I am describing here, by the way, is another reason not to do live telecasts of a church service. TV cameras, in my view, are sort of like what Jesus said about the Sabbath; they exist for us, not us for them. That's why our church videotapes the services and does the editing later, so television stations can air them on a seven-day delay.

Whatever distracts us from following God must be dealt with. People in the congregation can tell when we've got one eye on the clock and the other on the printed order of service. They know instinctively when everything is cut and dried. Even though we try to camouflage our bondage to a script, they can tell.

A friend told me about visiting a large church in the Chicago suburbs. It had good music and a biblically based sermon. "But there was something all the way through that seemed slightly rushed," my friend said. "The dead giveaway came right at the end, after the closing prayer, when the senior pastor apologized for running *four minutes late*. I looked at my watch, and—yes, it was now 12:19 p.m. This service, which had started at 10:45 a.m., was apparently to have run for exactly ninety minutes, concluding at 12:15. The pastor was so clock-conscious he felt he needed to apologize for going over by four minutes."

I tell my congregation, "Don't even think about putting a roast in the oven on Sunday morning. If you do, your chances of winding up with an Old Testament 'burnt offering' are good! I'm a Crock-Pot preacher, in case you hadn't already noticed."

When revival hit in the time of Nehemiah, "they read from the book of the law of the LORD their God for a fourth of the day; and for another fourth they confessed and worshiped the LORD their God" (9:3). I don't know if anybody got home by suppertime or not. That's how it goes in the presence of God. That's why eternity will be timeless. When we're with Jesus, we really don't care about the clock.

If we can't handle more than sixty minutes in church, what makes us think we'll like heaven? In fact, what makes us think we're even going there at all? God is looking for people with the spirit of Psalm 42:

> As the deer pants for the water brooks,
> So my soul pants for You, O God.
> My soul thirsts for God, for the living God;
> When shall I come and appear before God? (vv. 1–2)

I don't want to be too hard on my fellow pastors, because I understand their apprehensions. None of us like to get letters or e-mails from ruffled church members. We also wonder what our peers in the ministry will think if we stretch the traditions. But the greater point is, what does God think of our worship? What is He trying to accomplish in our lives? Paul wrote in Galatians 1:10, "For am I now seeking the favor of men, or of God? Or am I striving to please men? If I were still trying to please men, I would not be a bond-servant of Christ."

Most seminaries do not teach pastors how to lead worship. We spend a great deal more class time on Hebrew, Greek, systematic theology, and church history than on the dynamics of corporate worship. So pastors have to go out and learn on their own. I'm not criticizing any academic program; I am just stating the facts.

All of us in leadership need to pray along with the newly crowned Solomon, when God appeared to him at night and offered him a blank check for anything he wanted, "Give Your servant an understanding heart to judge Your people to discern between good and evil" (1 Kings 3:9). The Hebrew word for "understanding" here is *shamea*, a correlate of *shama*, which is translated "to hear" or "to hearken" more than nine hundred times. God can equip us with the sensitivity to hear in our spirits what is good and what is detrimental to the body of Christ. Much of that hearing will happen in advance of Sunday morning; some of it will happen on the spot, in the moment.

Entering into the flow of God's presence is a high privilege we must embrace. He has agreed to meet with us! This dialogue is one of the most valuable things in the world.

CHAPTER 11

Music: The Agony and the Ecstasy

Henry Wadsworth Longfellow, the great American poet who gave us "The Song of Hiawatha" and "Paul Revere's Ride," wrote in the 1830s, "Music is the universal language of mankind."[38] If he were around today, however, we'd have to inform the bearded gentleman that in our churches, music is not so much the universal language as the universal *aggravation*.

People get downright emotional about this topic, it seems. No longer (or at least not very often) do Christians seem to discuss doctrine like their parents used to do; now everybody's too worked up having *musical* debates. It is not a battle for righteousness or holiness but instead a struggle over formats and styles, rhythms and volumes, my way versus your way. Which instruments shall we use? How fast or slow shall we play them? How new or old shall the songs be? Can any good thing come out of Mobile, or Anaheim, or Australia, or the dusty hymnal?

Progressives feel impatient with the slowness of change, while traditionalists feel scorned and abandoned. Some church leaders have thrown up their hands and decided on a segregationist approach: one service for one group, another service for the other.

It is simply part of human nature that the older we get, the less thrilled we are about change. We start liking things to stay the way they've always been. Younger people, meanwhile, are all keyed up about innovation. They don't understand why in the world "Abide with Me" means so much to Granddad. That's because they weren't around when that hymn spoke deeply to Granddad during a spiritual crisis back when he was a young man. Neither party is wrong; they're both just coming from different angles.

I suppose there's a bit of comfort in realizing that church folk have been arguing about this for quite awhile—even before Longfellow's time. Listen to the official minutes of a business meeting at First Congregational Church of Windsor, Connecticut, dated Sunday, July 2, 1736 (forty years before the American Revolution):

> Society meeting, Capt. Pelatiah Allyn Moderator. The business of the meeting proceeded in the following manner: the Moderator proposed consideration of what should be done respecting that part of Publick Worship called Singing, whether in their Publick meetings on Sabbath day, they would sing the way Deacon Marshall usually sung in his lifetime, commonly called the "Old Way," *[i.e., singing by rote, from memory]* or whether they would sing the way taught by Mr. Beal, commonly called "Singing by Rule" *[i.e., by reading notes from a printed page].*
>
> And when the Society had discoursed the matter, the Moderator proposed to vote. But when the vote was passed, there being many voters, it was difficult to take the exact number of votes in order to determine on which side the major vote was; whereupon the Moderator ordered all the voters to go out of the seats and stand in the alleys *[aisles]*, and then those that were for Deacon Marshall's way should go into the men's seats, and those that were for Mr. Beal's way should go into the women's seats. The Moderator asked me *[the recording secretary]* how many there was for Deacon Marshall's way. I answered 42, and he said there was 63 or 64. Then we both counted again and agreed the number being 43.
>
> Then the Moderator proceeded and desired that those who were for singing in Publick the way that Mr. Beal taught would draw out of their seats and pass out of the door and be counted. They replied that they were ready to show their minds in any proper way where they were, if they might be directed thereto—but would not go out the door to do the

same, and desired that they might be led to a vote where they were, and they were ready to show their minds, which the Moderator refused to do and thereupon declared that it was voted that Deacon Marshall's way of singing, called the "Old Way," should be sung in Publick for the future.

He ordered me to record the same, which I refused to do under the circumstances thereof, and have recorded the facts and proceedings.[39]

Sounds like just a wonderful time of joy and peace in the Lord, doesn't it?!

The curious part is that while this nonsense was going on, a church only forty miles up the Connecticut River in the small town of Northampton, Massachusetts, was experiencing a revival from God. During the winter and spring of 1735, "more than three hundred souls were savingly brought home to Christ in this town, in the space of half a year," wrote the thirty-one-year-old pastor, Jonathan Edwards.[40] The Northampton church apparently had more important things to focus on than which style of singing would prevail.

So what do we do with our current differences? How do we calm down the worship wars?

The Missing Notes

Here is how I have chosen, as a pastor, to work with this issue. I believe and declare with all my heart that *you and I don't need to fuss about church music because we're not the audience, remember?* Singing in the house of God is not for our benefit! It is something we do as an offering to the Lord. The point is to please Him, not ourselves. If He is happy with our praise, that's all that really matters.

Have you ever thought about the fact that right smack in the middle of the Bible, God gave us a divinely inspired hymnal with 150 different songs—*but just the words.* No notes, no harmonies, no rhythms, no instrumentation, no chord charts. I think He left out that part on purpose. He didn't want to box us into one "right way" to worship Him. He only wanted to give us the important part, which was the content (approximately forty-five thousand words of content, in fact).

If you're telling yourself, "Well, I'm sure the Twenty-third Psalm was performed with lush strings and a background of soft trombones and French horns," you are clearly imposing your own Western cultural heritage on that psalm. Your Christian brother or sister who lives in India would say, "No, it needs the plucking of a sitar." Your fellow Christian in the Congo would say, "Well, you have to start with a rhythm pattern from hollow-log drums with goat-skin tops, and then the melody floats above that."

God is the God of the whole world, and He deliberately left out the musical details so that each culture and each generation could "sing to the LORD a new song" (Ps. 96:1). He welcomes each style, each format, as long as it comes from a sincere heart. He is glad to receive the adoration of His people.

The only remaining question is whether you and I, as opinionated human beings, will focus on worshipping Him as opposed to advancing our own personal preferences. This can be hard, I admit; it calls on us to yield, to bend, to flex, not always to get our own way. But isn't that the road of discipleship? Isn't that what Romans 12:10 means when it instructs us to "give preference to one another in honor"? In another place Paul writes: "Do nothing from selfishness or empty conceit, but with humility of mind regard one another as more important than yourselves" (Phil. 2:3). You probably hadn't thought of those Scriptures in connection with the "music wars." But they certainly apply.

> ☞ *God gave us a divinely inspired hymnal with 150 different songs—but just the words. No notes, no harmonies, no rhythms, no instrumentation, no chord charts. I think He left out that part on purpose.* ☜

The church of Jesus Christ always has to swim upstream against the prevailing culture by trying to be a *mix* of ages and stages. Just about every other grouping in our society is built for a *niche* of one kind or another. Take the radio dial, for example: you've got country stations, news/talk stations, classical stations, rock 'n' roll stations, oldies stations, African-American stations, Spanish-language stations, smooth jazz stations, National Public Radio (NPR) stations, and a dozen others. Or drive the avenue checking out restaurants: one offers Italian, the next one Chinese, the next one fast-food hamburgers, the next one fine dining with white tablecloths—you name it. We're spoiled here in America, always looking for goods and services that are tailored *just for me.*

Then on Sunday we come to church! It is by definition the *family* of God, which means we're not all alike. Some of us are male while others are female. Some of us are young while others are old. Some of us are comfortably fixed for money while others are struggling even to pay the electric bill. Some of us got to go to college; others of us did not. And here we are, all in the same place at the same time. How are we going to get along?

Dream with me for a moment: What if a rich entrepreneur told you he'd pick up the entire tab for a secular music concert in the city park if you would plan it—the only requirement being that everybody from age eight to eighty-eight would love every song? The teenagers, the old folks, the PhDs, the dropouts, the Southerners, the Yankees, the blacks, the whites, the Asians, the Hispanics—they'll all be there from all over town, and you have to please them all.

Impossible!

Every minister of music in every church knows what I'm talking about. If the goal is to satisfy each and every person who walks through the door, the future is doomed. We simply cannot keep everybody happy all the time, if the standard for happiness is their personal preference.

We have to rework the standard.

In one of my churches I was preaching from Acts 2:42–47. The passage tells a lot about the Jerusalem congregation, but it doesn't say much about their music. All it says in the last verse is that they were "praising God." I said to my listeners, "We have many people here today, and I for one have no intention of splitting this church into age brackets because of music or anything else. In fact, I want children to come to the same service as their grandparents. We need to be under the same roof together in the presence of the Lord.

"So in every service, we will have a blend of styles. I love the great hymns of the faith—'Holy, Holy, Holy' and 'Rock of Ages' and 'Great Is Thy Faithfulness.' Let me say to you young people, I hope you're willing to learn these songs. They have incredibly strong doctrine in their words. But we're also going to sing 'Shout to the Lord' and 'Friend of God' and 'Here I Am to Worship.' For all you saints and pillars of the congregation, these are good songs, too. The main thing is that they all are about Jesus, they're all scriptural, and they all glorify the Lord.

"We're not going to focus so much on what we *don't* like. Instead, we're going to focus on what we *do* like, which is one another! I may not love a particular beat, but I love *you*. And if I see you reaching out to the Lord through a particular song, whether it's on my personal hit list or not, I'm going to be thrilled about that."

What this has come to mean at my present church is a fifty-fifty blend. The music planners and I actually keep track. Half the selections are well-known hymns and gospel songs, while the other half are nontraditional praise-and-worship choruses. I'm not saying this is a rule for everyone. Each pastor and church should make its own decision on this, remembering that whatever ratios you choose, everyone is still going to have to bend a little. They're going to have to learn that if they don't care for a particular song, just stay calm and wait three or four minutes. The next one is likely to be much more palatable.

> *Some of the church's musical treasures were written long ago; others were written just last month. Let's not hide any of them on a dark shelf somewhere.*

Jesus said one time that anyone wanting to be "a disciple of the kingdom of heaven is like a head of a household, who brings out of his treasure things new and old" (Matt. 13:52). Some of the church's musical treasures were written long ago; others were written just last month. Let's not hide any of them on a dark shelf somewhere; let's use them all.

Some might say, "You can't teach an old dog new tricks." But we are Christians, and we can love our younger (or older) brothers and sisters in Christ enough to sing with them a new song to the Lord.

A tall young bass player in a Colorado church said, with wisdom beyond his years, "Can we all please understand that church was never meant to be your personal jukebox? Everybody has 165 *other* hours in the week to pick out just the songs you personally like." Go to your nearest Christian music supplier and load up on whatever you want. Play it nonstop from Monday to Saturday. The new technology of the iPod makes this even easier. You can select, download, and then replay your handpicked favorites as often as you want. But in the house of God, we have a different agenda. We're offering up praise and adoration for the pleasure of Someone else.

When C. S. Lewis finally surrendered to Christ at the age of thirty, he was already a brilliant professor of English literature at Oxford.

The idea of blending into a local church's worship was hard for him to swallow:

> I thought that I could do it on my own, by retiring to my room and reading theology, and wouldn't go to the church and Gospel Halls. . . . I disliked very much their hymns which I considered to be fifth-rate poems set to sixth-rate music. But as I went on I saw the merit of it. I came up against different people of quite different outlooks and different education, and then gradually my conceit just began peeling off. I realized that the hymns, which were just sixth-rate music, were, nevertheless, being sung with devotion and benefit by an old saint in elastic-side boots in the opposite pew, and then you realize that you aren't fit to clean those boots. It gets you out of your solitary conceit.[41]

Art for His Sake, Not Ours

Donna and I have four children, which at the present time means one in seminary, one in college, one in high school, and one in middle school. With joy and relief I can say every one of them listens to music about Jesus every day. I cannot say that I personally care for every one of their musical selections (to put it mildly!). But my wife and I are thrilled that they're focused on the Lord.

That is because we've never said during their growing-up years that, when it came to music, it was our way or the highway. We told ourselves that style and volume level weren't worth fighting about. If the words lifted up Jesus, we were content.

In the church most reactions I have received from members have been positive. After I had preached on musical worship, one dear saint wrote to say, "Brother Steve, before I saw what the Word of God says about 'psalms, hymns and spiritual songs,' I was close-minded regarding the newer music. But that message helped me see that God enjoys a variety of musical styles to be used in worshipping him." She went on to say, "It also thrills my soul to see our young people singing with all of their hearts not only the hymns but also the new songs. If they can learn the old songs, I can learn the new ones. Thank you for keeping us all together under one roof."

I've teased my church sometimes by saying, "Boy, you ought to be glad *I'm* not the one selecting all the music around here. If I were in charge, we'd have a banjo, a mandolin, a stand-up bass, a harmonica, and a couple of fiddle players—because according to me, bluegrass is the best music there is! How many of you would keep coming to church for that?" Out of a big congregation I usually get two hands waving wildly, as everybody laughs.

Half the time when Donna and I get in my SUV to go somewhere, she doesn't even have her seat belt buckled before she snaps, "Turn it off."

"What are you talking about?" I answer with a hurt look on my face. "You haven't even heard anything yet."

"I know it's there," she replies, glancing toward the CD deck. "The minute you turn that key, I'm going to get blasted with The Foggy Mountain Boys."

I smile. Some people just don't get it.

But when we go to church and begin worshipping the Lord, the priority is not really what Steve Gaines likes, or Donna Gaines, or the Gaines kids, or anybody else. We are all called to submit our personal tastes to the greater purpose of worship, which is to join together in exalting the honor of the True Audience. If He is pleased, then we can be pleased as well. We have given Him the recognition He deserves.

I fully admit that, to advance this purpose, we are using a human art form (music). And art forms are forever changing. That is just the nature of art. "Amazing Grace" is a classic hymn from John Newton, the vicious slave trader in the 1700s who gave his heart to the Lord and found salvation for "a wretch like me." But I can guarantee you that the way we sing it today is considerably different from its original form. If you doubt my word, have someone who can read music play it exactly as written in a hymnal. The pattern is straight, the chords simple; it has almost none of the soulful emotion we've come to add to "Amazing Grace" in recent times. We have adapted this classic to our present artistic climate, giving it almost a blues feel, while still keeping the same priceless lyrics.

Other hymns are now being massaged in a similar way, perhaps by adjusting the melody, adding a more rhythmic beat, or even inserting an all-new bridge passage or coda at the end. That's fine and useful. The best of the old is preserved even as new touches bring fresh enrichment.

If today's worshippers are able to do a better job of lifting up the Lord in this way, so be it.

What people sometimes don't realize is that *all* hymns were "contemporary songs" at one point—even "Joyful, Joyful We Adore Thee" and "Come, Thou Fount of Every Blessing" and "O Worship the King." Through decades and centuries of use, they have now become classics. The same will happen to the latest praise choruses just now coming out. Some will be quickly forgotten, while a few will become "the old favorites" over time.

It's kind of like our cars. None of us, technically speaking, drives a "new car." It's a "used car" two seconds after we drive off the dealer's lot. (Just check the current wholesale value of your car if you doubt what I'm saying.) In the same way every song is on its way to becoming "old" in human terms; some are just further along that trail than others.

The hymnal, being a collection of time-tested songs from the past, is not to be compared with the latest CD sampler from a contemporary music house. It's apples versus oranges. Charles Wesley, it is said, wrote 7,270 different hymns—many of them scratched onto small pieces of paper while his brother, John Wesley, was preaching in the open air, so Charles would have something new to sing at the close of the meeting. How many of those hymns do we still use today? "Rejoice, the Lord Is King," "O for a Thousand Tongues," "Hark, the Herald Angels Sing," "Christ the Lord Is Risen Today," "And Can It Be that I Should Gain?" and a few dozen others. The other seven thousand have apparently fallen by the wayside since the 1700s. We've kept the best and respectfully laid aside the others.

> *What people sometimes don't realize is that all hymns were "contemporary songs" at one point—even "O Worship the King."*

This process happens to every songwriter's work. It will happen to today's choruses as well. The wheat gets sifted from the chaff. We should not expect any songwriter to produce wheat every time.

Meanwhile, this teaches us that the age of a song is irrelevant to its value. What matters is whether it lifts up the Lord. If we worshippers are keyed on exalting the name of Jesus Christ, we would do well to use material from a wide variety of sources, regardless of the copyright date.

See the River

In one sense the current fixation with style and rhythm and instrumentation in today's churches is a distraction from the real beauty of worship. Think of worship as a boat trip down a beautiful river. The psalmist even wrote once, "There is a river whose streams make glad the city of God, the holy dwelling places of the Most High" (46:4). If you and I are involved in bringing gladness to the heart of God, every minute we spend studying the gangplank of the boat, the engine, the rudder, the curve of the gunwales is a moment lost from the scenery of the river. As long as we are thinking about the *music* and particularly its contours, we're not thinking about the Lord.

We do not truly worship until we get *beyond* the music, per se. Only when we rise above the notes and time signatures and rhythm patterns do we become "lost in wonder, love, and praise," as Wesley wrote at the end of his hymn "Love Divine, All Loves Excelling." That is where we belong, not fussing over the details of an art form. We are the church of the living God, not a music society.

Music is like technology: it makes a wonderful servant but a terrible master. Its purpose is not to make us happy or proud of ourselves; it is rather a language for us to employ in lifting up the Lord. We use it, rather than expecting it to gratify us. Does the carpenter analyze the aesthetic beauty of the screwdriver? "My, what a lovely handle this screwdriver has. But I wish it were a bit more orange instead of yellow." No, he puts it to use in making a beautiful cabinet. What the tool does is far more significant than how it looks (or sounds). Music is a means to an end. It is a vehicle to get us to the destination—the Lord Himself. The way we worship can become an idol if it does not lead us to the Person we worship.

Perhaps the most musical of the Psalms is the last one, Psalm 150. It mentions using just about every instrument in the orchestra, from trumpets to pipes to "loud cymbals" (v. 5). It comes to its crescendo with this stirring finale: "Let everything that has breath praise the LORD" (v. 6).

It does *not* say, "Let everything that has breath criticize the music." God didn't give us breath to complain. If we have breath at all, we are to be praising God with it! That is the true purpose of the gift of music, and the solution for the unnecessary conflicts of our day.

CHAPTER 12

Praying Together

Prayer in the church? Well, of course. No Christian is *against* prayer. In terms of approval, prayer is right up there with motherhood, apple pie, and the flag.

But how many of us are fervently *for* it? How many of us believe that prayer is vital, and that without it our efforts to build the kingdom of God will fail?

I'm talking about using prayer as far more than a spacer in church programming, a polite little sixty-second speech to God that casts a reflective mood over the congregation before the next song or the sermon.

I'm talking about more than a handy silencer to get the crowd to quiet down at the start of a church potluck or Sunday school class. You know the routine: The place is buzzing with chitchat, and the moderator wants to get everybody to stop and pay attention. What is the easiest way to accomplish that bit of crowd control? Just step up to the microphone and say, "Let's all bow our heads for a word of prayer." People instinctively hush up. It's a social courtesy rather than anyone actually wanting to talk to God at that moment.

We in the modern church may be blasé about prayer, but I can tell you two others who definitely are not. One is God. He has made Himself abundantly clear that He wants to hear from us. I've heard some Christians brush off the idea of prayer by saying, "Well, God's going to do whatever God's going to do." A similar line is this: "Prayer doesn't change anything. It just changes the person who prays."

I don't believe that. Here is the bigger picture:

- Some things God will do all by Himself, whether we pray or not. For example, the sun will rise again tomorrow morning because "in Him all things hold together" (Col. 1:17).
- Some things will *not* happen no matter how hard we pray. God is an intelligent Father who knows that children have to be told no once in a while.
- *But some things will happen only IF we pray!* That was certainly true for Abraham when his nephew Lot was at risk down in Sodom, for Hannah wanting a baby, for David seeking protection from his enemies, for the Jerusalem church trying to get Peter out of jail—and it's true for you and me today. In cases such as these, God acts if we pray and doesn't if we don't. Now if that concept doesn't square with your theology, then you might need to adjust your theology.

Jesus was totally clear on this. The whole point of His story about the widow and the judge (Luke 18:1–8) was "to show that at all times they ought to pray and not to lose heart" (v. 1). Only the widow's persistence brought results.

Andrew Murray, the eminent South African church leader and writer a century ago, wrote, "The man who mobilizes the Christian church to pray will make the greatest contribution to world evangelization in history."[42]

The second being who takes prayer seriously is the devil. I preached a sermon one time entitled "Are You Known in Hell?" My text was Acts 19:11–17, the story of some folks in Ephesus who tried to cast out a demon without the power of prayer. The evil spirit promptly gave them a good old-fashioned whipping as it snarled, "I recognize Jesus, and I know about Paul, but who are you?" (v. 15). The devil and his minions were wisely afraid of the Son of God and of those in close contact with Him. They knew all about this power. Any other fellows who came along just spouting religious talk, however, were nothing to worry about.

Heaven knows who you and I are. But do the demons? What we do on our knees pushes back the kingdom of darkness.

More Than a Specialty

In recent times it seems that more and more Christians have strayed off into viewing prayer as *the specialty of a few* rather than the calling of us all. It's for the "prayer warriors" of the congregation, they say—those devout folk who really "get into" that sort of thing. The rationalization goes like this: Some of us are good at teaching, some of us are good at organizing, some of us make good ushers, some of us can sing well or play an instrument, and then some people do their thing in the prayer closet. How nice. That way, the rest of us are off the hook.

Where does the Bible teach this? Is prayer in the list of "spiritual gifts" that the Spirit gives out to various Christians as He sees fit? No. Paul wrote to the Ephesian church to "pray at all times in the Spirit, and with this in view, be on the alert with all perseverance and petition for all the saints" (6:18). Jude gave a similar, far-reaching instruction: "But you, beloved, building yourselves up on your most holy faith, praying in the Holy Spirit, keep yourselves in the love of God" (vv. 20–21).

> More and more Christians have strayed off into viewing prayer as the specialty of a few rather than the calling of us all.

When preaching evangelistically, we often say that the ground is level at the foot of the cross, meaning that anyone from any background is welcome. Let me add, in the present discussion, that the ground is also level at the prayer closet. A person who has been saved just five minutes can talk to God as directly as someone who has been walking with the Lord for forty years. You don't have to work your way up some seniority ladder. You don't have to earn an extra access card to the courts of heaven. You don't have to punch in some four-digit PIN, like at an ATM. God is waiting to hear from you and me at all times, without hindrance.

Prayer, in fact, is meant to be the breathing instinct of the Christian life. When I was in college, I signed up for voice lessons. I had always enjoyed singing, but I wanted to learn to do it properly. The instructor walked in the first day and said, "OK, sing something for me."

I got through the first verse of a song, and he promptly said, "You're singing all wrong."

Oh, really? "What do you mean?" I asked.

"You're not breathing diaphramatically" (whatever that signified). "You're breathing up here in your chest, not down in your stomach. Let me show you what I mean. Lie down on the floor."

I stretched out while he took his penny loafers off. Then he proceeded to step up on top of my stomach! (Fortunately, he was a little guy.) "Now make me go up and down by your breathing," he ordered.

"Do what?"

"Just try it."

I sucked in as much air as I could—and in fact, I did manage to raise him up a half-inch or so. I took in another gulp. Soon he was saying, "That's it! You're using your diaphragm. And that's how to support your singing. You can't sing until you learn how to breathe."

> ☙ *No church is going to grow strong and healthy without the inhale/exhale rhythm of prayer. Fancy programs and systems aren't going to do it long-term. We pray, or we shrivel.* ❧

I've thought over the years about the parallel to preaching. You can't preach until you learn how to pray. If you don't pray right, you won't preach right, you won't live right, and you won't do right. For Christians to perform at their best, they have to breathe in the life of God through prayer. Likewise, no church is going to grow strong and healthy without the inhale/exhale rhythm of prayer. Fancy programs and systems aren't going to do it long-term. We pray, or we shrivel.

And not just the "prayer warriors." All of us.

Prayer in the Sanctuary

I already wrote in chapter 10 about my starting every service with a season of prayer. It is deliberately more than just, "Let's open with a word of prayer." And it's more than just one guy with a microphone. It is an unhurried time for everyone present—pastors, musicians, those in the pew—to humble ourselves and call upon the Lord, inviting His manifest presence into our midst.

But actually, our quest to be "a house of prayer for all the nations" (Mark 11:17) begins several hours ahead of this. At seven a.m. each

Sunday, the full ministerial staff of Bellevue meets me in the sanctuary to pray. We each take a section and go row by row, asking God to make Himself real to whoever sits there today. "Lord, come and be present in this place," we pray. "Let the Spirit of God open each person's heart as they worship and hear the preaching of Your Word. We pray for those who are not Christians, that Your Spirit will convict them— that they'll turn to You and be saved. We pray for every Christian who isn't completely surrendered to you. Help them repent and return to You."

Yes, it's early in the morning, and we've all got a long day ahead of us with many demands for energy. But I can't think of anything more important for us to do. We are turning on the "prayer conditioning" in this place, as the old saying goes. Where prayer is focused, God's power falls.

When we finish, we come together at the altar area, praying that people will find Christ there. We go up to the platform, asking God to bless the preaching of the Word on this day. It's a valuable time. We finish with holding hands and singing a worship chorus or hymn a capella. The whole process takes us close to half an hour.

From there, the staff then spreads out to get ready for their various duties, since classes begin at eight o'clock, followed by two main services at nine-thirty and eleven. We have started our day, however, with the most important thing: calling out to God.

In the services themselves I'm a firm believer that not every prayer time has to be scripted. People come to church carrying all kinds of silent burdens. Joseph Parker, the British pulpiteer of the later 1800s, said, "There is a hidden hurt in every pew." I have visited at least a couple of churches where the pastor called forward a line of trained prayer counselors to stand across the front and then said to the congregation, "If you have a need in your life today, come and pray with one of us." Folks have immediately begun to stream forward by the dozens simply to take a stranger's hand and tell their deepest need. In fact, I've done it myself. The counselors had been coached to listen quietly and then go straight to God in prayer. The whole process took maybe five minutes, during which time the rest of the congregation sang songs of worship. It was a precious atmosphere.

How many of the problems and burdens that people carry around in life could be alleviated simply by praying together in a church service? We have not because we ask not (see James 4:2).

We hear a lot of talk in some circles these days about spiritual warfare and "wrestling with God." I'd like to put in a word for "nestling with God," just coming up close to Him to talk, to share what's in our hearts, to love Him, and to be honest with Him. I believe in spiritual warfare, but I personally don't want to spend my prayer time focusing on the devil; I'd rather focus on my loving heavenly Father. He's much stronger than the evil one. He can well take care of the devil directly. That's what the angel said in Zechariah 3:2: "The LORD rebuke you, Satan!"

I will never forget one Friday night during a tour of Israel a few years ago. We were staying at the Jerusalem Holiday Inn, and the restaurant was full that evening, since *Shabbat* (the Sabbath) had begun at sundown. The Orthodox Jews were all dressed up: men in black suits, women in elegant black dresses, and children in their best attire as well.

Israeli restaurants often have a big salad buffet. I was standing in line, waiting my turn, behind an Orthodox man. Suddenly a call came from his little girl in a high chair across the room: *"Abba! Abba!"*

I had known for years that the Hebrew word *abba* means "daddy"— but in this moment, I was struck afresh with the reality. I have three daughters of my own who mean the world to me. Here this little girl was crying out to her papa. When Jesus cried out "Abba!" in the garden of Gethsemane (see Mark 14:36), He was desperate, like that little girl: "Help! I'm going to get arrested any minute!" Paul wrote to the Romans, "For you have not received a spirit of slavery leading to fear again, but you have received a spirit of adoption as sons by which we cry out, 'Abba! Father!'" (Rom. 8:15; see also Gal. 4:6).

God is our loving, concerned, wonderfully attentive *Abba*. He welcomes us to nestle up close to Him and receive His love. What better place to do this than in church?

One of the reasons the rabbis had a hard time with Jesus was that He sounded way too intimate with God. Seldom in the Old Testament had God been spoken of as "Father." Now here came Jesus doing it all the time. The Pharisees challenged His credentials, and He replied:

"In your law it has been written that the testimony of two men is true. I am He who testifies about Myself, and the Father who sent Me testifies about Me."

So they were saying to Him, "Where is Your Father?"

Jesus answered, "You know neither Me nor My Father; if you knew Me, you would know My Father also." (John 8:17–19)

People today are starving for the warm embrace of a Father they can trust. The more we realize what a Father He is to us, the more we will want to talk with Him in prayer and guide others to do the same.

Another great occasion for praying in church comes at the very end—after the benediction, in fact. Inevitably, as I just wait around and walk slowly through the crowd, somebody comes up to me and says, "Would you pray for me? I'm having medical tests this week," or, "My son is being sent to Iraq," or even things like, "My marriage isn't doing so hot."

> *We hear a lot of talk in some circles these days about "spiritual warfare" and "wrestling with God." I'd like to put in a word for "nestling with God."*

I've learned to listen to their description of the details and then say, "OK, let's pray right now." Not sometime later, but here in the moment. I take them by the hand and begin to intercede right there in the aisle or the church lobby. Why not? That's what this building is for.

This way people know I'm taking their needs seriously. I'm not going to forget. It's far too easy to say, "Oh, yes, I'll pray for you," and in fact never get around to it later. Better to pray spontaneously at the time.

I've prayed for people in airports, in parking lots, at Wal-Mart, anywhere they bring up a need. *Abba* is always available to hear us, and the person is standing right there—so why delay?

Prayer beyond the Sanctuary

Some people in every church, of course, are a little nervous about praying in a large group. They worry about "not sounding right" when talking to God. They need gentle instruction in a nonthreatening environment on the ways of prayer.

Occasionally I've said to six or eight men in my congregation, "Hey, how about meeting me once a week for a time of prayer? We could do it at my office early some morning before you go to work. Just a small group of us." This has turned out to be a mentoring time, because one of the best ways to learn to pray is to hang out with somebody who already is comfortable doing so. The practice of prayer is as much caught as it is taught.

At times, of course, direct instruction is appropriate. For example, a group may need to be reminded that we're here mainly to pray, not to socialize. The tendency often is to talk with one another for forty-five minutes and then pray for only fifteen. We can spend three times as long *describing* a "prayer request" to the others in the room as we spend actually talking to God about it. If this is going to be a prayer group, then I want at least 75 percent of the time to be spent in actual praying.

Once in a while, people need to be taught to share the prayer time with others. That may sound a little bold, but it's better than letting everybody else in the room get frustrated.

> *One of the best ways to learn to pray is to hang out with somebody who already is comfortable doing so.*

Don Miller has done a wonderful teaching on "How to Spend an Hour with God" (see box on next page). People say, "An hour—are you kidding? What in the world would I say for all that long? I'd run out of topics in ten minutes." Well, there are some good answers for that.

Jesus in the garden said to His three disciples almost nonchalantly, "So, you men could not keep watch with Me for one hour?" (Matt. 26:40). The tone almost seems to be *Come on, guys—an hour is no big deal.*

If you're married, think back to your engagement period. An hour spent with the one you loved was like a snap of the finger. The time flew by—it was midnight before you knew it. Why should an hour with God be any different? We say He's the one we love more than any other.

How to Spend an Hour with God
based on a chart by Don Miller*

Give five minutes each to the following twelve activities:
1. Praise the Lord for who He is (Heb. 13:15).
2. Read the Word (Ps. 119:105).
3. Meditate on what you have just read (Josh. 1:8).
4. Confess your sins and shortcomings (1 John 1:9).
5. Intercede for others (1 Sam. 12:18).
6. Listen for God's voice (Ps. 46:10).
7. Pray using the language of the Word (Ps. 22:1).
8. Petition God for your own needs (James 4:2).
9. Pray for your pastor (1 Thess. 5:12–13).
10. Pray for your church (Eph. 5:25).
11. Pray for public and corporate leaders (1 Tim. 2:1–8).
12. Give thanks (Ps. 136).

*Available from Bible-Based Prayer Ministries, Box 8911, Fort Worth, TX 76124. Phone: 817-429-6917.

Spurgeon said once, "I would rather teach one man to pray than ten men to preach."[43] By word and by example, we can draw people into an intimate dialogue with God that will enrich not only their own lives but the church as well.

Prayer is contagious. When I hear a preacher say, "Well, you know, this congregation just doesn't seem to want to pray very much," I don't entirely buy it. A church's prayer life will never rise above the leader's prayer life. The more we pastors engage in open prayer and invite others to join us, the more the rest of the church will become praying people.

One time in Gardendale, we prepared ourselves for a series of evangelistic meetings by doing two things the week before. First, we cleared off the stage and, starting at eight o'clock Sunday evening, we read the Bible aloud straight through for the next 120 hours, from Genesis all the way to Revelation. People signed up to be readers during time slots up to Thursday evening. Ephesians 5:26 talks about Christ "sanctify[ing] her [the church], having cleansed her by the washing of water with the word." We pretty much doused every square inch of that sanctuary with the Word of God.

Then, on Friday night, we brought on the "second bath" in that place: twenty-four hours of prayer. We prayed over every pew and every corner. "God, we need You. We invite You to come down in this place—especially next week during the special meetings. We need You to save lost people. We need You to change our hearts. We want a fresh touch of Your hand upon our lives and our church." This kept going through the night and all day Saturday. At seven o'clock that evening, I led a prayer walk around the whole church property, as we quietly asked God to move in our midst. We ended up on the front steps of the church at eight o'clock for a closing time of praise and singing. We then went home in full expectation that God was going to do great things.

The next day the sanctuary was packed three times. The worship and the singing were electrifying. And when the preacher got to the invitation, non-Christians flooded to the altars and gave their hearts to Christ in every service. Don't tell me prayer doesn't work!

If this sounds extreme, it is modest compared to what happens at the Brooklyn Tabernacle, where a prayer band is in session 24/7 year-round. Pastor Jim Cymbala tells in his book *Fresh Wind, Fresh Fire* about how the group started years ago on Friday nights, then added the other weeknights as well, then expanded to pray whenever a service was going on. Today people come to the designated room for their three-hour shifts of prayer at all hours, not fearing the dangerous streets and subways of New York City; they want to call on the name of the Lord. They go through stacks of requests turned in on small cards written by Sunday attenders at the church, asking God to intervene in everything from employment needs to wayward children. They pray for God's outpouring in the public services of the church.[44]

Prayer is what makes for a growing church, a holy church, a tithing church, a worshipping church. Sunday prayer, weeknight prayer, small-group prayer, individual prayer—it's all valuable. It is the key that unlocks so many doors. Prayer needs to be a priority in every Sunday school class, every deacons' meeting, every choir rehearsal, every committee meeting, every staff meeting—and above all, every worship service. The more central it becomes to our congregational life, the more God's will can be done on earth as in heaven.

Samuel Chadwick (1860–1932) was a godly Methodist preacher and college president in England. His words ring as true today as when he wrote them: "The one concern of the devil is to keep Christians from praying. He fears nothing from prayerless studies, prayerless work and prayerless religion. He laughs at our toil, mocks at our wisdom, but he trembles when we pray."[45]

CHAPTER 13

A Word from Above

Does preaching have a place in our quest for the manifest presence of God? Or is the sermon on a different plane? Readers may have assumed up to this point that I think God shows up as we sing and close our eyes and meditate and pray and maybe even lift our hands; but as soon as the preacher says, "Open your Bibles, please, to Romans 15," the mood changes. What has so far been a *vertical* experience, reaching up to God, now turns *horizontal*. The human speaker behind a pulpit begins informing the minds of his fellow human beings in the pew.

No, that is not my view at all. Preaching, if done correctly, has the potential to be the pinnacle of the worship service. It is intended to be *God* speaking to us, and what could be more vertical than that? In fact, what God has to say to us is more important than what we have to say to Him. The dialogue begun through singing and other means now reaches its greatest potency.

I will go so far as to say that preaching is meant to be more than an encounter with the Word of God. It is to be an encounter with the God of the Word. The Word can be a powerful conduit of its author. It's more than a thousand-page book. It is the inspired utterance—the "breathings" of Almighty God.

Perhaps that explains what happened to me as an eighteen-year-old college student, when I started reading the Bible seriously for the first time in my life. I'd been a regular church kid growing up, but I'd never actually committed my life to the Christ I heard about every Sunday.

Now I was a six-foot four-inch defensive end, and in the evenings after football practice and my studies were finished, I was reading through the Gospel of John.

I got to the dramatic account in chapters 18 and 19 of Jesus being arrested, hauled from one tribunal to another, and finally winding up before the Roman magistrate Pontius Pilate. He questioned Jesus on whether He was actually a "king" or something else. He asked his now-famous query, "What is truth?" The rabble kept screaming for the death penalty. Pilate was clearly flustered. He wanted to get out of this mess, but he also was intrigued with this defendant from Galilee.

He brought Jesus out to the seething crowd and declared, with a mix of perplexity and deep respect, "Behold, the Man!" (John 19:5).

That statement suddenly gripped my heart. I had thought that to be a real man, you had to bench-press three hundred pounds or knock an offensive tackle off balance and blindside the quarterback for a sack. Now it dawned on me that Jesus was not only the God-man, but He was also truly a man's man. He had taken a nasty whipping throughout the night and was still able to keep His head clear while talking with Pilate, eventually winning His admiration.

Within a few days I surrendered my life to the Lord and received him as my Savior. I discovered that to be a real man meant becoming a man of God.

What caused this? The God of the Word broke through at last. When we let the power of Scripture (what Ephesians 6:17 calls "the sword of the Spirit") cut loose to impact our lives, we are changed forever. The best preaching is that which brings the Word and its Author to bear upon the listener in an immediate, compelling way. Heaven touches earth, and sparks fly.

What We Want Most

This, in fact, is what people are earnestly seeking. They may (or may not) have heard lots of sermons in the past. But what they crave, in order to get through the coming week, is the eternal truth presented with power. They are like King Zedekiah in the darkest hours of Jerusalem's history when he was surrounded by Babylonian troops, and he knew he was in big trouble. His whole world was about to crash down on his head. In desperation he sent a secret messenger to get the prophet Jeremiah out of a dungeon. The king then sneaked him into the palace by some kind of back door and whispered anxiously, "Is there a word from the LORD?" (Jer. 37:17).

This wicked king was finally asking the right question. Millions of people today are wondering the same thing.

Fortunately for Zedekiah, this prophet of God did not scratch his head and mumble, "I dunno." The next sentence in verse 17 records, "Jeremiah said, 'There is!'" and goes on to tell a clear message from God. Jeremiah, having been filled up with God back in the dungeon, now turned himself loose. This was, after all, the man who had said earlier that if he ever tried to squelch the word of the Lord, "In my heart it becomes like a burning fire shut up in my bones; and I am weary of holding it in, and I cannot endure it" (20:9).

Jeremiah's message this time happened not to be very good news for the king: he would soon lose his throne. But at least it was direct and understandable. Zedekiah knew where he stood with God.

People want to know where they stand with God, even if it's not ideal. The faithful preacher will open the Word of God and let them know.

One hundred fifty years after Zedekiah's time, when the people of Israel had endured a long captivity in Babylon and were starting to rebuild their country again, they still showed this passion to hear from God. "All the people gathered as one man at the square . . . and *they asked Ezra* the scribe to bring the book of the law of Moses" (Neh. 8:1). Notice their hunger for the Word of God. Ezra didn't nag or browbeat the people to listen to a sermon; *they asked him!* "Ezra, can we please hear something from God's Word? We really need it. We're out here by ourselves trying to rebuild this city before the Ammonites and the Arabs all around us knock us down. Give us something solid to hold on to!"

The Bible says that Ezra declared God's Word "from early morning until midday, in the presence of men and women, those who could understand; and all the people were attentive to the book of the law. . . . When he opened it, all the people stood up. Then Ezra blessed the LORD the great God. And all the people answered, 'Amen! Amen!' while lifting up their hands; then they bowed low and worshiped the LORD with their faces to the ground" (vv. 3, 5–6).

This kind of hunger for the Word of God demands the substantive provision of biblical preaching. We are just as vulnerable as the people in Ezra's and Nehemiah's day. We've got our own set of enemies and dangers on every side. We need the fortitude that only God can give us through His Word.

Conception and Delivery

This is why preachers absolutely must take their preparation seriously. It is far more than just getting up "a little talk" for next Sunday. It is far more than filling a half-hour slot in a program. It is finding out what God wants to say on this particular occasion and then doing our best to be His mouthpiece.

Stephen Olford, the great expository preacher who came from England long ago and spent his final years here in Memphis, said that preaching is a lot like pregnancy. God implants a seed in the preacher's heart, a sermon idea from the Word of God. The preacher then goes through days of study and prayer, a period of gestation and growth. By the time he gets up to preach, he's full of the message. He is even uncomfortable. He cannot wait to deliver this word to the people. *Deliver*—yes, that's a fitting term.

> Preaching is meant to be more than an encounter with the Word of God. It is to be an encounter with the God of the Word.

Delivery is intense. It's sometimes a little messy. It's definitely painful. But it produces a wonderful result.

There is no shortcut for this vertical impartation from God into the preacher's inner being. It certainly doesn't work to go borrowing a sermon outline from somebody else. I am amazed, even scared, at how many preachers these days are plagiarizing one another rather than hearing from God. It used to be a matter of buying books of sermons; now the practice is even more rampant with the Internet offering hundreds of outlines for sale or even free. Such sermons enter through the preacher's eyes and exit the mouth without ever passing through the head or the heart.

I am not saying that research is wrong; I do a ton of it myself during the "pregnancy." By the time I'm ready to preach, I've got eight to twelve pages of notes that include wisdom and insight from a number of authors, all properly credited. But the main concept has been birthed out of a text that I believe God identified for this congregation on this particular day.

Otherwise, I'd be just "baby snatching" from other preachers. I don't want to get even close to what God condemned in Jeremiah 23:30: "Therefore behold, I am against the prophets . . . who steal My words from each other." Oh, that couldn't mean borrowing a sermon outline, could it? My reply is: Yes, it could. Stealing is stealing is stealing, whether it's cheating on a test in school or passing off somebody else's sermon as your own. God doesn't need pirates in His pulpits who offload stolen goods, nor does He need parrots who simply quote commentaries and other resources. Instead, He wants prophets who declare, "Thus saith the Lord."

> *People want to know where they stand with God, even if it's not ideal.*

If we who stand in the pulpit are too busy to hear from God and thoroughly prepare a message, we're filling up our week with the wrong things. Preaching has to remain a top priority of every pastor. Paul commended "those who work hard at preaching and teaching" (1 Tim. 5:17). I started out in a church of 150 people, and the load has increased dramatically over the years, but it doesn't matter. I'm determined not to take shortcuts in sermon preparation. Every week I must seek God for His choice of a text, then dive into it with full attention. The goal is more than just getting hold of the text; it's that the text gets hold of me, of my heart, my soul, my mind, my whole being. Only then can I draw listeners close to the Father who wants to speak to us all.

Scripture-Soaked

The main text needs to be buttressed with many other supporting Scriptures so that the sermon fairly oozes with the direct Word of God. In the process of explaining the text, illustrating it and applying it, what wise quotations could I possibly find that would be as valuable as those coming from God Himself? The best commentary on Scripture is other Scripture. I believe in packing the sermon full of verses from across the Bible, Old Testament as well as New, that reinforce the point of the main text.

This is what penetrates the heart. Hebrews 4:12 says, "The word of God is living and active and sharper than any two-edged sword, and piercing as far as the division of soul and spirit, of both joints and marrow, and able to judge the thoughts and intentions of the heart." Scripture has an uncanny way of getting right to the point that needs to be exposed. It's like a laser that goes straight for the hidden tumors in the soul. It wastes no time or motion.

I've heard preachers say, "Well, next Sunday I'll be preaching from this text . . ." and the longer they preach, the further *from* the text they get! They don't realize they're actually preaching away from the text. The Scripture gets featured in the first two minutes but little thereafter. No wonder the vertical component is lacking.

Any sermon that rests on human wisdom, no matter how eloquent, is nothing more than a speech. On the other extreme, any so-called movement of God that is not squarely based on what the Bible says is a house built on shifting sand. Some people are driving hundreds of miles to hear modern-day "prophets of God" who fascinate crowds with their pronouncements, but the scriptural underpinning is absent. We will never be smart enough to replace God's words with ours. Only the authoritative, inspired, inerrant truth of Scripture deserves our trust.

Contemporary illustrations have their place, so long as they do not overshadow the Word of God. I certainly believe in painting visual pictures for the listeners, so they can see the truth being applied to daily living. But I wouldn't spend most of a sermon telling stories. Illustrations serve as spotlights to illumine the central text of Scripture, bringing it alive in fresh and relevant ways.

One Mother's Day I was preaching on Hannah in the Old Testament under the title of "The Power of a Godly Woman." My first point was: even godly women have problems in this life. I elaborated on the fact that just because you pray and worship the Lord, as she did, does not prevent you from going through difficulties. Hannah's problem was her inability to conceive a child. Barrenness was viewed as a curse in her day.

To illustrate this point in the message, I told about another godly woman in the 1700s named Susannah Wesley. She loved the Lord passionately, yet she encountered many hardships. Her problem was not infertility; in fact, she bore nineteen children, but nine of them died in infancy. One of those was smothered by a maid. Another was permanently crippled in an accident.

Yet she lived long enough to see the fruit of her labor as a mother. Just before her death, her son John preached a great revival meeting in the family hometown of Epworth. The crowds were the largest in that town's history. God went on to use him and his brother, Charles, to lead a great spiritual awakening that blazed across England and came even to the thirteen colonies in America just prior to the Revolutionary War. Both John and Charles credit their mother, Susannah, as the greatest Christian influence in their lives.

When I finished telling that story, it was obvious from the expressions on the faces of the congregation that they understood more about Hannah because of Mrs. Wesley. The illustration illumined the biblical text.

The best preaching is far more than an intellectual exercise. It appeals to the heart as well as the mind. It is a call for action as well as understanding. It moves the emotions as well as the intellect.

Some preachers are afraid to speak to the listeners in terms of "you." They think that's too confrontational. They feel better generalizing along the lines of "We all need to be more faithful." Jesus, on the other hand, had no qualms about saying directly to Nicodemus, "You must be born again" (John 3:7). During the Sermon on the Mount, He looked across the hillside at the crowds and boldly proclaimed, "Unless your righteousness surpasses that of the scribes and Pharisees, you will not enter the kingdom of heaven" (Matt. 5:20). He wasn't trying to be abrasive; He was simply speaking on behalf of His Father, which is what every preacher should seek to do.

No wonder that when Jesus finished that day, "the crowds were amazed at His teaching; for He was teaching them as one having authority, and not as their scribes" (Matt. 7:28–29). They had heard plenty of dull, boring sermons in their lives. But this man was different. On a later occasion even the tough military guards sent to arrest Jesus in the temple came back shaking their heads. The chief priests wanted to know why they were empty-handed. "Never has a man spoken the way this man speaks," they answered (John 7:46).

Preaching that is God-ordained lands with an impact. It drills the truth of God directly into the human heart, and the listener is never quite the same.

Softening Up

Of course, it is easier to penetrate a softened heart than a heart of stone. That is why the earlier time of praise and worship in a service is so strategic. People who come into the sanctuary in a distracted or frustrated frame of mind, who have been busy all week with the demands of job and household, can start focusing on the Lord during the singing and prayer. The whole tenor of the service says, *OK, this is about God now. It's time to forget about ourselves and concentrate on Him.*

We pray together to the Lord, we exalt Him musically, we give our offerings to His work . . . and now we're ready to hear what He wants to tell us. It is all woven together in a single fabric.

I love the integration of the old hymn:

> *Brethren, we have met to worship*
> *And adore the Lord our God;*
> *Will you pray with all your power*
> *While we try to preach the Word?*
> *All is vain unless the Spirit*
> *Of the Holy One comes down;*
> *Brethren, pray, and holy manna*
> *Will be showered all around.*

George Atkins, who wrote those lyrics way back in 1819, knew that worship and prayer are what make for powerful preaching. Otherwise, "all is vain." Without the Holy Spirit coming down, nothing the preacher says or does is worthwhile. But when God's anointing falls on the preaching of His holy Word, the entire congregation is showered with spiritual food.

In such a climate, what we do not need are preachers who interrupt this focus by talking at length about themselves, promoting themselves, making sure everybody knows about their achievements, and so on. Yes, pastors are the divinely chosen leaders of the church, but it's still not *their* church. It's God's. We preachers need to say along with John the Baptist, "He must increase, but I must decrease" (John 3:30). May God deliver us from prima donnas in the pulpit who have some psychological need to be in the spotlight all the time. I've known some pastors who seemed to want to be the bride at every wedding and the corpse at every funeral!

Every minute that people spend thinking about how cool we preachers are, how eloquent, how funny, or how bright is a minute lost to hearing from the God we say we serve. He is the true source of life and hope, not me. I'm just one of the junior staff in God's kingdom, which means I can be real and admit my shortcomings from time to time as I preach. When I say, "You know, Donna and I actually do get upset with each other sometimes!" people more easily believe me. I go on, "And this affects my prayer life. I can't be the pastor God wants me to be when I'm at odds with my wife. We have to confess what we've done wrong in order to restore harmony in our relationship." I may then give attention to 1 Peter 3:7, which says that marital discord is a cause of unanswered prayer.

But the point is not to be cute or to build a personality attraction. The point is to highlight what it means to be in rhythm with God. That is the goal for the entire church. We must want whatever He wants. We must tune our ears and our lives to His voice. He speaks to us through the preaching of His Word, and we respond to His call.

> ☞ *The best preaching is far more than an intellectual exercise. It appeals to the heart as well as the mind.* ☜

In fact, some congregations these days are even moving back into a second time of worship following the sermon and invitation, as a response to what God has said. I can see definite value in that. God spoke through the Word; now what are we going to do about it? Our minds have been challenged and our hearts stirred. Maybe this is a good time to say, "Lord, I hear You loud and clear. I intend to follow and obey what You have said today."

Preaching is not meant to be a stand-alone event by any means. It is an integral component of experiencing the presence of God in the house of God. Our lives are filled with other forms of communication, from cell phones to e-mail to pagers to elaborate PDAs. But what we desperately need to hear is a word from God. Preachers must preach in such a way as to maximize the message and minimize the messenger. When people come to church, they do not need to be impressed by the choir, the building, the program, or even the speaker. They need to hear a word from above.

CHAPTER 14

Calling People to the Savior

A great gulf has opened up in many parts of the church these days between worship and evangelism. Worship, it is assumed, is what we do by ourselves on Sunday mornings (and at other times); we gather, just us saints, to lift up the Lord and receive "deep" teaching from His Word. Evangelism, on the other hand, is what happens in the stadium, the civic arena, the workplace, out in the neighborhoods, wherever Christians encounter those who have no relationship with Jesus. Once in a great while, we might use our church buildings for a special occasion of evangelism (a musical at Christmas or Easter, for example), at which time all worship is laid to the side. But generally speaking, east is east and west is west, and never the twain shall meet.

The only trouble is, nobody remembered to tell the public about this. Secular people who feel some kind of inner need in their life, who wonder if maybe God could help with their marriage or their parenting or their nagging sense of guilt for things they've done, blithely say, *I think I'll go to church next Sunday morning.* After all, that's the place where spiritual answers are supposed to be waiting, right?

Yes, they could delay until some kind of citywide crusade comes along. Or they could get up the nerve to ask a coworker who seems to be "religious." But the easiest, least threatening thing to do is simply to slip into a back pew at a church and see if it might help the pain inside.

Always Pursuing

That is why I believe in calling people to the Savior *as part of* a worship service. If we know anything about God, we know He is always planning for men, women, and young people to be saved. It is never away from His mind. He's thinking about it fifty-two weeks a year, not just when we happen to schedule our annual outreach.

God is always in process with people. He's working on them, pursuing them to turn to Him. As the British poet (and onetime opium addict) Francis Thompson wrote in his famous work "The Hound of Heaven," God never stops pursuing the lost and disoriented.

> Still with unhurrying chase,
> And unperturbèd pace,
> Deliberate speed, majestic instancy,
> Came on the following Feet,
> And a Voice above their beat—
> "Naught shelters thee, who wilt not shelter Me."[46]

When was the last time somebody with *absolutely no idea* of God or Jesus Christ walked into your church service? Probably never, especially here in North America. Many of the visitors to our church (and yours) have heard sermon after sermon in the past. The Holy Spirit has been dealing with them before they ever walked through our door. In fact, a number of them come to the service for the express purpose of giving their heart to Jesus Christ. They can't wait for me to stop preaching and give an invitation so they can make their move!

> ☞ *Our lives are filled with other forms of communication, from cell phones to e-mail to pagers to elaborate PDAs. But what we desperately need to hear is a word from God.* ☜

That is why I believe that the public invitation is an indispensable part of the sermon. I have been practicing this my whole ministry, and I always will. I could not live with myself if I came down to the end of a message and did not do two things: (1) ask Christians to apply the main point of the sermon to their lives, and (2) give lost people a chance to be saved. Who knows when the seeker reaches the last step of the journey and is now ready to cross the line from darkness to light? I certainly don't, and I'm not going to risk missing that delicate moment.

The appeal to come to Christ can be worded many ways, of course. What I usually say is this. (By the way, I do *not* close my Bible or signal in any other way that the service is near its finish. In fact, a strategic part is just about to begin. Our members have been instructed that no one should leave the sanctuary at this holy moment unless there's a legitimate emergency.)

"Would you bow your heads with me in an attitude of prayer, please?

"Probably many of you today are Christians, and in response to what I've just been preaching, you need to _____"
(whatever has been my theme on this occasion).

"But some of you are not in contact with Jesus at all. Let me tell you, first of all, that God loves you. He is on your side. Even though all of us have sinned against Him, He sent His Son, Jesus, who was sinless, to pay our sin debt. He was our great sacrifice on the cross.

"Not only did He die, but He was raised from the dead to give us the gift of eternal life. It's pretty amazing when you think about it. He did something for us that we had no hope of gaining on our own.

"How do you receive this gift? You repent of your sin and put your trust in Jesus. That's what the Bible teaches: 'As many as received Him, to them He gave the right to become children of God, even to those who believe in His name' (John 1:12). In another place it says, 'Whoever will call on the name of the Lord will be saved' (Rom. 10:13). This is something you can do right here, today.

"I'm going to lead in a prayer, a phrase at a time. You can ask Christ to come into your heart right where you are. Pray this with me: 'Dear Lord Jesus, . . . thank You for loving me. . . . I know that I'm a sinner, . . . and I cannot save myself. . . . Thank You for dying on the cross . . . as an atoning sacrifice for my sins. . . . I believe that God raised You from the dead and that You're alive. . . . I repent of my sin. . . . I turn to You, . . . and I turn away from sin. . . . I put my faith in You. . . . SAVE ME RIGHT NOW, LORD JESUS. . . . Wash me and cleanse me in Your blood. . . . Fill me with Your Spirit . . . and help me to live for You for the rest of my life. . . . In Jesus' name, amen.'"

Then I ask everyone in the building to stand.

"If today you prayed to receive Christ, heaven is rejoicing right now, and we'd like to rejoice with you as well. We are about to sing our song of invitation. I'm going to ask you at the moment we begin to sing to step out into the aisle and come to the front of the sanctuary to meet one of our pastors. Tell them about your decision to receive Christ. They want to rejoice with you, pray with you, and give you some material on how to grow in your new faith. If you need a Bible, we will give you a free copy.

"Just as a newborn baby needs immediate care, you are a newborn child of God. You need immediate care to get started in the right direction.

"Also, let me add something to those who have made this decision in the past, but you've never been baptized. Baptism is the way you tell the world that you belong to Jesus. It's like putting on a wedding ring. The ring doesn't make you married; it simply announces that you are. Baptism doesn't save you, but it shows that you are saved. It's how you profess the faith you already possess.

"It's the first step in obedience to God. If you don't obey God in baptism, what is to say you'll obey Him in anything else? Come and speak with one of our counselors here to set up a time right away for your baptism.

"Third, maybe you're here today and you're sensing that it's about time to settle down in one church home. If you would like to join this church and put down your spiritual roots here, I invite you to come as well and start the process.

"Please step out—for any of these three reasons—and come as the rest of us sing."

As you can see, this part of the worship service is not rushed. It takes maybe five minutes altogether. That's OK. People need an opportunity to do business with God.

Theirs to Decide

I use a normal tone of voice—no hysterics, no manipulation, no melodramatic sob stories. I simply lift up the opportunity and let people make their own decisions. If the Holy Spirit has been dealing with a person, he or she simply needs to be guided, not beguiled. We don't need any "cleverness of speech" (1 Cor. 1:17).

We even extend this invitation at the close of our Wednesday night service, and people come. Church members know the speaker is going to do this *every time*, which encourages them to invite their unsaved friends and relatives to any service. This serves to increase the pool of those who need the Lord.

I know what some preachers are thinking right now: *What if I preach my heart out, and nobody responds at the end?* That, however, does not constitute failure on the preacher's part, provided he has made the gospel clear. It is not my job to force numerical results. All I must do is make the offer of Christ available. The Holy Spirit will do the rest in His own timing. He doesn't need me to make people feel guilty. He only wants me politely, tactfully, and warmly to explain what they need to do to make a decision. If I do that, they take action on their own.

Acts 2:40 says that at the end of Peter's sermon on the Day of Pentecost, "with many other words he solemnly testified and *kept on exhorting* them, saying, 'Be saved from this perverse generation!'" The Greek word for "exhorting" here is *parakaleo*, literally, "to call for." Peter was giving an altar call there. In response, the next verse reports that "that day there were added about three thousand souls" (v. 41). It was like a Billy Graham crusade! The audience didn't just listen and walk away; they made definite commitments to follow this Christ.

For people in my church who are too timid to step out in front of a large crowd, I say at the end, "Now we're about to conclude this service. My invitation is over at this point— but God's invitation is never over until your death, or until Christ returns to earth in the future. If you still need to make any of these three decisions— to be saved, to be baptized, or to join this church—some of our counselors are going to stay standing here at the front to meet you. Just come up to one of them, take their hand, and tell what you want to do. Maybe you just need someone to pray with you about a situation in your life. Whatever you do, please don't leave here without Jesus."

> *If we know anything about God, we know He is always planning for men, women, and young people to be saved. It is never away from His mind.*

People respond to this "P.S." almost every week.

I am not saying that a person has to walk a church aisle to be saved. Other preachers direct people to a counseling room instead, and that's fine. I only say that if someone is going to do something as momentous and life-changing as becoming a child of God, it's highly valuable to let somebody know about it. A public profession of faith is healthy.

In fact, some of the people who come forward in our church have already been led to Christ during the week by a friend at work, someone who visited them at home, or one of our outreach teams. Now they just want a public place to seal that. I could never deny them that opportunity.

Sometimes people's response has little or nothing to do with my preaching at all. In some cases, it's the music that touches the sensitive spot deep inside. I'll never forget the Sunday morning when someone responded to a song before I had even started my sermon. The choir was singing a moving arrangement of "Lord, Have Mercy" when, unbidden, a young man in his late twenties approached the altar and knelt. I glanced his way and could tell he was crying.

As the song continued, one of our associate pastors went over to kneel beside him and pray with him. In the course of further conversation, we found out the background of his decision. He had gone through a great many difficulties, and now a friend had invited him to church. Listening to the choir's message of repentance, he simply had to respond on the spot.

Part and Parcel

Does what I've been describing here serve to derail the worship experience? Not at all. Guiding new people into the presence of God is a vital part of worship. If the main reason we come to church is to meet with God, why not extend that wonderful privilege to everyone?

This does not mean that I skew my sermons toward the unsaved. Probably 95 percent of the time, I preach to Christians. In any sermon the Holy Spirit can use the Word of God to prick the human heart, even when the basics of the gospel are not articulated until the invitation. There is power in the Word of God, and He says, "It will not return to Me empty, without accomplishing what I desire, and without succeeding in the matter for which I sent it" (Isa. 55:11).

John Bisagno, pastor for thirty years of a great evangelistic church in Houston, told me once about preaching a finance message entitled, "The Sermon on the Amount." He traced all the places in Matthew 5–7 where Jesus mentioned money. The whole point was that Christians need to honor the Lord in their giving.

Still, when John got to the invitation for salvation, eighteen people came forward to be saved that day! The Holy Spirit had convicted them to follow Christ not only with their wallets but with their whole lives. This response was no doubt the culmination of many messages that people had heard previously.

That encouraged me not to worry about whether every sentence out of my mouth in the pulpit is crystal-clear for the unbeliever who is listening. I certainly don't try to confuse them, but neither do I feel obligated to stop and define every biblical term for their benefit. This would distract many of the Christians who are listening. The Bible is what it is, and God is well capable of using His Word to connect with people at all ages and stages of spiritual development.

God at Work

Our counselors are trained to ask a key question as soon as they meet a person responding to the invitation: "What is your decision?" In other words, they are not to waste time on peripheral details, where the person lives, what their religious background is, and so forth. They are to get right to the main point.

I'll never forget the Sunday morning I met a young woman myself at the front. She was quietly crying; her makeup had already started to run. I spoke in a quiet voice, not wanting to upset her any more.

"What is your decision?" I asked.

"I want it all!" she blurted through her tears.

What was *that* supposed to mean? I didn't know what to make of her statement. I backpedaled just a bit.

"You 'want it all'? I guess I'm trying to understand. . . ."

"All that stuff you just talked about!" she said. "To be saved, baptized, join the church—I need it all! The whole works!"

She had come seeking the grand package. With all her heart she wanted to be a fully devoted and obedient child of God. The Spirit of God had touched her deeply, and no half measures were good enough.

One of our counselors sat down with her and led her in the direction of a whole new life in Christ.

> ☞ *No hysterics, no manipulation, no melodramatic sob stories. I simply lift up the opportunity and let people make their own decisions.* ☜

This kind of encounter with God is as important as any worship chorus we could sing or any prayer we could pray. In fact, it is evidence of something I mentioned in an earlier chapter: *Give me a church where at least some things fall into the category of what only God can do.* When He penetrates the human heart and draws people to Himself, we know He is at work among us in the most powerful way of all.

PART THREE

Hindrances to Overcome

If God truly desires to visit us with His divine presence and we yearn to have Him come, then it might be assumed that the path is open. Both parties are willing, even eager. A free flow between heaven and earth should be assured.

But we know that this is not entirely the case. Blockages, built up subconsciously over many years, serve to impede our most sincere wishes. Habits of church life have become deeply entrenched. What we want is often derailed by who we are.

In this section we shine a light on five "-isms" that must be dismantled to permit God's best in the hearts and lives of His people.

CHAPTER 15

Formalism

Of all the differences between the Old and New Testaments, one of the least noticed is the contrast in worship style. Old Testament worship in the tabernacle (and then the temple) was exceedingly structured. The priests had to wear just the right garments in just the right colors, and their movements were tightly programmed. The blood of the animal sacrifices had to be handled in a precise way. The prayers and blessings were carefully scripted. When we read the book of Leviticus today, we sometimes get weary with the formality of it all.

Worship in the New Testament, on the other hand, is another story altogether. We find little detail on procedure. We see sincerity and genuine reverence for the Lord, of course. But if you're looking for prim and proper formalism, you'll come up empty. The apostle Paul gives a summary statement that "all things must be done properly and in an orderly manner" (1 Cor. 14:40), and not much more is said. Certainly nothing about the life of the early church appears to be proud or stiff.

Jesus and His Disciples Lived Informally

Jesus Himself grew up in the humble home of a young tradesman and his wife who lived in the relatively obscure village of Nazareth in the rural area of Galilee. Like His stepfather, His earthly trade was carpentry. Jesus understood the plight of the poor because He was raised in what we might call a blue-collar home.

When Jesus began His public ministry at age thirty, "the common people heard him gladly" (Mark 12:37 KJV). His disciples likewise were nothing more than fishermen, tax collectors, political zealots, and other run-of-the mill, average people. Those who had been forgiven for scandalous sins such as adultery followed Him. He touched lepers and healed them. He touched corpses and raised them. In fact, Jesus spent most of His time in the quaint, rural areas surrounding the Sea of Galilee, where few people of affluence and influence lived.

Jesus even stressed that it was difficult for rich people to follow Him and enter into heaven. Yes, a rich person could go to heaven, because all things are possible with God—but Jesus warned that an overemphasis on riches and an unhealthy focus on money would prevent many from entering the kingdom of God.

The lower-class tilt to the makeup of Christ's followers didn't change much as the years passed by. A few decades after Jesus' ascension back to heaven, Paul wrote in his first letter to the church in Corinth that there were still "not many wise according to the flesh, not many mighty, not many noble" among the Christians (1 Cor. 1:26). Apparently the congregation held few scholars, politicians, aristocrats, or societal movers and shakers. "But," Paul went on, "God has chosen the foolish things of the world to shame the wise, and God has chosen the weak things of the world to shame the things which are strong, and the base things of the world and the despised God has chosen, the things that are not, so that He may nullify the things that are, so that no man may boast before God" (1 Cor. 1:27–29). It was these common, informal believers whom the Jewish religious leaders scorned as "men who have upset the world" (Acts 17:6).

Jesus and His Disciples Ministered and Worshipped Informally

On a personal level Jesus gave little emphasis to formality in worship. When He and His disciples retreated to pray, they usually went to a mountainside or a garden. They ministered primarily in remote areas. Yet masses of spiritually hungry people flocked to them and received help and healing. Often the worship services for these crowds were held outdoors beside the Sea of Galilee in an open field. In such a setting, Jesus naturally used such agricultural references like "observe how the lilies of the field grow" and "the sower went out to sow" and "look at the birds of the air." It was all simple, plain, down-to-earth language. There was no show, no pretense, no pomposity in Jesus' ministry.

Jesus rebuked the Jewish religious leaders of His day for formally and ritualistically "practicing your righteousness before men to be noticed by them" (Matt. 6:1). They loved their titles and places of honor before the people. They loved the procedures of their religious rules and customs. These formality-focused fanatics always washed their hands with elaborate ceremony before eating a meal, according to the tradition of the elders. Yet Jesus denounced their duplicity, pointing out that their hearts were still contaminated with the sin of hypocrisy.

Jesus knew that formality for the sake of formality was lethal when it came to worshipping God. On one occasion He spoke in prayer to His Father about this.

> At that very time He rejoiced greatly in the Holy Spirit, and said, "I praise You, O Father, Lord of heaven and earth, that You have hidden these things from the wise and intelligent and have revealed them to infants. Yes, Father, for this way was well-pleasing in Your sight." (Luke 10:21)

Those who approached God with simple childlike sincerity and faith, without excessive religious formality, were the ones who would find acceptance.

Quiet + Still = Reverence?

If Jesus and His disciples were not formal in their worship, why are we? Why do people in churches today insist on man-made, man-exalting formality? Unfortunately, churches and individual Christians often equate formality with reverence.

As a young child I was taught that when you entered the sanctuary for worship, you were supposed to be quiet and sit still. Those two traits, being *quiet* and *still*, were considered irrefutable proof that a person was genuinely worshipping the Lord. As a young boy sitting on the pew next to my mother, I got pinched on the leg more than once for daring to make any noise or movement!

But is this what truly constitutes reverence? Not necessarily. When I was a teenager, my mother started a janitorial service. She eventually employed more than fifty people and was very successful. One of her earliest customers was Curry's Funeral Home. I went there many times around six o'clock in the morning to vacuum. People would ask me if I was awake at that hour. I'd always respond, "Man, when you're in a funeral home early in the morning with nobody but dead people around, you're wide awake!" If anybody had flinched, I would have been out of there in a flash.

The point is, those corpses were being still and quiet, all right. But it had nothing to do with being reverent.

I fear that the same is true in many of our churches. They're still and quiet—not because they're reverent—but because they are spiritually dead.

It reminds me of the story of the father and son who were touring a great cathedral in Vancouver, British Columbia. The father pointed out the exquisite stained-glass windows. "Those are memorials to our Canadian soldiers who died in the service," he explained.

"Which one?" the boy wanted to know. "The morning service or the evening service?"

Silence and immobility do *not* automatically indicate reverential worship. Even the Old Testament prophet Isaiah said things such as, "Lift up your voice mightily, O Jerusalem, bearer of good news; lift it up, do not fear" (Isa. 40:9). He encouraged vocal praise and rejoicing before the Lord.

Ice or Fire?

Excessive formality in worship cannot help but create a climate of spiritual coldness. My evangelism professor in seminary, Dr. Roy Fish, used to say, "You can't hatch eggs in a refrigerator." How true.

Scripture refers to God as "a consuming *fire*" (Heb. 12:29). When Moses led the people of Israel out of Egyptian bondage, the Lord went before them in "a pillar of *fire*" (Exod. 13:21). When Jesus reappeared in His resurrected state to the two disciples at Emmaus, they responded by saying, "Were not our hearts *burning* within us while He was speaking to us on the road, while He was explaining the Scriptures to us?"

(Luke 24:32). When the Holy Spirit came from heaven to that small band of praying Christians in the upper room on the day of Pentecost, He came with tongues of *fire,* not icicles (Acts 2:3)! God's presence creates spiritual warmth, not spiritual chill.

Perhaps much of what we call "reverence" in our churches is little more than pretentious religiosity. Those in love with formality in religion are akin to the Jewish religious leaders whom Jesus scolded, comparing them to "whitewashed tombs" (Matt. 23:27). On the outside they appeared fine and clean. But on the inside, they were filled with spiritual death and decay. God sends fire, not ice.

Years ago a lady said to me, "Pastor, if my dear sweet mother could see us clapping our hands in church and saying amen, she'd roll over in her grave."

"Is she in heaven?" I asked.

"Oh, yes."

"Then don't worry," I replied. "She's already doing those things herself!"

How Can We Become Less Formal?

What are some simple ways to make our churches warmer in order to attract God's presence and also reach a culture that has grown less and less formal in the past few decades?

Don't Let "The Saints Go Marching In"

A great place to begin is to eliminate the "grand entrance" by leaders at the start of a worship service. When pastors and other dignitaries file in as if at a graduation ceremony, it feels like what one writer called "the parade of the pious." Such showiness doesn't go over very well in our society.

I much prefer to enter the worship center several minutes *before* the service begins. That way I can walk slowly through the crowd, looking individuals in the eye, conversing and sometimes even praying with those who have a need. After the service concludes, it's not good for the pastor to bolt through the door, hop in his car, and head for the restaurant. Instead, he and the staff members should remain in the sanctuary, talking and ministering to people for awhile. Such simple gestures bless the church members and greatly endear the pastor and the staff members to them.

PASTOR, SIT WITH YOUR FAMILY

The pastor should also seriously consider sitting on the front row with his family and the rest of the congregation, rather than mounting the platform for the entire worship service. Sitting in the congregation sends a message to the people: *I'm not only a shepherd; I'm also a sheep. I'm one of you.* I find it easier to participate in genuine worship of the Lord when I'm not on display. I'm not distracted by the thought that people are watching me! It also means something to Donna and any of the children who are with us, who appreciate having the family united during times of musical praise.

THE CHURCH IS NOT AN OPERA

The more classical and high-church the music becomes, the harder it gets for the average person in the pew to make the connection. If the church's music is so highbrow that the average person can't relate to it, we have failed. Church musicians should not try to imitate the sound of a baroque fugue. Instead, they need to choose simple, scriptural, Christ-centered songs that touch the heart as well as the head.

The way to a person's head, in fact, is through his heart. Music touches the heart and the emotions, and *then* it speaks to the head and the mind. Few people, if any, will be debated and talked into the kingdom of God. But when their hearts, like John Wesley's that night back in London, are "strangely warmed" by God's Spirit, their minds open up to the truths of the gospel.

TALK NORMALLY

Simply put, the key to less formality in a church is the leader. If the pastor is stiff and starchy, formality will rule the day. But if he is down-to-earth, genuine, and believable, people will follow along. Such informality will help the church accomplish its mission of glorifying God and reaching people for Christ.

Have you ever been turned off by a preacher's "ministerial voice"? I've been a guest preacher in many places through the years, and I've noticed an odd switch in some of my hosts. Before the service begins, the pastor and I will talk in a normal speaking voice. "How are the kids,

Sam?" "Great, Steve. They're growing up so fast!" Or I'll say, "Wow, there are a lot of people here tonight for the service." "Yeah, we've been praying for the Lord to bless our time together tonight." Then all of a sudden, the choir enters, the organist begins to play, and the same pastor steps to the pulpit with a totally dif-ferent tone: "Gooooood eeeeevening. It is sooooooo gooooood to be in the hooooooo-ouse of the Loooord!"

What in the world happened to him?! I say to myself. He was normal just a few seconds ago, but now he's turned into somebody else. This church must have Dr. Jekyll and Mr. Hyde for their pastor.

Today's "get-real" world fully expects a normal tone of voice from anyone they listen to.

> *On a personal level Jesus gave little emphasis to formality in worship. When He and His disciples retreated to pray, they usually went to a mountainside or a garden.*

Formal Is Fading; Casual Is Coming

The American culture is getting less and less formal. Nowhere is that seen more clearly than in the area of clothing. Go to a shopping mall and see for yourself. Notice how many more clothing stores focus on selling casual clothes rather than dress clothes. When I was a kid, if you wanted to buy a pair of jeans, you had only one option: straight-legged blue jeans made by Levi's. Today things have changed radically. Jeans come in every shape, color, and style. One popular cut even carries the name "Relaxed Fit"!

In the workplace, employees are all but demanding freedom to shed the neckties and high heels so they can be more comfortable. Businesses today have to define the differences between "business casual," "nice casual," and "regular casual" as opposed to downright sloppy. Oftentimes even companies who require traditional wear as the norm still allow for "dress-down Fridays." Here at our church, employees are allowed to wear casual clothing every day except Sundays and Wednesdays, the days of our worship services.

All this is in sharp contrast to the days when people dressed up to go to church. No one asked what they were supposed to wear. Women and girls wore dresses; men and boys wore suits with neckties. One

of the Sunday morning rituals at my house when I was a kid was to
spread out the newspaper so I could shine my shoes for church. It was,
without question, a formal event. Preachers would make statements like
"God deserves your very best, and that includes the clothes you wear to
His house."

Indeed, God does deserve our best worship. But His emphasis is
always on the person's *interior.* The Lord told Samuel that "God sees
not as man sees, for man looks at the outward appearance, but the LORD
looks at the heart" (1 Sam. 16:7). We need to remember that Jesus actually castigated the Jewish religious leaders for their love of wearing long,
ornate robes in order to distinguish themselves as significant religious
figures (Mark 12:38).

I'll be frank with you: When it comes to wearing ties, I have a
natural aversion. I'm a former football player with a twenty-inch neck.
When I get to heaven, I'll be looking for the guy who invented these
things; and if I find him, I'll have a long talk with him!

When we lived in Texas, a restaurant called the Trail Dust
Steakhouse advertised that the only type of acceptable dress was casual;
if anyone wore a necktie, it would literally be cut in half. They were
serious about it. Hundreds of men had showed up over the years in old neckties they no longer wanted, allowing workers to cut them in two and staple
them to the walls. The owner of each tie signed his name with the date of the
cutting. Those hundreds of sliced ties looked like scalps across the wall.

> ☙ *Many of our*
> *churches are still and*
> *quiet—not because*
> *they're reverent but*
> *because they are*
> *spiritually dead.* ☙

Centuries ago, I'm told, neckties
started out as bibs during meals. Isn't
that just like formality? It takes something with a perfectly good *func-*
tion and transforms it into an annoying *form!*

Don't get me wrong: I'm not advocating the inauguration of a tie-
cutting brigade in your church. But I am suggesting that people should
be allowed to dress less formally. What does it matter if men wear open
collars instead of neckties? Will God think less of a woman who wears
a pantsuit than He does of one who wears a dress? Should a person have
to buy a suit before he can darken the door of our churches? Would
Jesus, the humble carpenter and friend of the common person, require

such as that? The answer is obviously no. As long as someone's heart is hungry for the Lord, what he or she wears is secondary.

Use Common Sense

As I say all of this, I realize that a word of caution is necessary. While casual dress should be permitted in our churches even on Sunday, casual dress should never degenerate into immodesty. Overly revealing clothing is not merely a matter of poor style; it is a dishonor to the God who created our bodies. A Christian should dress morally, never allowing his or her clothing to become a display of carnality.

Let's be specific. Men and boys should not seek to display their physique by what they wear. Godly ladies and girls should not wear sexually suggestive clothing at any time, whether it's a formal or casual occasion. To be frank, I've seen some formal wedding dresses that were downright lewd.

I know of an African-American pastor who has a group of saintly women who help him at this point. When a girl sits on the front row of the church with a short, revealing skirt or dress, one of the ladies takes a blanket and says, "I'm covering you on behalf of Jesus and my pastor!" May the numbers of such bold, godly people increase. Modesty is always the best policy for the child of God, regardless of the occasion.

How Close?

I can hear some readers thinking, *But if formality is out, isn't there a danger of becoming too casual with God?* To be sure, too many people are flippant and frivolous in their spiritual relationship. This should not lead us, however, to hold God at a distance.

Bill Reynolds chaired the committee that put together *The Baptist Hymnal,* which was published in 1976. During their deliberations a debate broke out about preserving the old song "In the Garden." One member complained that it was simply "too personal and casual" in its references to God. "Listen to the lyrics," he said. "'And He walks with *me,* and He talks with *me,* and He tells *me I* am His own.' That language is too relaxed to be used in reference to God. Let's leave it out."

The discussion went back and forth until one man raised his hand in the back of the room. When Dr. Reynolds recognized him, the man simply quoted these words: "The Lord is *my* shepherd; *I* shall not want. He maketh *me* to lie down in green pastures; He leadeth *me* beside the still waters. He restoreth *my* soul." When he had completed the entire Twenty-third Psalm, he sat down without saying another word.

The place broke out in applause. Within minutes the song was overwhelmingly approved to be in the new hymnal.

God deeply loves us. He does not want us to be cold and formal with Him. We should love Him intimately, passionately, and devotedly. After all, He's our Father.

Some people seem to love formality and dignity more than they love the Lord Himself. It's hard to focus on human dignity and heavenly deity at the same time. By nature, worship is an act of humbling oneself before the Lord.

When the Israelites were bringing up the Ark of the Covenant to Jerusalem, King David worshipped the Lord with complete abandonment of personal pride and self-interest. "David was dancing before the Lord with all his might, and David was wearing a linen ephod. So David and all the house of Israel were bringing up the ark of the Lord with shouting and the sound of the trumpet" (2 Sam. 6:14–15).

The only trouble was, David was married to a lady named Michal. She was the daughter of Saul, the former king of Israel. She had been brought up as an aristocratic blueblood. She didn't care for David's display of emotion. She "looked out of the window and saw King David leaping and dancing before the Lord; and she despised him in her heart" (v. 16).

After the Ark was safely in its place in Jerusalem, David dismissed all the people who had assisted him and sent each of them home with a gift of food. When he arrived at his own home, Michal was there to meet him with gold-plated sarcasm. "How the king of Israel distinguished himself today!" she hissed. "He uncovered himself today in the eyes of his servants' maids as one of the foolish ones shamelessly uncovers himself!" (v. 20).

David was not apologetic. He said, "It was before the Lord, who chose me above your father and above all his house, to appoint me ruler over the people of the Lord, over Israel; therefore I will celebrate before the Lord. I will be more lightly esteemed than this and will be humble in my own eyes, but with the maids of whom you have spoken, with them I will be distinguished" (vv. 21–22). The New International Version sheds light by translating verse 22 this way: "I will become even more undignified than this, and I will be humiliated in my own eyes."

As you know, the Lord agreed with David's perspective 100 percent. He punished Michal for her attitude by permanently withholding the gift of motherhood (see v. 23).

When God's people abandon biblical, heartfelt, sincere, humble worship and replace it with man-exalting formality, God curses their disobedience. God sets the rules for worship; we don't. If we insist on maintaining our dignity and formality, God will allow us to reap the harvest of spiritual sterility. God is looking for people who are interested in pleasing Him with childlike faith and worship that esteems Him, not their pride.

> ✍ *Church musicians should not try to imitate the sound of a baroque fugue.* ✍

Formalism is a mask, a guise, to cover up a lack of substance. Jesus said that people who practiced their piety with formality, to be seen by others, were nothing more than hypocrites, or "mask wearers" (see Matt. 6:1–8, 16–18). They were praying, giving, and fasting in order to be noticed. That's formalism.

This hinders revival because it makes things unreal, artificial, overly polished, unnatural. May God deliver us from this enemy of revival.

CHAPTER 16

Faticism

While the church of the Lord Jesus Christ must avoid the pitfall of formalism, she also must steer clear of the ditch on the other side of the road, which is fanaticism. Today in the church, fanatics are overreacting to formalism, while formalists are overreacting to fanaticism. God wants to send revival to His people, but Satan desires to give them his cheap substitutes. When Christians begin to gravitate toward "spiritual experiences" that are not clearly mentioned anywhere in Scripture, they are treading on extremely dangerous ground.

Emotions Versus Emotionalism

Jesus warned that to chase after signs was a dead-end street (see Matt. 12:39; 16:4). We are not to be driven by our fleshly feelings. Yes, Jesus commanded us to love God with all our heart and soul, but He also commanded us to love the Lord with our minds.

My predecessor, Adrian Rogers, once said, "If God tells us we have 'the mind of Christ' (1 Cor. 2:16), then by all means we should use it!" While nothing is wrong with loving God with our *emotions* (i.e., "heart and soul"), we must avoid the extremes of radical *emotionalism*.

When I first became a Christian, a friend of mine and I began to sing in various churches. We were so eager to share Christ through our testimonies and music that we would go virtually anyplace, anytime. On a few occasions we encountered what I now know was religious fanaticism.

Once after my friend and I had sung and the preacher had started his message, an elderly woman stood up and started running up and down the aisle. My young eighteen-year-old eyes had never witnessed anything like that in a worship service before. I leaned over and asked someone what in the world she was doing. I was told, "She can't help herself. She's just 'running in the Spirit.'"

It wasn't long before some other folks stood up and began to engage in strange behavior. One lady was basically jerking in her seat. Again I asked, "What's wrong with her?" Again, the Holy Spirit was blamed for causing her peculiar actions.

Soon the chaos intensified. Some people were yelling, others were moaning, some were jumping, others were contorting, and most all of them were acting, for lack of a better word, *different*.

> *If something isn't in the Bible, it's neither of God nor from God. After all, He inspired the book.*

I remember rushing back to my room after that service, opening my Bible, and searching to find out whether what I had seen that night was in the pages of the New Testament. I couldn't find it anywhere. I concluded that those things weren't biblical but rather examples of fanaticism.

Did God *Really* Do That?

The Lord gets blamed for a lot of things He doesn't have anything to do with. Years ago a woman came up to me with a piece of paper, saying, "Brother Steve, God gave me these words. It's a song I'd like to sing sometime in church."

Well, I'd heard her try to sing, and I knew she probably shouldn't. But I took a look at the lyrics anyway. They were a mess. I didn't have the heart to tell her what I was thinking, which was this: *You know, God wrote the book of Psalms, and He can do a whole lot better than what's on this paper!*

If something isn't in the Bible, it's neither of God nor from God. The reason I say that is because the Holy Spirit inspired the Book. "All

Scripture is inspired by God and profitable for teaching, for reproof, for correction, for training in righteousness" (2 Tim. 3:16). Peter said, "But know this first of all, that no prophecy of Scripture is a matter of one's own interpretation, for no prophecy was ever made by an act of human will, but men moved by the Holy Spirit spoke from God" (2 Pet. 1:20–21). If someone says they are being "led by the Spirit" to do something that is never found in or supported by Scripture, then the activity is purely theirs, not the Spirit's.

It really is amazing how strange some people can get when they enter into the realm of religious fanaticism. Here are a few of the most extreme examples:

Gold in Them Thar Hands?

A preacher in Georgia once claimed to have a special anointing from the Lord to pray successfully for people who needed physical healing. The preacher said that when the Lord's healing anointing was upon him, gold dust appeared on the palms of his hands. He, in fact, was not the only one making such a claim.

The primary proponent of this alleged phenomenon was Ruth Ward Heflin, who for a time operated Mount Zion Miracle Chapel in Israel, and also directed the Calvary Pentecostal Campground in Ashland, Virginia.[47] In 1998 newspapers across the nation began to report Mrs. Heflin's claim that gold dust was being distributed by God during her services. Another female preacher at that time named Silvania Machado claimed that while she ministered, "holy gold flakes" would appear on her face, and then oil began to flow supernaturally from her body.

Soon after these claims, Mrs. Heflin died at the age of sixty from cancer. *Charisma* magazine described her death with a full-page article that said in part:

> During her nearly 40 years of ministry, Heflin's bur-
> den for Israel and for evangelism and discipleship took her
> around the world. Heflin also was the founder and director
> of Mount Zion Fellowship, an international prayer ministry
> in Jerusalem, where she lived for more than 25 years before

returning to the United States. . . . Heflin suffered a broken ankle in an automobile accident last year. In April, doctors diagnosed her with breast cancer that already had spread into her bones. Heflin underwent a mastectomy on April 25, but refused chemotherapy or further cancer treatment because she said the Lord told her to refuse, according to Connie Wilson, her personal assistant. . . . Heflin recently has been a central figure in the so-called gold dust revival. People who attended her camp meetings said they saw gold dust appear on their faces and hands, and some reported that God put gold fillings in their teeth. Some said they even saw diamonds, rubies or feathers appear.[48]

Why should we be concerned with such claims? Because they are extrabiblical and sensational.

When I think of people claiming that God put gold dust in their hands, I can't help but remember the apostle Peter's famous words to the beggar at the Beautiful Gate of the Jewish temple in Jerusalem: *"I do not possess silver and gold,* but what I do have I give to you: In the name of Jesus Christ the Nazarene—walk!" (Acts 3:6). Indeed, God's anointing for healing flowed through Peter's hands. No gold dust was mentioned.

Spurious claims are unfortunate and serve as a detriment to the cause of Jesus Christ. When a person maintains that he or she has experienced that which is impossible to support scripturally, attributing it to the working of the Holy Spirit, people turn sour toward the things of God.

Prayer Rugs?

I also wonder what God thinks about a mailing operation[49] that currently sends out "Holy Ghost Bible Prayer Rugs" for people to kneel on, or lay across their knees, in search of healing, financial windfalls, new cars, and the like. Actually, the "rug" is not made of fabric at all; it is rather an eleven-by-seventeen-inch piece of thin paper with a picture of Jesus on it, surrounded by a Persian-rug design. After praying in a quiet room on the "rug," you must then store it overnight in your Bible;

if you don't have a Bible, you're allowed to place it under your mattress. But you can't keep the paper more than twenty-four hours; you have to mail it back the next morning (preferably with a "seed gift" of money) for someone else to use.

(Some will say this is an echo of the method Paul used in Ephesus to extend his healing ministry through "handkerchiefs or aprons"—Acts 19:12. But the Bible says nothing about people needing to send the cloths *back* to Paul with a donation.)

Please understand me—I believe in physical healing! While God does not promise perfect health in this life, He is still Jehovah-Rapha, "the LORD, who heals" (Exod. 15:26 NIV). My own mother was miraculously healed of breast cancer when she was only twenty-four years old. She had already lost one breast, and the other was scheduled to be taken soon. But something remarkable happened that changed her life forever.

> *The Lord gets blamed for a lot of things He doesn't have anything to do with.*

Mom was sharing a hospital room with an elderly Baptist lady who was recovering from a recent double mastectomy herself. The night before my mother's second surgery, that little lady climbed up into her bed, placed my mother's head in her lap, and prayed *all night* for the Lord to heal her. My mom was semi-sedated during those hours, coming in and out of consciousness. Each time she would awaken, she would hear the voice of that dear saint crying out to the Lord on her behalf.

And when the doctors came in the next morning, all the cancer was gone.

That Baptist lady went on to share the gospel there in the hospital, and my mother prayed to receive Christ as her Savior and Lord. When she returned home, she was soon baptized in a Baptist church. My dad was also saved and baptized. That is exactly how the Gaineses became a Christian family.

Indeed, I know that God can and often does heal people physically. Nevertheless, as I read the New Testament, I never see the Lord Jesus or any of His disciples turning any healing into a production. In fact, when He healed the paralyzed man beside the pool of Bethesda, He was so low-key about it that the fellow didn't even catch Jesus' name. He got up and started walking, and when he looked around, the "healing evangelist" was gone. John 5:13 says, "The man who was healed did not know who it was, for Jesus had slipped away while there was a crowd in that place."

The genuine presence of God is not a theatrical spectacular. It isn't flashy or gaudy. When we try to present Jesus Christ in a glitzy manner, it simply doesn't work.

When Satan tempted Jesus to have a sensational ministry and attract a crowd by jumping from the pinnacle of the temple so the angels could catch Him and then lower Him to the ground, He refused. Such activity would have been nothing short of putting God to the test, He said (Luke 4:12). Jesus was not a showman.

Once again the Bible gives us clear guidance on what is in and out of bounds. We have no right to permit what the apostles would have shut down.

The Virgin Mary in an Alabama Field?

When we lived near Birmingham, Alabama, a woman named Marija Lunetti made national news by claiming to have seen the Virgin Mary in a local field. Greg Garrison, a religion reporter for *The Birmingham News*, interviewed her and wrote how she, one of six Yugoslavs who claimed to see Mary back in the village of Medjugorje starting in 1981, was now saying the same thing about her visits to our area. Every time she came to see her brother in the hospital and stayed in a certain home in Shelby County, she insisted that Mary showed up in an adjacent field.

Pilgrims began coming from all over the United States and even as far away as Northern Ireland to spend time praying with Ms. Lunetti.

> After kneeling and praying with them on Monday morning, Lunetti spoke to a crowd of pilgrims for about 15 minutes. She said that Mary helps Christians get closer to her son, Jesus. "To be ready, we need our hearts open," Lunetti said. "God gives us his beautiful grace to be here and pray together." . . .
>
> She said her visions of the Virgin Mary have been continuing daily, including Monday at 6:40 p.m., and that Mary

brings simple messages of prayer and peace. "She asks that we pray for peace," Lunetti said.[50]

Such sightings are prime examples of religious fanaticism. They have no scriptural substantiation whatsoever. The New Testament does not mention a single appearance of Mary to anyone following her death. Nor does the New Testament ever command or even encourage us to worship Mary or address her in prayer.

Spiritual but Not "of the Spirit"

Everything that is spiritual is not necessarily of God. That is why the apostle John urged us, "Beloved, do not believe every spirit, but test the spirits to see whether they are from God, because many false prophets have gone out into the world" (1 John 4:1).

While the previous examples in this chapter have reflected simple naiveté and gullibility, there is another level that gets into far deeper water. The devil likes to imitate God's supernatural power. Christians need to be careful to be scriptural in every spiritual experience.

Moses was called by God to go to the king of Egypt and demand the release of his Hebrew brothers and sisters, who served as slaves. When Moses and his brother, Aaron, arrived, they were to perform several miracles to show that their calling and authority came from Jehovah and not themselves. Interestingly, the magicians who served in Pharaoh's court were able to execute several of the same miracles. They used their "secret arts" to cause their staffs to turn into serpents. They also used those same powers to cause water to turn into blood and to make frogs come up out of the Nile (see Exod. 7:11, 22; 8:7).

> ☞ *The Bible gives us clear guidance on what is in and out of bounds. We have no right to permit what the apostles would have shut down.* ☜

Where did they get such "secret" powers? From Satan. While Satan is not all-powerful, he *is* powerful. The Bible teaches that Satan can empower people who yield to him to perform "signs" and various "miracles." We see that happening today in the casting of spells by witches involved in the Wiccan religion as well as other New Age circles. That is why in the Old Testament the Lord condemned the practice of witch-craft and divination.

> When you enter the land which the LORD your God gives
> you, you shall not learn to imitate the detestable things of
> those nations. There shall not be found among you anyone
> who makes his son or his daughter pass through the fire, one
> who uses divination, one who practices witchcraft, or one who
> interprets omens, or a sorcerer, or one who casts a spell, or a
> medium, or a spiritist, or one who calls up the dead. For who-
> ever does these things is detestable to the LORD; and because
> of these detestable things the LORD your God will drive them
> out before you. You shall be blameless before the LORD your
> God. For those nations, which you shall dispossess, listen to
> those who practice witchcraft and to diviners, but as for you,
> the LORD your God has not allowed you to do so.
> (Deut. 18:9–14)

Such demonic practices were not limited to Old Testament times. Many pagans during the New Testament period practiced sorcery as well. When Paul preached at Ephesus, the Lord sent revival, and many people were saved. They were also set free from various occultic activities.

> Many also of those who had believed kept coming, con-
> fessing and disclosing their practices. And many of those
> who practiced magic brought their books together and began
> burning them in the sight of everyone; and they counted up
> the price of them and found it fifty thousand pieces of silver.
> So the word of the Lord was growing mightily and prevailing.
> (Acts 19:18–20)

Satan has always worked miraculously through his servants. The apostle Paul referred to this when he said:

> For such men are false apostles, deceitful workers, disguis-
> ing themselves as apostles of Christ. No wonder, for even
> Satan disguises himself as an angel of light. Therefore it is not
> surprising if his servants also disguise themselves as servants
> of righteousness, whose end will be according to their deeds.
> (2 Cor. 11:13–15)

According to Scripture, Satan will work this way until the end of time. During the period of the great tribulation, Satan will empower the Antichrist and his workers to perform many miraculous signs and wonders (see Rev. 13). Unfortunately, many people will fall for his deception.

The Greatest Miracle of All

Lest you read this chapter and erroneously surmise that I don't believe in the supernatural power of God, please hear my heart! I do believe God can and will do things that cannot be explained by human beings. At times He will do miraculous things. I'm certainly not put off by that. In no way am I ashamed of an all-powerful God who can do anything He pleases.

But whatever God *does* will always be in perfect harmony with what He *says* in the pages of Scripture. When it comes to miracles, we must always focus on biblical phenomena.

I also believe that we need to remember constantly that the greatest miracle of all is conversion. That is the miracle of all miracles, when a soul corroded with sin comes to Jesus for forgiveness. When that person repents and puts his faith in what Jesus did for him on the cross and at the empty tomb, his soul is plunged into the redeeming blood of Jesus and made as white as snow.

The sweetest words we can ever hear are the words in Matthew 9:2 when Jesus said, "Take courage, son; your sins are forgiven." This outweighs any surge of emotion, any spectacular healing, any religious drama. We don't need formalism, but we don't need fanaticism either.

Fanaticism is not revival. This distortion is, in fact, a hindrance to genuine revival. God never does today that which would contradict what He did and said yesterday; He is "the same yesterday and today and forever" (Heb. 13:8). The manifestations of Scripture are, in fact, exciting enough as they stand. They don't need any embellishments from us. If we open our hearts and minds to receive the manifest presence of God as evidenced in the Bible, we will have more than enough.

CHAPTER 17

Liberalism

You may find it strange for me to include this kind of chapter in a book on seeking the manifest presence of God. The intensely personal quest to reach out and draw near to the Lord isn't really affected by the theological debates of the ivory tower, is it? Let the intellectuals write their papers and give their lectures; meanwhile, can't we just concentrate on welcoming the touch of God and the wind of His Spirit in our meetings?

If that is your wish, I need to tell you with all seriousness that there *is* a real connection between what you believe (or don't believe) and how you worship. If you don't believe in the Word of God, you won't believe in the God of the Word. The Word takes us to God Himself. If the Scripture is not your governing bedrock, you have no basis to seek revival. The pastor will have nothing solid to preach. The church has no guidelines for operation. We have no Great Commission. We won't know that humanity is really lost without Christ. There is no gospel.

Liberalism is not just a political philosophy or a cultural preference. When the term is used in the spiritual arena, it means taking *liberties* with foundational truth. It means questioning that which God already nailed down long ago. As a result, the whole house begins shaking and rattling in the breeze. The concrete footings and the four-by-six timbers that were meant to hold everything else in place can no longer be relied upon.

In my denomination we've had more experience with liberalism and its effects than many of us ever wanted. So I speak with some experience on this subject (I'll give details later in this chapter). Thank God we're doing much better these days. Other church groups have gone through similar struggles. They have learned along with us that liberalism is not a danger to be ignored.

In my opinion theological liberalism has sent more people to hell than the effects of secular humanism and radical atheism combined. When Christian leaders, whether pastors or seminary professors, begin to call into question the accuracy and trustworthiness of the Bible, the results are devastating.

Jude warned of such problems in his short epistle:

> Beloved, while I was making every effort to write you
> about our common salvation, I felt the necessity to write to
> you appealing that you contend earnestly for the faith which
> was once for all handed down to the saints. For certain per-
> sons have crept in unnoticed, those who were long beforehand
> marked out for this condemnation, ungodly persons who turn
> the grace of our God into licentiousness and deny our only
> Master and Lord, Jesus Christ. (Jude 3–4)

This early-church leader was telling his readers that whenever false prophets and teachers creep in among Christians, it is time to go to war. Those who believe God's Word must not sit idly by and allow liberalism to take over. Instead, they must "contend earnestly for the faith" and take back their churches, institutions, and seminaries before it is too late.

A number of Christian denominations in America have chosen not to contend for "the faith which was once for all handed down to the saints," and they have suffered for it. They have dwindled in both spiritual power and in membership. At one time they were great missionary organizations sending out men and women who were called of God to share the gospel of Christ with lost people in foreign lands. But when their theology was corrupted by liberalism, it ate away at their theological foundations, causing their evangelistic and missionary zeal to implode and disappear.

Not a New Invention

If you think liberalism is a recent hazard that just cropped up in the last fifty or a hundred years, that's not true. This problem goes back at least to Jesus' time. The theological liberals then were called Sadducees. Luke, the lone Gentile writer of Scripture, pointed out their disbelief in any type of bodily resurrection after a person dies. Note his parenthetical statement in Luke 20:27. "Now there came to Him some of the Sadducees (who say that there is no resurrection)." The same writer later elaborated on the Sadducees' liberalism by contrasting them with the opposite group of Jewish leaders during that time period, the Pharisees. "For the Sadducees say that there is no resurrection, nor an angel, nor a spirit, but the Pharisees acknowledge them all" (Acts 23:8).

Sadly, the Sadducees were known during the New Testament period primarily for what they *did not* believe. Their dismissal of any resurrection, of course, could hardly square with Daniel's prophecy that says:

Now at that time Michael, the great prince who stands guard over the sons of your people, will arise. And there will be a time of distress such as never occurred since there was a nation until that time; and at that time your people, everyone who is found written in the book, will be rescued. Many of those who sleep in the dust of the ground will awake, these to everlasting life, but the others to disgrace and everlasting contempt. (Dan. 12:1–2)

Perhaps the Sadducees didn't like the idea of eternal rewards for the righteous and eternal judgment for the wicked. It was hard for them to believe that God would sentence even the most sinful Jew to any form of eternal punishment, no matter how wicked he had been during this life. After all, Jews were the "children of Abraham" (Acts 13:26 NIV).

According to Luke, the Sadducees also refused to believe in angels. That gave them trouble with any number of Old Testament accounts where angels showed up (e.g., Hagar in the desert, Balaam, Gideon, Samson's parents, David, Elijah, and the prophet Zechariah, among others). Perhaps these were just religious myths or legends.

If the Sadducees dismissed any type of spirit, how did they explain the "evil spirit" that terrorized King Saul (1 Sam. 16:14–23)? Perhaps they taught their rabbinical students and other listeners that this was merely some sort of mental illness and that the biblical writer was simply using language that would accommodate the popular, superstitious beliefs of Saul's day.

John the Baptist and Theological Liberals

Even before Jesus began His public ministry, the Sadducees showed up in the Judean wilderness at the Jordan River just north of the Dead Sea to check out John the Baptist. They said they wanted to be baptized by him. But when John saw them, he rebuked them (along with the legalistic Pharisees) by saying:

> "You brood of vipers, who warned you to flee from the
> wrath to come? Therefore bear fruit in keeping with repen-
> tance; and do not suppose that you can say to yourselves, 'We
> have Abraham for our father'; for I say to you that from these
> stones God is able to raise up children to Abraham. The axe
> is already laid at the root of the trees; therefore every tree
> that does not bear good fruit is cut down and thrown into the
> fire." (Matt. 3:7–10)

Can you imagine calling a group of baptismal candidates a "brood of vipers" (i.e., "a barrel of snakes")? Those were incredibly strong words of denunciation. John was telling both the legalistic Pharisees and the liberal Sadducees that just because they were Jewish did not automatically guarantee that they were right with the Lord. They needed more than their Jewish heritage, lineage, and pedigree to be God's children. They needed to repent of their sins and live lives of holiness that bore witness to the fact that they had indeed repented. They also needed to put their faith in the coming Messiah (Jesus), to whom John referred when he went on to say:

> "As for me, I baptize you with water for repentance, but
> He who is coming after me is mightier than I, and I am not
> fit to remove His sandals; He will baptize you with the Holy
> Spirit and fire. His winnowing fork is in His hand, and He
> will thoroughly clear His threshing floor; and He will gather
> His wheat into the barn, but He will burn up the chaff with
> unquenchable fire." (Matt. 3:11–12)

John was telling the Sadducees that unless they embraced Jesus as the Christ and repented of their sins, they would spend eternity in hell!

Two-Time Losers

The week before Jesus was crucified, the liberal Sadducees challenged Him to a theological debate. They posed a rather far-fetched "what if?" They told about a woman whom they said had outlived seven husbands, all brothers, and finally died herself in her old age without ever having children. (Somebody should have called the Guinness Book of World Records.) The Sadducees wanted Jesus to declare which husband would be hers in heaven after the resurrection (which, of course, the Sadducees did not accept in the first place). What a preposterous example.

> Jesus said to them, "Is this not the reason you are mistaken, that you do not understand the Scriptures or the power of God? For when they rise from the dead, they neither marry nor are given in marriage, but are like angels in heaven. But regarding the fact that the dead rise again, have you not read in the book of Moses, in the passage about the burning bush, how God spoke to him, saying, 'I am the God of Abraham, and the God of Isaac, and the God of Jacob'? He is not the God of the dead, but of the living; you are greatly mistaken." (Mark 12:24–27)

> ☞   *If the Scripture is not your governing bedrock, you have no basis to seek revival.*

Ouch! That had to hurt! Jesus told these highly intellectual, theological "experts" who had dedicated their entire lives to an intensive study of the Old Testament that they actually were two-time losers: (1) they didn't have a clue when it came to understanding the Scriptures, and (2) they were equally clueless about the mighty power of God, through which anything is possible.

Can't you just imagine what they were thinking when they heard His scathing rebuke? *"Who do you think you are, you untrained, country, itinerant rabbi-wannabe? How dare you try to lecture us concerning biblical matters! Don't you know who we are? We're the Sadducees!"* They had tried to embarrass Him in front of His followers by stumping Him with a hypothetical example that would unravel any idea of the resurrection of the dead, and they failed. Instead, Jesus' reply was so compelling that they were the ones embarrassed and silenced before the listening crowds. It was a fairly brief debate.

Theological liberalism always subtracts from the Word of God. The Sadducees didn't believe in the resurrection, despite the fact that the Old Testament Scriptures taught such a doctrine. Jesus stressed that God did not say to Moses, "I *was* the God of Abraham, Isaac, and Jacob." Instead, He said, "I *am* the God of Abraham, Isaac, and Jacob"— even right now. That set up His clincher: "He is not the God of the dead, but of the living; you are greatly mistaken."

Where Liberalism Started

Have you ever wondered how theological liberalism got going in the first place? The answer is found in the first book of the Bible. According to Genesis 3, the first liberal was the devil himself. He posed the question "Indeed, has God said?" (Gen. 3:1). That made Satan the first person ever to question the Word of God.

His question is at the heart of liberalism. Instead of submitting to the Scriptures, a liberal attempts to rule over them. Instead of allowing the Bible to judge him, he decides he's going to judge the Bible.

When people question the validity and truthfulness of God's Word, they start denying it next. That's what the devil did with Eve. After his opening question, he then grew more bold to say, "You surely will not die!" (Gen. 3:4), a direct contradiction of God's earlier warning to Adam.

This questioning of God's Word did not end in the garden. The devil tried to tempt Jesus in the same way immediately after His baptism. When Jesus was baptized, God clearly declared from heaven, "This is My beloved Son, in whom I am well-pleased" (Matt. 3:17). Right away, the devil said to Jesus, "If you are the Son of God . . ." (Matt. 4:3, 6).

What was Satan doing? The same thing he had done in the garden of Eden with Adam and Eve. He was calling God's statement into question.

Like Satan, theological liberals first question God's Word. Pretty soon, they deny it altogether. When that happens, they become a ship without a rudder, floating on a sea of theological, ethical, and moral relativism. They no longer know what's right or wrong; and what's worse, they really don't care to know. They give up on any form of absolute truth. Instead they say, "What's right for you isn't necessarily right for me."

Liberals start out denying the *accuracy* of Scripture, and before long they're denying the *authority* of Scripture. "We don't care what the Bible actually says about this or that; we're going to do what we think is best." It all begins with the fiery dart of Satan's question, "Indeed, has God said?" A person is never more like the devil than when he or she denies the reliability and trust-worthiness of the Bible, God's holy Word.

This line of thinking holds no power to nurture the soul. E. Stanley Jones, the old-time Methodist

> *Liberalism is not a recent hazard that just cropped up in the last fifty or a hundred years. This problem goes back at least to Jesus' time.*

missionary to India, wrote a devotional back in the early 1940s entitled "We Cannot Live by a 'No.'" Listen to his poignant words:

Modern man is beginning to see that he cannot live, as he once thought, on the denial of other people's faith. The generation of people that lived on denials soon found themselves disillusioned even with their disillusionments. They had "three sneers for everything and three cheers for nothing." And they soon found they couldn't live by sneers—to live by sneers is poor fare. If we should walk to the table each day and look over the food and then turn away in high disdain, we could get away with this disdainful attitude for awhile—but only for awhile. In the end, hunger would bite us and drive us to affirm something about food and to act on our affirmation. Both physically and spiritually we are positive beings and cannot live on a negation. We cannot live by a "No"; we must live by a "Yes." And that "Yes" must be God, or it will let us down.

The future of the world is in the hands of believers, for the nonbelievers cannot act. They are suffering from "the paralysis of analysis." They can only deny.[51]

A person is not necessarily smart just because he asks a question about God or the Bible that is hard to answer. Any three-year-old can perplex his parents with "When I blow out my birthday candles, where does the fire go?" but that doesn't make him wiser than mom or dad. Neither is liberalism validated by its ability simply to cast uncertainty. We need the sure voice of God's truth to make sense of our complicated world.

How to Detect a Theological Liberal

How can you recognize a modern-day Sadducee? What are some of the core teachings that one *must* believe in order to be accurately classified as a Bible-believing Christian? Here are three crucial questions that sort out the matter in quick order.

1. WHO IS JESUS?

What does the New Testament say about Him? It clearly calls Him the eternal, *divine* Son of God. Mormons and others falsely teach that Jesus was a man who became God. According to Scripture, just the opposite is true. Jesus existed as God the Son before He was born in Bethlehem (John 1:1–5). When He was born, Jesus was God in the flesh (John 1:14; Col. 2:9). Jesus is also the *virgin-born* Son of God (Matt. 1:23–25). He was born of a virgin so He would not receive a sinful nature like every other person after Adam and Eve has received at conception (Rom. 5:12).

Jesus is also the *sinless* Son of God. Although He was tempted in all ways like we are, He never once yielded to a single temptation (Heb. 4:15). That qualified Jesus to be the *sacrificial* Son of God. He died as an atoning sacrifice (i.e., propitiation) on the cross to pay the penalty for our sins. He died in our place.

Jesus is also the *resurrected* Son of God. He rose bodily, victoriously, and eternally from the grave (Rev. 1:18). He is even the *returning* Son of God. He will come back to this earth one day as King of kings and Lord of lords (Phil. 2:9–11; Rev. 19:11–16). Finally, Jesus is the *saving* Son of God (John 3:16). He came to the earth in order to seek and to save that which was spiritually lost (Luke 19:10).

If your pastor, church, or denomination does not adhere to these straightforward, biblical beliefs concerning Jesus Christ, you need to find another church. If what they believe about Jesus is incorrect, nothing else they believe really matters.

2. WHAT IS THE BIBLE?

The Christian's authority under Christ is the written Word of God, the Bible. The Bible itself claims to be the Word of God. It restores and replenishes a person's soul with spiritual strength because, as the psalmist said, it is "perfect" (Ps. 19:7). God "inspired" every verse of Scripture in both the Old and New Testaments (2 Tim. 3:16). That term is more appropriately translated "God-breathed" (see the NIV). Since God "breathed" Scripture into existence, it must be error-free due to the fact that it originates in the heart and mind of a perfect God who is incapable of lying (Titus 1:2).

While God did not dictate the Scriptures to human beings, He did superintend the process in such a way that no human error tainted the absolute purity and perfection of the finished product. Peter affirms this by saying, "But know this first of all, that no prophecy of Scripture is a matter of one's own interpretation, for no prophecy was ever made by an act of human will, but men moved by the Holy Spirit spoke from God" (2 Pet. 1:20–21). The word *moved* in verse 21 means "to bear; to carry." That is, God bore men along and carried them in His arms in such a way that no error entered as He inspired them to record His written Word.

Regardless of what subject the Bible addresses, it is absolutely accurate. For instance, while the Bible is not primarily a history book, whatever it says concerning history is without error. Likewise, the Bible is not chiefly a book of science. Nevertheless, when it speaks regarding scientific matters, it does so with 100 percent accuracy.

If your pastor, church, or denomination cannot say that the Bible is God's inspired, inerrant, infallible Word, you should recognize that they are tainted by theological liberalism.

3. HOW IMPORTANT IS SALVATION?

Anyone who says that everyone is going to heaven, regardless of what he or she believes about Jesus Christ, is a universalist and is theologically liberal. Since salvation is so crucial, it is important to adhere to the following four theological tenets in order not only to be correct but also to know God personally.

You must be born again. Ask your pastor if he believes that one must be "born again" (John 3:3) in order to go to heaven after death. If he responds negatively, sarcastically, or with the slightest hesitation, or if he offers any answer short of an unqualified yes, he is a theological liberal.

Each individual must repent of his sins. He must believe that Jesus died and shed His blood for his sins. He must also believe that Jesus was raised from the dead. That person must then willfully surrender his life to Jesus and receive Him by faith as Savior and Lord.

Someone has well said that God has no spiritual grandchildren, only children. That is, no one will go to heaven simply because his parents were Christians. Each of us must receive Christ personally and be "born of the Spirit" (John 3:1–8) if we want to know God personally and go to heaven when we die.

Salvation is by grace alone. The Bible plainly teaches that no one will ever be saved because of his or her "good works." Rather, we are saved only by the grace of God. It is "by *His* doing [that we] are in Christ Jesus" (1 Cor. 1:30). When someone refuses to submit to the Lord's righteousness, he actually seeks to establish his own (Rom. 10:3). The problem is that our righteousness (i.e., the very best we can do) is like filthy rags of a leper compared to God's (Isa. 64:6). Our best efforts simply aren't good enough to save us. Therefore, God saves us the only way He can—by His grace and mercy.

> ☞ *Instead of submitting to the Scriptures, a liberal attempts to rule over them. Instead of allowing the Bible to judge him, he decides he's going to judge the Bible.* ☜

That is why Paul said, "For by grace you have been saved through faith; and that not of yourselves, it is the gift of God" (Eph. 2:8). He also said, "He saved us, not on the basis of deeds which we have done in righteousness, but according to His mercy, by the washing of regeneration and renewing by the Holy Spirit" (Titus 3:5).

Salvation is through faith alone. We are saved *through faith* (Eph. 2:8) by *believing* on the Lord Jesus Christ (Acts 16:30–31). We must believe that Jesus is God's Son, who died for our sins, and that He rose from the dead. Salvation occurs when a person willfully believes in Christ and receives Him into his or her life (John 1:12). At that moment, the person is instantaneously, supernaturally, and eternally transformed into "a new creature" (2 Cor. 5:17).

Again, good works are not enough to get us into heaven. We must not trust in what we *do* but what Jesus has *done* for us on the cross and at the empty tomb. Only then can we be saved.

Salvation is in Christ alone. Jesus is not merely one way among many ways to God. Nor is Jesus even the best way to God. Jesus is the *only* Savior and the *only* way to God.

Jesus Himself emphatically made this claim when He said to Thomas, "I am the way, and the truth, and the life; no one comes to the Father but through Me" (John 14:6). Likewise, when Peter preached to the Jewish religious leaders of his day, he emphatically declared that "there is salvation in no one else; for there is no other name under heaven that has been given among men by which we must be saved" (Acts 4:12).

Later on when Paul wrote his first letter to Timothy, he included these sobering words: "For there is one God, and one mediator also between God and men, the man Christ Jesus" (1 Tim. 2:5). All religions do not lead to God. No one will spend eternity in heaven unless he is saved through Jesus Christ—no one!

Why All This Matters So Much

Theological liberalism destroys the vitality of any Christian, any local church, or any denomination. In fact, it is fair to say that theological liberalism never grows a church (or anything else, for that matter). Rather, liberalism is parasitic in nature. It lives off other things. It sucks out the life, then goes on to a new host to repeat the process.

I believe that when Satan gets ready to destroy the vitality of a Bible-believing, Christ-honoring, soul-winning body, he begins by planting his insidious seeds of theological liberalism in the colleges and seminaries that help train the preachers of tomorrow. If he can successfully infect the professors, he will be able to change the thought processes of the students. The heresy perpetuated in the classroom will soon be propagated from the pulpits. Such liberalism will soon empty the pews, because when people lose faith in God and the truthfulness of His Word, they no longer sense a need for the Lord or His church. That is when all hope is gone and all hell breaks loose.

I am a Christian by conversion and a Southern Baptist by choice. Like most Christian denominations in America, Southern Baptists had begun to drift into theological liberalism in the mid- to late 1900s. A few of our seminaries had begun to embrace the European higher-critical method of interpreting Scripture. Some of our preachers, though passionate for evangelism, Christ, and the Bible when they started their studies, were weakened in their faith by the time they graduated. They had been told that the Bible contains errors, its history is mythological, and its miracles are not real.

In 1979 my predecessor at Bellevue Baptist Church, Dr. Adrian Rogers, was elected president of the Southern Baptist Convention. When asked to compromise for the sake of peace, he wisely and boldly declared, "We don't have to get together. We don't have to survive. I don't have to be the pastor of Bellevue. I don't have to live! But I'm not going to compromise the Word of God."

His election began a succession of elections of theologically conservative presidents, who used their appointive powers to get conservative trustees onto the various boards of our Southern Baptist agencies and entities, including the six seminaries. Those trustees began to hire conservative seminary presidents and professors, who in turn began to teach aspiring young preachers from a conservative vantage point. As a result, the Southern Baptist world changed its course and turned back to its roots.

That phenomenon is unique. While I certainly know that Southern Baptists are not the only theological conservatives in this nation, I do believe it is fair to say we are the only major denomination in Christian history that pulled itself back from a drift in the liberal direction. We're still not everything we ought to be, but at least we're not where we were headed. I shudder to think what would have happened to the Southern Baptist Convention if the conservative resurgence had not started in 1979.

Here's the Church, Here's the Steeple, Open the Door, but Where Are the People?

During the closing years of Spurgeon's ministry, Baptists in England began to embrace what Spurgeon called "the down-grade" of theological liberalism. He fought tenaciously against it and lost. He eventually had to take himself and his church, London's Metropolitan Tabernacle, out of the Baptist Union. More than likely Spurgeon's intense efforts to combat theological liberalism in his homeland led to his decline in health and his untimely death at the age of fifty-eight.

British Baptist churches that once emphasized Bible preaching and soul winning went on to trade in their conservative beliefs for the newer, more liberal social gospel that almost exclusively stressed the meeting of physical needs as opposed to spiritual needs. Soon universalism, the belief that all people will go to heaven, became the theological norm. The tragic result was that the people lost hope and stopped seeing the need to attend worship services in their churches.

Several years ago the Gardendale church I was serving surprised my wife and me on my fifth anniversary as their pastor by giving us an all-expenses-paid trip to England. We got to see many of the famous Spurgeon sites. We also decided to take a high-speed train to Paris and back, passing through the famous thirty-one-mile Chunnel, the second-longest rail tunnel in the world. Once we came out the other end and began racing across the beautiful French countryside at 183 miles per hour, we passed village after village, each of which seemed to contain an ornate Catholic cathedral.

> *It is fair to say that theological liberalism never grows a church (or anything else, for that matter). Rather, liberalism is parasitic in nature. It lives off other things.*

My brother, who has visited France on numerous occasions, informed me later that they are by and large hollow shells with only a few elderly people attending. Meanwhile, the Protestant churches in most towns are gone altogether, victims of liberal theology and secularism. What happened? The poison of theological liberalism infected their seminaries, then their pulpits, and ultimately, the people in the pews. Sadly, the same sort of thing is happening in many denominations in our own country today.

Theological liberalism is a curse. It takes away from the Word of God. I have often thought that if a liberal in our day had found the woman caught in adultery (see John 8:1–11), he would have felt comfortable saying, "Neither do I condemn you," but I doubt he would have finished Jesus' sentence with the convicting words, "Go and sin no more." He would have tried to lift up the fallen without also lifting up the standard of God's Word.

Again I say, if atheism and humanism have slain their thousands, theological liberalism has slain its tens of thousands. Christians who yearn for the presence of the living God must be on guard against this subtle, sinister enemy.

CHAPTER 18

Legalism

On the other hand, we also need to look at the opposite of theological liberalism, which is legalism. This is just as great a hindrance to revival. If liberalism subtracts from the Word of God, legalism is guilty of adding to it. While liberalism is a ditch on the left that fails to believe what God said in His written Word, legalism is a ditch on the right that goes beyond the commandments of God to tack on human inventions.

The problem here is that we human beings are not as wise as God, and when we start adding our own rules, we bog ourselves down in institutional paralysis. We no longer focus vertically on God and His wonderful character; instead, we get consumed with debating what is allowed and what is out of bounds. We've moved from *relationship* to *regulation*. We're so obsessed with controlling behavior that we lose our momentum. Heavy black lines are drawn and enforced, consuming all the available energy.

Legalism never brings vitality. In fact, "the letter kills, but the Spirit gives life" (2 Cor. 3:6). While liberalism breeds heresy, legalism breeds hardness.

What actually matters is whether things are the Bible way. The Bible is our authority, not the pronouncements of any group. Where the Bible lays down a rule or a practice, we need to follow it faithfully. We dare not cut corners. Sometimes Christians who feel like obeying only about 70 percent of the Bible will look at those trying to obey 100 percent of it and call them "legalists."

No, a legalist is what might be described as a "120 percenter." This kind of person wants to push not only what the Bible says but also what he has chosen to add on the side. If we lack biblical underpinning for our declarations, we have no right to pretend otherwise.

Legalism in Jesus' Day

The classic legalists mentioned in the New Testament were, of course, the Pharisees. They were in many respects the most influential Jewish religious party in Jesus' day. Unlike the Sadducees, whom we considered in the previous chapter on liberalism, the Pharisees believed God had inspired not only the first five books of the Old Testament (the Torah, or Pentateuch) but also the Prophets (the prophetic books) and the Writings (the wisdom literature including Psalms and Proverbs).

> *If liberalism subtracts from the Word of God, legalism is guilty of adding to it. While liberalism is a ditch on the left, legalism is a ditch on the right.*

As a result, the Pharisees enthusiastically believed in life after death, which the Sadducees denied. The Pharisees affirmed that at the end of time, a resurrection would occur, and the righteous would be eternally rewarded while the unrighteous would be eternally punished. They also believed in angelic beings and the spiritual nature of mankind.

While the Pharisees numbered only approximately six thousand in Jesus' day, they held tremendous respect and influence among the masses. Unlike the aristocratic Sadducees, the Pharisees appealed to the common people. They were viewed as the workingman's religious party. Their name, *Pharisee*, meant "separation." Their roots traced back to the days of Ezra and Nehemiah in the fifth century BC, when a strong movement among the Jews in Jerusalem pushed to separate from the Gentiles who had infiltrated the Holy Land during the exile a century earlier. Those early Jewish separatists were the ideological, philosophical, and theological ancestors of the Pharisees, who came into existence as an official group sometime during the second century BC.

Unlike the more radical Essenes, who withdrew from Jewish religious life to live in the Judean wilderness, the Pharisees were involved in society. They desired to purify and revamp the religious life of Judaism rather than abandon it altogether.

As you might expect, they didn't think much of their religious rivals, the Sadducees. The Sadducees were more politically motivated and served as the principal leaders of the official Jewish judiciary body known as the Sanhedrin. But that august group had a number of Pharisees in its ranks as well. This was the body that tried Jesus and pronounced Him worthy of death.

The Pharisees were seemingly sincere and at least outwardly devout. They sought to live according to the teachings of the Jewish Scriptures. In fact, they were so earnest about this that they committed the cardinal error of legalists: they started adding to the Word of God. To make sure they didn't violate a divine commandment, they made up extra rules around the edges so they wouldn't get even close to an infraction. God had said, for example, to keep the Sabbath as a holy day to the Lord. The Pharisees decided that meant no one should light a cooking fire or walk more than a certain distance on the day. These became the tradition of the elders (Mark 7:3), which were equally authoritative regarding all matters of faith and practice. In their eyes their rules were just as inspired and binding as God's written Word.

Legalism in Our Time

We look at all their regulations from a distance of two thousand years and think, *How silly. They were so busy trying to police the people that they missed the main point of God's truth.* But maybe it would do us good to pause and ask whether we, too, have built up extrabiblical "traditions of the elders" in our day. What do we do that has gotten cast in stone over the decades without a biblical justification?

I made the mistake in one church of moving the offering from the middle of the Sunday morning service to the end. I thought it made good sense at the time. Some people got downright upset about that!

A bigger example comes from those who say the only truly inspired translation of the Bible is the 1611 King James Version (KJV). Now before those of you who cherish the KJV get mad and set this book aside for good, please listen to my heart. In no way would I ever denigrate this wonderful translation. In fact, I have read it from cover to cover on several occasions, and I have also memorized many verses from it. Some passages such as Psalm 23 and John 3:16, if quoted from any version other than the KJV, sound a little awkward to me.

But that is due to my personal heritage, not because the KJV is the only inspired version of Scripture. The simple fact is, I learned those key verses as a child from the version our pastor used, the King James.

While the KJV is a wonderful, time-honored translation of the Bible, it is definitely not the only inspired Bible in existence today. To insist otherwise is a clear indication of legalism.

Have you ever thought about the fact that God did not give us any of His written Word in English? I personally wish He had; it would have made this discussion a lot simpler for Americans and other English-speaking people around the world. But the plain fact of the matter is that He gave us His Word in Hebrew, Aramaic, and Greek. That means the rest of us, who speak English, Spanish, German, Swahili, Japanese, and all the other languages, have to utilize translations of His original Word.

Some proponents of the KJV attempt to say that the manuscripts from which other versions of the Bible are translated are inferior to those that drove the KJV. The fact of the matter, however, is that since 1611, many older manuscripts of both the Old and New Testaments have been discovered, some portions now going back much closer to the apostolic era. (We have no *original* manuscripts of the Bible in any library or museum today—not a single papyrus upon which David or Isaiah or Matthew or Paul wrote. Again, I wish we did. But the best we have are handwritten copies of those original documents. In reality, they are copies of copies of the originals.)

We must be careful not to view the whole world through the lens of the English language. Our brothers and sisters in Latin America as well as much of Africa and Asia will never master the subtleties of seventeenth-century Elizabethan English—nor should they have to. God is no doubt entirely wiling to communicate His truth to them through quality translations in their mother tongues.

Furthermore, KJV-only adherents must recognize that over the past four centuries, linguistic scholars have learned much about the original texts of Scripture. Archaeologists have shed new light on passages that used to be obscure; computer technology has made analysis and comparison much faster and more accurate. We are closer today than ever to the original intent of the biblical writers. While the KJV is a wonderful translation, it is simply not the only version through which the Holy Spirit speaks today.[52]

Jesus' Response to Legalism

While Jesus affirmed the inspiration and authority of Scripture (see Matt. 5:17–19), He did not believe that human rules were equal in authority to the Scriptures themselves. He emphasized this when he said, "Unless your righteousness surpasses that of the scribes and Pharisees, you will not enter the kingdom of heaven" (Matt. 5:20). Although the Pharisees gave strict attention to obeying the Law and their revered commandments with minute detail, Jesus indicated that they were not on their way to heaven.

The classic confrontation between Jesus and the Pharisees is found in Mark's gospel. One day when Jesus and His disciples were together, a representative group of Pharisees from Jerusalem confronted them. They had noticed that His disciples had begun to eat a meal without first ceremonially washing their hands. The legalistic Pharisees would have never made such a "mistake." As Mark explains:

> *Legalism keeps people at a distance from the One who waits to feed their souls.*

For the Pharisees and all the Jews do not eat unless they carefully wash their hands, thus observing the traditions of the elders; and when they come from the market place, they do not eat unless they cleanse themselves; and there are many other things which they have received in order to observe, such as the washing of cups and pitchers and copper pots. (Mark 7:3–4)

Indeed, the Pharisees were concerned about observing the religious minutiae that had been painstakingly prescribed by their legalistic ancestors.

Now the Pharisees immediately questioned Jesus, "Why do Your disciples not walk according to the tradition of the elders, but eat their bread with impure hands?" (v. 5).

Jesus rebuked them quickly and concisely: "He said to them, 'Rightly did Isaiah prophesy of you hypocrites, as it is written: "This people honors Me with their lips, but their heart is far away from Me. But in vain do they worship Me, teaching as doctrines the precepts of men." Neglecting the commandment of God, you hold to the tradition of men'" (vv. 6–9).

Jesus' indictment was sharp and simple: God's Word is more important and authoritative than human interpretations of Scripture. Jesus affirmed the Word of God, but He refused to submit to legalistic man-made rules.

In fact, He wasn't finished. Jesus went on to humiliate the Pharisees by showing them just how unbiblical they had become. He continued:

> You are experts at setting aside the commandment of God in order to keep your tradition. For Moses said, "Honor your father and your mother"; and, "He who speaks evil of father or mother, is to be put to death"; but you say, "If a man says to his father or his mother, whatever I have that would help you is Corban (that is to say, given to God)," you no longer permit him to do anything for his father or his mother; thus invalidating the word of God by your tradition which you have handed down; and you do many things such as that.
> (vv. 9–13)

The Pharisees had actually used their legalistic requirements to excuse people from supporting their aging parents when they needed financial assistance. The Pharisees worded their excuse in such a way that their disobedience sounded (at least in their own ears) righteous and pleasing to God. Jesus said to them, "Guys, you don't have a clue. You're totally missing the will of God because you're more interested in what people say than what God says."

Paul's Response to Legalism

Such theological legalism was opposed by Jesus' followers as well. The apostle Paul was called to be an apostle to the Gentiles (Acts 9:15; Rom. 11:13; 1 Tim. 2:7). While he believed that the gospel of Jesus Christ should be preached "to the Jew first," he firmly believed that God wanted to save the Gentiles as well (Rom. 1:16).

Not every Christian of his day agreed with him.

As Paul traveled on his missionary journeys, he led multitudes of Gentiles to faith in Jesus Christ. But many of the Jews who had become Christians in and around Jerusalem believed that once a Gentile was converted to Jesus, he needed to convert to Judaism as well. These Judaizers basically said, "You can be saved through Jesus, but you also need to be circumcised and follow all the teachings of Moses" (see Acts 15:1). Paul disagreed vehemently.

The debate became so heated that Paul and Barnabas (Paul's missionary partner) went to Jerusalem to meet with the apostles and the pastors (elders) to discuss the issue. When they arrived, they reported all that the Lord had done through them to win multitudes of Gentiles to faith in Christ.

While they were speaking, "Some of the sect of the Pharisees who had believed stood up, saying, 'It is necessary to circumcise them and to direct them to observe the Law of Moses'" (Acts 15:5). Note: the Pharisees were at the heart of this legalism. Although these had been saved by God's grace in Christ, they were still hanging on to their legalistic ways. They wanted to add to the gospel by forcing the Gentile converts to be circumcised, which was a symbol of the Old Testament covenant with God. They also wanted them to adhere to the teachings of Moses (the Torah). It is also more than probable that they desired to have these Gentiles embrace the rules of the Jewish elders as well.

At that important meeting of the greatest minds in Christianity in that day, the apostle Peter weighed in with a compelling argument. He reminded the entire group of how the Lord had taken the gospel to the Gentiles by sending him to Caesarea to witness to a Roman centurion named Cornelius and his family (see Acts 10). Peter said, "Brethren, you know that in the early days God made a choice among you, that by my mouth the Gentiles would hear the word of the gospel and believe. And God, who knows the heart, testified to them giving them the Holy Spirit, just as He also did to us; and He made no distinction between us and them, cleansing their hearts by faith" (Acts 15:7–9). Indeed, Cornelius' entire family was saved, and each of them was baptized.

Peter then asked a probing question: "Now therefore why do you put God to the test by placing upon the neck of the disciples a yoke which neither our fathers nor we have been able to bear?" (v. 10). Peter was saying, "We couldn't obey all of the laws in the Old Testament ourselves, much less the additions of the elders! If we couldn't do it, why should we put that same albatross around the Gentiles' necks?"

That historic meeting ended with a devastating blow to the legalism of the Judaizers. It was agreed not to force the Gentile Christians to be circumcised or to become adherents of Judaism. James, the senior pastor of the church at Jerusalem, after hearing all sides of the debate, suggested a solution. "It is my judgment that we do not trouble those who are turning to God from among the Gentiles, but that we write to them that they abstain from things contaminated by idols and from fornication and from what is strangled and from blood" (vv. 19–20). He further reasoned that any Gentile who wanted to learn more about Judaism could easily do so. He said, "Moses from ancient generations has in every city those who preach him, since he is read in the synagogues every Sabbath" (v. 21).

> ⌖ *If someone's baptism is good enough for God, shouldn't it be good enough for us?* ⌖

Open or Closed?

This kind of clearheaded reasoning set a whole new course for the spread of the gospel in the first century. We dare not lose our grip on this principle today. Are we going to continue to be an open church that welcomes all to the feet of Jesus, or are we going to saddle them with additional requirements not based in the Word of God?

I remember one day when my wife and I decided to try out a new Mexican restaurant. I absolutely love Mexican food, by the way. The sign on the door said "Abierto," which in Spanish means "Open." I eagerly marched up to the door, my taste buds already warming up for some great fajitas.

The only trouble was, the door was locked! I was a ready and willing customer—but in the end I had to retreat to my car and go somewhere else. Needless to say, I was not a happy camper.

Some of our churches today pose as if they are "open" to serve hungry humanity with the Bread of Life, but in fact they've got a whole extra set of requirements that complicate the process. Trying to get a good meal of spiritual nutrition in these places turns out to be a frustration. Legalism keeps people at a distance from the One who waits to feed their souls.

Both the Old and New Testaments clearly condemn adding to Scripture. The writer of Proverbs says, "Every word of God is tested; He is a shield to those who take refuge in Him. Do not add to His words or He will reprove you, and you will be proved a liar" (Prov. 30:5–6). The apostle John concurred by saying, "I testify to everyone who hears the words of the prophecy of this book: if anyone adds to them, God will add to him the plagues which are written in this book" (Rev. 22:18). While this verse applies specifically to the book of Revelation, it is also appropriate (especially in light of Proverbs 30:5–6) to view this warning in reference to the entire Bible.

"Be Baptized in Our Water!"

Where can you find legalism today? You don't have to look far. There are still many Christians who, either knowingly or unknowingly, seek to add to the teachings of the Word of God. Let me cite just one further example:

More than a few denominations say, in effect, "Getting saved and baptized in water is not enough; you need to be baptized in *our* tank." In saying this they are adding to Scripture as the Pharisees did.

Now I fully admit that biblical baptism has some definition to it. The Bible teaches that it is an intentional act by a *believer* in Jesus Christ to be *immersed* in water *in the name of the Father, Son, and Holy Spirit* as a *symbol* of his or her salvation. Each of the italicized words in the previous sentence is important, because the Bible says so. I could go into a lengthy exposition on each of them, quoting chapter and verse.

But I can't find any Scripture that sets rules for the *location* of water baptism. It is pure legalism when a church or denomination says, "Even though you have been baptized scripturally in another denomination, you must be baptized again if you desire to join our church."

Again, I must emphasize the word *scripturally*. People who have experienced only sprinkling as an infant, or others who have been baptized in an environment that made it intrinsic to salvation (rather than a symbol of salvation already complete) have not been baptized scripturally. They should be baptized with a correct understanding.

But if a believer has been baptized by immersion in the name of the triune God as a symbol of their salvation, there is no basis to force a rebaptism in order to enter a certain denomination or church. Such a requirement makes a mockery of that person's New Testament baptism.

A rule regarding the location of baptism is not only unfortunate, but it is also a classic case of legalism. If someone's baptism is performed according to Scripture, then it is valid in God's sight. If someone's baptism is good enough for God, shouldn't it be good enough for us? Show me a chapter and verse that says someone must believe *exactly* as we do on every issue concerning salvation before we can agree that their baptism is valid.

When you stop to think about it, new believers in the time of the New Testament weren't baptized in anyone's tank, since churches didn't own any buildings! Those who repented of their sins and accepted Christ were baptized under God's clear blue sky in rivers and lakes or perhaps in a private home. We dare not set up more restrictions than the New Testament employed.

A Poor Substitute for Walking in the Spirit

I could go on with other examples of current legalism, from hair length requirements (both male and female) to the wearing of jewelry and makeup, to clothing regulations. Granted, we have a biblical injunction to avoid all immorality, but some of the rules seem to go far beyond that concern.

Both Peter and Paul emphasized that men and women are designed by God to be delightfully different. Neither is inferior to the other, but they are not identical. In order to avoid every form and appearance of evil (see 1 Thess. 5:22), Christians both male and female should dress modestly and discreetly in such a manner that they do not draw undue attention to themselves. All of this is to be guided by the leadership of the indwelling Holy Spirit rather than man-made rules that are legalistic additions to the Word of God.

These are sometimes simply a human way to avoid walking in and being led by the Spirit of God. Legalism puts great emphasis on the outward appearance of ritualistic religion. That's why the Pharisees cared more about their ceremonial customs than having a broken and contrite spirit before God. Indeed, human beings have a tendency to look at the externals while the Lord always looks first at the heart (see 1 Sam. 16:7).

God wants to have a relationship with us that involves moment-by-moment prompting by the Holy Spirit. When Scripture is specific about a matter, it is easy for a Christian to know what to do. But when the Scriptures are not as specific as we desire, it is sometimes hard to discern what the Spirit would have us do. Should I listen to this song or not? Should our family watch that movie or not? In all such decisions we have to go to the effort of hearing God's direction.

Legalism suppresses revival because it focuses on obeying a set of human rules instead of pursuing a dynamic, daily relationship with a living God who relates to us as a heavenly Father.

What would a legalist have said to the woman caught in adultery (John 8)? He would have relished the part of Jesus' statement that said, "Go and sin no more!" But he would likely have skipped over the loving words that preceded it: "Neither do I condemn you." The legalist, like the liberal, would have conveyed only his favorite half of the message Jesus delivered, conveniently omitting the other side.

> *Legalism suppresses revival because it focuses on obeying a set of human rules instead of pursuing a dynamic, daily relationship with a living God.*

Legalism condemns a person; love converts him. The legalist binds you instead of setting you free. Yes, there are valid biblical rules that Christians should obey. But if they are not obeyed out of a heart of love, the relationship won't be healthy. When we focus on the relationship, the rules will largely take care of themselves. You can do all the rules and still be cold toward Jesus. The warmth of His presence will stay at a distance.

May God deliver us from both of these dangerous hindrances to revival.

CHAPTER 19

Traditionalism

Closely related to the problem of legalism is *traditionalism*; in fact, they are first cousins. Both serve to trap the people of God in rigid molds. The main difference is this:

Legalism claims a biblical basis for its rules, when in fact there isn't any.

Traditionalism insists on something because "we've always done it this way." The corollary of this statement is, "We've never done it that way, and we're not about to start now."

I heard about one fellow who had just gotten saved and walked into a fairly uptight church the next Sunday, excited about Jesus. The choir sang a good song, and when they finished, the young man exclaimed, "All right!" (He hadn't yet learned the religious term "Amen!") People all around glared at him.

The preacher began his sermon and, when he made his first solid point, the guy piped up again. "Yeah!" he said. Again, cold stares came his way.

Soon the preacher made another good statement, and this time the young man cut loose with "Right on!"

That was enough to make an usher walk over and tap him on the shoulder. "Young man, you're going to have to tone it down," he admonished with a stern face.

"What are you talking about?" the fellow answered. "I'm a new Christian, and I've got the joy of the Lord!"

"Well," said the usher, "you sure didn't get it here. So be quiet!"

Almost Everything Changes

Here is a sweeping statement that may sound excessive. But I believe I can make it stick. *Except for God and His Word, the only thing that never changes is the fact that everything always changes!* Even on Sunday mornings, it's true.

Think about the startling changes that hit you the day you entered this world. You started out the day enjoying a safe, warm, dark environment with a simple daily routine that had been familiar for nine months. Then you found yourself in the hands of a strange person wearing a mask who promptly smacked you on the bottom! People started shouting, laughing, crying, and standing in line to hold you. The air was cold, the lights were bright, your vision was blurred, your face was swollen, and you were totally at the mercy of others. Your daily routine had been altered forever. They should have put up a sign that read, "Welcome to Earth— the place where everything *always* changes!"

You and I have lived through hundreds of changes since that day, most of which were not enjoyable or comfortable, at least at first. When it comes to the routines of our churches and the way we worship and serve the Lord, each generation does church in specific ways until it becomes comfortable with them. We find ourselves happy and content, getting to the point that we really don't want to stop doing it the way we've always done it. We even become defensive of our church traditions. We repeat seemingly wise phrases such as, "If it ain't broke, don't fix it." Meanwhile, we conveniently forget about the other saying that defines a rut: it's basically "a grave with the ends kicked out."

The Way We Were

When we stop a minute and look back twenty or thirty or forty years, however, we have to admit that at least some traditions needed to be changed. I don't know what kind of church environment you grew up in, but just for fun, let me recount what it was like for me as a kid in a small West Tennessee church that was typical of most conservative and traditional churches in that day. Actually, it wasn't all that different from the way my aunt's church operated in Chicago and the way my cousin's church functioned in Alabama. Don't get me wrong—there wasn't anything innately wrong with the way we did things. But folks pretty much agreed with the Duke of Cambridge, who in the late 1800s once said to those critical of his military administration, "Any change, at any time, for any reason is to be deplored." (He eventually got fired, by the way, after thirty-nine years as commander in chief of the British army.)

The Way We Worshipped

First and foremost, there was a detailed "order of service." It was the unchangeable road map on any given Sunday. From the prelude to the postlude, it told you exactly what was going to take place. There was to be no such thing as a deviation from the "order of service," and that's an order!

The morning service always began with the Sunday school superintendent making his way to the pulpit to announce how many people had been in Bible study classes that morning. After his report, the piano and organ (our only musical instruments) began to play jubilantly as the adult choir entered the *sanctuary* (no one called it a "worship center" in those days). Everyone in the congregation sat quietly as the pastor and minister of music ascended the platform. When the pastor sat down, the choir then sang an opening anthem we labeled "the call to worship." The pastor then prayed, we sang three hymns (usually omitting the third verse of each to save time), and then followed up with the doxology.

After that the ushers (including my dad) came forward to pass the offering plates while the organist played. Next the choir sang its "special music." Then the pastor preached his sermon. When he concluded, he invited people to come to the front of the sanctuary to receive Christ as their personal Savior and Lord and/or to join our church. After this invitation was over, the choir sang a final song. One of those concluding songs was an Irish blessing that started off with "May the road rise up to meet you, may the wind be always at your back."

Each of those Sunday services began promptly at 10:50 a.m. and concluded punctually at 12:00 noon. The pattern was fixed, and nothing changed.

The Way We Learned

Sunday school had its own set of traditions in those days. Boys and girls were in separate classes. Even adults were split up: most men attended classes with other men while women were with other women. Few churches offered coed classes at any age level.

Classes were age graded all the way up the line. If you were an adult, you found your proper place in the class for those twenty to twenty-nine years old, or thirty to thirty-nine, etc. We had an annual "Promotion Sunday," on which everyone advanced to their new classes for the new Sunday school year. I remember distinctly some of our older members not wanting to "promote" to our oldest class, which was listed simply as seventy-five plus. I can't say that I blame them. I'm sure they realized that the only way they were going to "promote" out of that class was to die!

Once inside the classroom door, all proceedings were governed by the appropriate Sunday school quarterly, purchased from the denominational publishing house. It contained three months of lessons, and each person was expected to keep up with it and read every word of it to prepare for class on Sunday.

The Way We Dressed

With all of this protocol firmly in place, it should not be surprising that there was also an unwritten, yet firmly established dress code for churchgoers in those days. Men and boys were expected to wear dark suits, white shirts, and neckties (boys could wear the clip-on kind, thank goodness). Dark leather shoes, which had been polished that morning, were also a standard. Meanwhile, women and girls wore *dresses*. Women and girls did not wear pants to church. On special occasions, some of the women wore hats, a custom I remember loving as a child. I made a point to try to sit behind a woman with a big hat so the preacher couldn't see if I was doing something besides listening to him!

Why did we dress that way? Again, the standard answer went something like this: "God deserves your best. Your best is not casual attire. Casual attire in church is a display of disrespect for the Lord. Put on your 'Sunday best' when you come to the house of God." Most everyone went along with that logic. It was just the way we had always done it.

The Way We Gave

Our church had a multipurpose offering envelope (again, prepared by the denominational publishing house) waiting in every pew. It was of course a weekly reminder to give financially to the church's budget. The second function of that little envelope was to keep track of a list of weekly religious "ought-to-dos" that were printed on the outside. Each member was expected to mark little boxes such as "Giving," "Read your Bible each day," "Attended Sunday school," and "Attended Sunday worship."

I filled out hundreds of those envelopes when I was growing up. I never remember a single occasion when I could check *every* box! I would have considered anyone who did to be a super-Christian, at least for that week.

When Change Came

Such were the widespread traditions of the American religious world during my childhood. They successfully programmed me on how a local church ought to operate. Things were simple and uncomplicated. I knew what to expect. Worshipping God was entirely predictable. Nothing was going to change.

Then the Jesus Movement came along in the late 1960s and early 1970s. Suddenly all kinds of traditions began to shake, first in the areas of youth ministry and music, then gradually spreading out to other parts of church life as well. By the time I was in high school, I went to a combined Sunday school class that put boys and girls together (much to my delight). The adults likewise had mixed classes. Many of the teachers started using study helps and materials not written or printed at the denominational press. Few adult classes paid much attention to Promotion Sunday any longer. Instead, they felt free to attend any class they wished. The "75+" sign was thrown away.

> *Except for God and His Word, the only thing that never changes is the fact that everything always changes!*

To be sure, some folks didn't like all the changes that took place. Some believed that churches were compromising with the world and becoming corrupt. Indeed, some churches did go too far and watered down the demands of the gospel. But most churches were simply shedding the traditionalism that had bound them for decades and had rendered them incapable of reaching their culture for Christ.

As Christians, we must come to grips with a vital lesson at this point: *We are called to take a never-changing gospel to an ever-changing culture.* While the content of the gospel message does not change from one generation to the next, the leaders of every local church must learn to think like missionaries and seek to be culturally relevant to the people they are trying to reach for Christ.

The updates of the sixties and seventies were not the last ones needed by any means. Here in the early twenty-first century, we can sit back and smile at the traditions of that long-ago time without realizing that we, too, stand in need of change. Society is always changing. To fulfill our calling as we share the gospel and practice our faith, we must not allow traditions of the past to limit our effectiveness. If we are obsessed with defending the methods of our past, we will miss the fresh opportunities of the present.

Suggestions for Healthy Change in Today's Church

Here are some ways any church can make healthy changes in order to share the gospel more effectively with each generation. If your church has already made these adjustments, you will no doubt respond, "Well, obviously! We did that ten years ago." Bear with me, however, for the sake of others who are still in process.

And consider what new departures from *your* tradition might still be warranted. The goal for us all is to be as receptive as possible to God's leading in the current environment.

Don't Embarrass Your Guests

When people visit your church, most don't want to be singled out. They don't want to raise their hands or wear some special lapel pin that shows everyone they are an outsider. Yet, for the purposes of follow-up, churches need to know who is a guest in their worship services. Is there a way to find them and welcome them without embarrassing them? Yes.

Invite visitors to fill out an information form that is attached to the bulletin and turn it in at a hospitality table in the foyer at the end of the service. In exchange they will be given a gift bag that contains a CD of the church's choir and orchestra. (Trust me, guests will like the music better than a CD of the pastor's sermon!) Our gift bag at Bellevue also contains a pen with our church's name on it, a coffee mug, a nice brochure about the church, a discount card for the church bookstore, a copy of our doctrinal statement, and a GooGoo cluster (the greatest chocolate candy ever!). Gift bags are a big hit with guests. The number of visitors who willingly identify themselves in this way can easily double with this one simple alteration.

SIMPLIFY THE LORD'S SUPPER

Have you ever been to a worship service where the passing of the bread and juice seemed to take forever? Or maybe those who were distributing the Lord's Supper filed up and down the aisles in perfect synchronization like a disciplined unit of soldiers. I have to believe that when Jesus instituted this ordinance with His disciples on the night before He was crucified, things were more simple and informal.

Too many churches equate formality with reverence, especially when it comes to the Lord's Supper. The fact is, Christians can be reverent without being stiff and regimented. In order to expedite the distribution of the elements, choose a serving tray that accommodates both elements. There are several on the market. That way, the serving time can be cut in half. And tell the servers to relax as they accomplish their task efficiently.

I'd also encourage you to offer the Lord's Supper on Sunday mornings, not just Sunday nights—even though it entails more work. Many senior adults don't drive at night and can't attend the evening worship services. The Lord's Supper is important to *all* believers.

BLEND THE MUSIC

I made this recommendation in chapter 11, but this area is so important that I want to reemphasize it here. In each service let the praise music be a blend of both the great hymns of the faith and the newer choruses. This allows each worshipper to enjoy at least some of the music he or she prefers. Young people need to learn the hymns, and older folks need to learn the newer songs. All of the music should be in line with Scripture.

Remember that hymns don't always have to be sung to their traditional tunes. Spice them up sometimes with accompaniments that are more similar to the music people listen to today.

UNSHACKLE THE HANDS

If you've done any church visiting in recent years, you know that more and more worshippers are expressing themselves to the Lord by lifting their hands or by clapping. This has not been part of my Baptist tradition. The unwritten rule has been to keep your hands in your lap!

But where does the Bible say that? In fact, it says the opposite at times. Psalm 47 starts out, "O clap your hands, all peoples." Everyone is invited to share in this expression of joy and praise.

The more I observe the younger generation in my church, the more I notice that clapping is their equivalent to saying "Amen." It is their way of affirming what has just happened. I can't really see what's wrong with that.

Isn't it odd that we encourage kids to clap in time with the music during children's church or a children's choir—but then discourage the practice as soon as they reach "big church"? What a conflicting message.

Similarly, I find at least eleven Scripture references about lifting hands to the Lord (2 Chron. 6:12–13; Neh. 8:6; Ps. 28:2; 63:4; 119:48; 134:2; 141:2; 143:6; Lam. 2:19; 3:41; 1 Tim. 2:8). This last reference is a clear instruction from the apostle Paul: "I want the men in every place to pray, lifting up holy hands, without wrath and dissension."

I preached an entire sermon once on what lifting hands to the Lord really means. I pointed out that it's the universal symbol for "I surrender," which is a not a bad posture for us to assume before God.

How does a preschool child communicate "Daddy, hold me"? He lifts up his hands. When we come to the Lord, this is one way to indicate our desire for closeness with Him.

It also signifies an offering of ourselves. People in Old Testament times brought their animal sacrifices to the temple altar, where a priest lifted them up to God. Maybe that's the origin of Hebrews 13:15, which says, "Through Him then, let us continually offer up a sacrifice of praise to God, that is, the fruit of lips that give thanks to His name."

At the end of the message, I didn't force anybody to do anything. I simply said, "Let's stand together. We're going to sing a song to the Lord, and if you have liberty, go ahead and lift your hands to worship Him as you sing." Many people did that day and have felt free to keep doing so afterward. They just needed permission from their leader to do it. They broke out of their tradition that had constrained them up to that point.

Why do people recoil from the idea of lifting hands to the Lord in worship? Some say it brings too much attention to the worshipper. I guess I see it differently. When I raise my hands to the Lord, I'm actually pointing people upward to Him, not drawing attention to myself. For me personally, lifting holy hands to the Lord is a fulfilling, intimate means of worshipping Him. I've never allowed the traditions of others to prevent me from worshipping God that way.

> *Isn't it odd that we encourage kids to clap in time with the music during children's church or a children's choir—but then discourage the practice as soon as they reach "big church"?*

These two practices should not be forbidden in a Christian worship service. They may not be in accordance with your church's tradition, but they are in accordance with the Word of God. The Bible is the authority for every local church in matters of faith and practice. I find it interesting that many of the same people who oppose clapping and lifting hands in a worship service will do both at a football or basketball game. Isn't it an indictment against our pride and tradition when we express ourselves more biblically at an athletic event than we do in the presence of the King of kings?

A TIME TO DANCE?

I have seen the Lord use interpretive dance to enrich Easter and Christmas musicals presented by church choirs and orchestras. My own daughters took ballet and interpretive dance classes, which equipped them to contribute to those settings at church. For such dancing to bring glory to the Lord, the participants obviously need to dress modestly, and their movements must in no way be provocative.

In the Old Testament, it is obvious that God's people worshipped Him through some form of dance. See such Scriptures as Exodus 15:20

(Miriam and her troupe); 2 Samuel 6 (David's rejoicing before the ark); Psalm 30:11; 149:3; 150:4 ("Praise Him with the timbrel and dancing"); and Ecclesiastes 3:4 ("a time to mourn and a time to dance").

If practiced in an appropriate setting and in an appropriate manner, God can use this art form to give visual aid to a song about the gospel of Jesus Christ.

Traditionalists Couldn't Win a Super Bowl

Imagine a group of old-time traditionalists trying to coach a modern NFL team. The offensive line coach would insist that linemen weighing 220 pounds were big enough. After all, that's what they weighed in the 1960s, so that's good enough for today, right?

Likewise, the kicking coach would refuse to use a soccer-style technique for kickoffs and extra points. Why, everyone knows that when you play football, you're supposed to kick the ball with your toes, not the inside of your foot.

The quarterback coach would have his players concentrate on handing the ball off to the running backs. After all, throwing passes to receivers brings the risk of interceptions; everyone knows that football games are won primarily on the ground (three yards and a cloud of dust).

Would a group of coaches who were this fossilized win even one NFL game, much less the Super Bowl? I don't think so.

Effective churches know how to start a ministry, and they also know how to end one. Ineffective churches take too long to start good ministries, and they delay in doing away with ministries that have lost their value. When I was a child, most Baptist churches had a bus ministry. Teams would go out on Saturday mornings and invite boys and girls to Sunday school. Then on Sunday mornings they would pick them up and take them to church. That worked in the 1970s. But with all the heightened worry about "stranger danger" for children these days, few churches (if any) are still running buses with any success. It was hard for some churches to let go of the bus ministry. Some church traditions die a slow and painful death.

The bigger point is to get in step with what God wants to accomplish today. When we concentrate on Him instead of our traditions, we find life and vitality. God once declared through the prophet Jeremiah,

"My people have committed two evils: They have forsaken Me, the fountain of living waters, to hew for themselves cisterns, broken cisterns that can hold no water" (Jer. 2:13). When we want to do things our traditional way instead of God's way, we are left thirsty, without His living water. When we open up ourselves to the fresh flow of His Spirit, we are refreshed and rejuvenated. We are also made far more effective in doing what He has called us to do.

> *We are called to take a never-changing gospel to an ever-changing culture.*

PART FOUR

Pressing On

CHAPTER 20

Discontented

Two words in the English language are close to each other in meaning, but one is thought to be negative while the other is positive. It's a bad thing to be *complacent*, we say. But it's good to be *content*. The first carries the notion of being sleepy, not paying attention to important issues. The second implies coming to terms with the way things are.

I'm not sure I want to be either one—at least in the spiritual realm.

Late in his life, writing from a musty Roman prison cell, the apostle Paul told the Philippians, "I have learned to be content in whatever circumstances I am. I know how to get along with humble means, and I also know how to live in prosperity; in any and every circumstance I have learned the secret of being filled and going hungry, both of having abundance and suffering need. I can do all things through Him who strengthens me" (Phil. 4:11–13).

Yet in just the chapter before, the apostle—now well into his fifties, if not sixties—aspired passionately to know Christ better. "I press on so that I may lay hold of that for which also I was laid hold of by Christ Jesus. Brethren, I do not regard myself as having laid hold of it yet; but one thing I do: forgetting what lies behind and reaching forward to what lies ahead, I press on toward the goal for the prize of the upward call of God in Christ Jesus" (Phil. 3:12–14).

We may summarize in this way: Paul was *content materially* but *discontent spiritually*. On the physical plane he traveled light. He didn't become attached to the creature comforts of this world. On the spiritual plane, however, it was a whole different story.

In our day I am afraid that too many of us Christians are *content spiritually* and *discontent materially*. Our walk with God rocks along comfortably with just the minimal investment of time and energy. Meanwhile, we feel a need to trade up to a bigger house, a newer car, and when can we start planning that next vacation trip?

This is a dangerous way to live. The *Rocky III* movie has a poignant scene where Mickey Goldmill, the trainer, says to the now success-ful and somewhat lethargic champion, "Three years ago, you were supernatural. You were hard and you were nasty. You had this cast-iron jaw. But then, the worst thing happened to you that could happen to a fighter. You got civilized." He was trying to tell the man that he wasn't hungry anymore. He'd lost that fire in the eye.

> *Discontentment can actually be a spiritual blessing. That's what I feel every time I read the book of Acts.*

This happens all the time to pastors and church members. We start out with a blaze in our hearts. Everything is dynamic and new. It feels like the first love of early marriage. But somewhere along the way we settle into the religious routine. We start going through the motions. We know how to do church, how to get by, how to maintain the facade. We go on autopilot. Everything still looks good to observers, but deep inside, we know we've lost something we used to have.

When I was first saved during college, all I wanted to do every day was read my Bible, pray, listen to Christian music, and tell people about Jesus. The question that haunts me today is whether I still have that pas-sion. Yes, my relationship with God should have matured by now, and it has. I have greater understanding and theological background. But have these taken the place of an inner thirst for the presence of God? If so, I have become *content* in an unhealthy way.

What about our churches? Are we content to have just a few more people in the pews this year than last? If the budget income goes up by, say, 4 percent, does that equal success? The culture around us is growing more carnal and darker every week. Are we content to settle for just a tiny sliver of growth?

Go for the Original

Discontentment can actually be a spiritual blessing. That's what I feel every time I read the book of Acts. I can't get through a chapter without thinking, *Why don't our churches today look like that?* We're busy running from one conference to another seeking to copy the "successful" congregations of our time. Seminars for church leaders are big business these days.

Instead of copying one another, why don't we copy the original? Someone has well said, "It's about time for us to get our noses out of the book of Numbers and into the book of Acts." J. B. Phillips, the Anglican clergyman who paraphrased the New Testament back in the 1950s, wrote a stunning preface when his first edition of Acts came onto the market. He got honest about how his work had impacted him personally.

It is impossible to spend several months in close study of [this] remarkable short book . . . without being profoundly stirred and, to be honest, disturbed. The reader is stirred because he is seeing Christianity, the real thing, in action for the first time in human history. The newborn Church, as vulnerable as any human child, having neither money, influence nor power in the ordinary sense, is setting forth joyfully and courageously to win the pagan world for God through Christ. The young Church, like all young creatures, is appealing in its simplicity and singleheartedness. . . .

Yet we cannot help feeling disturbed as well as moved, for this surely is the Church as it was meant to be. It is vigorous and flexible, for these are the days before it ever became fat and short of breath through prosperity, or muscle-bound by overorganization. These men did not make "acts of faith," they believed; they did not "say their prayers," they really prayed. They did not hold conferences on psychosomatic medicine, they simply healed the sick. But if they were uncomplicated and naïve by modern standards, we have ruefully to admit that they were open on the God-ward side in a way that is almost unknown today.[53]

The church today needs to look more like that church. When God comes to church, He is the answer for all our problems. We don't need another program; we need His presence. We don't need better personalities in the spotlight; we need His presence. We don't need slick marketing; we need His presence. Lights, cameras, and Web sites don't matter nearly as much as the power of God. The Holy Spirit is our primary draw. When He touches people, they're never the same.

Some will say, "Well, Acts was a special case. God gave them special power to get the church up and rolling. He's not doing that anymore." I'm sorry, but that sounds like a cop-out to me. Why would God put us on earth at this point of history and withhold from us the same power He gave the early Christians? Our surrounding culture is as bad as the one they faced. He wants to redeem people in our time as much as He did back then.

No, the shortage is not with God. The shortage is with us. We're not hungry enough, obedient enough, committed enough. Peter called us "aliens and strangers" (1 Pet. 2:11). This world is not our home, a place to try to get comfortable. Instead, we're supposed to be soldiers behind enemy lines.

We have to admit that, too often, what we're doing in the church today is not working. One classic definition of insanity is "doing the same thing again and again while expecting different results." If nice sermons and polished songs could save America, the nation would have been saved a long time ago. We need an outpouring of divine power. We need God a whole lot more than God needs us.

Surprises in Unlikely Places

When God shows up in a church, people will beat down the door to get there, even if it's out in the wilderness somewhere like John the Baptist was. Location won't matter. They will be drawn like a magnet to the glory of God in the house of God.

I can think of at least two examples in my own experience:

Back in 1996, we took our children on an East Coast vacation. We started at Williamsburg, then proceeded north to the monuments of Washington, then on to Philadelphia, New York, Boston, and Plymouth

Rock. During our time in New York City, we saw *Beauty and the Beast* on Broadway, the Empire State Building, Central Park, and other great sights. On Sunday we went to the Brooklyn Tabernacle because we had listened to the music of their Grammy Award-winning choir for years and wanted to hear them live.

We arrived an hour early for the twelve o'clock service, only to find ourselves joining a long line of people out on the sidewalk along Flatbush Avenue waiting to get inside the fifteen-hundred-seat building. I studied the situation and then walked up to the front of the line to talk with an usher.

"Does the big choir sing in this service?" I asked.

"No, the noon service will be the youth choir," he answered. "You're looking for the three-thirty or the seven-thirty instead. But you need to be here early for those too."

I chatted with him a bit longer and found out he was an ex-cocaine addict from New Jersey whose life had been radically rescued through this church. He had now moved across the Hudson River to be nearby so he could usher and also sing in the choir.

> *We're busy running from one conference to another seeking to copy the "successful" congregations of our time. Instead of copying one another, why don't we copy the original?*

With time to kill, our family caught a cab and went over to the World Trade Center to show the kids the view from the observation deck up on top (an experience no longer available now, since September 11, 2001). We got back to the Brooklyn Tabernacle around two-thirty.

Even the choir's warm-up, ahead of the service, was wonderful. They wore no robes; they sang with gusto from their hearts. We looked around our row to see a mixed, eclectic congregation: blacks, whites, Hispanics from the Caribbean, Asians, the rich, the poor. You could tell that all felt welcome here.

The worship began, and we were immediately swept up in an awesome atmosphere of praise. The choir's music was incredible. Even the announcements in this church were a blessing! For example, they announced a special time that week for parents to bring their school-age children for prayer regarding the upcoming school year. "Would you like us to pray over your children for safety as they head back to the classroom? If so, bring them." In such a high-crime area of the city, I could tell this was a definite concern.

Pastor Jim Cymbala preached a good, biblical message and called for response at the end. I went up with many others and, when it was appropriate, introduced myself to an associate. I asked if Jim would pray for me. When he came my way, I could tell by his face that he was exhausted from three services already that day. Yet he prayed earnestly for several minutes that God would bless my ministry. It was a sweet time. If it hadn't been for our young children running out of steam by that hour, Donna and I would probably have stayed for the evening service as well. The presence of God was obviously in that place. They weren't Baptists like us; I may not have agreed with every part of their theology. But God was moving there. We headed back to our hotel feeling loved, accepted, and nurtured.

The building had been congested, the street was noisy, the church had *no* parking provision—not a single space to call their own. Jim Cymbala has been quoted as saying, "Sometimes I think we're the most seeker-*UN*friendly church in America!" Yet the presence of God seemed to override all that.

A few years later, I experienced almost the exact opposite of the Brooklyn Tabernacle. I was invited to preach on what turned out to be a cold, rainy night at Bethlehem Baptist Church, northwest of Huntsville, where the NASA research center is. It's one mile from the Tennessee state line, out in the middle of almost nothing but cotton patches and cornfields. The small cluster of farmhouses there form an unincorporated community called—no joke—Lickskillet, Alabama.

> *Lights, camera, and Web sites don't matter nearly as much as the power of God. When He touches people, they're never the same.*

With a couple of my daughters plus my mother, we drove up to a little country church with a sanctuary that would hold no more than 150 people. I took one look and thought, *What am I doing up here on a cold Sunday night? Why did I accept this invitation, anyway?*

We pulled on our coats and went inside. There I found that the sanctuary had been converted into educational space. The service would be held further back in what used to be their gymnasium.

I came through the door, and there were some four hundred people, beaming with the joy of the Lord! The morning attendance, I found out, had been seven hundred. Now on this chilly evening, they began to worship God. The leader with a guitar reminded me of Ronnie Dunn of the country duo Brooks & Dunn. Nothing here resembled Brooklyn, that was for sure. But as they lifted up songs like "These Are the Days of Elijah" and a number of other praise songs, we were swept into the presence of God. I couldn't believe it.

Pastor Joel Carwile had been an evangelist before becoming pastor of this church. The minute he opened his mouth, you could tell he had a happy, precious spirit. He introduced a woman named "Claire," who had been playing with the praise band, to sing a song. The minute she said her first sentence as an introduction, it rang a bell. *I know that voice!* I told myself. Within seconds I found out it was Claire Lynch, a Grammy-winning bluegrass artist. That of course got my attention.

I stopped the whole service and asked if I could sing a song with her. "Sure—come on up!" she replied. So I picked up an extra guitar, and we sang an old hymn together. Then she did her own song, after which I preached. People made decisions to follow Christ that night; others joined the church. It was an awesome evening, right there in Lickskillet.

I came back a year later, and the church was still going strong. On Easter, more than a thousand people had attended. The church was baptizing more than a hundred people a year out there in the cotton patch. People were driving from towns all around to get to this church because it was on fire for God. It reminded me of Jerry Falwell's line, "I'd rather drive across town and be fed than walk across the street and be fooled."

Once again I saw that the externals don't really matter that much. Location is beside the point. Outward appearance doesn't tell you what's on the inside. Looks, in fact, can be deceiving. The lawn may be immaculately groomed, the building may be worthy of an architectural award, but the presence of God can be totally missing. On the other hand, the address may be hard to find, the carpet may be worn, the steeple may be a little crooked (or missing altogether), but the Spirit of God can be filling every cubic inch.

What Does Jesus See in Us?

When the One whose eyes were like fire wrote to the church at Ephesus (Rev. 2:1–7), He looked right through the externals to the heart of this congregation. They had a great heritage, of course. This had been one of the apostle Paul's strongest churches. But now it was in danger of losing its lampstand (see v. 5). Why? "I know your deeds," said Jesus (v. 2).

Oil is often mentioned in Scripture as a metaphor for the Holy Spirit. A church without oil for its lampstand is nothing but a liability to God. Without fuel to light the way, it might as well be shuttered.

Jesus knows what's really going on in my church and in yours. He walks through every room, every office, down every corridor, across the parking lot. He knows what's said in every class, every committee meeting, every counseling session, every casual conversation. Dare we brag to one another when He is listening?

Is there a spirit of prayer and humility or a spirit of arrogance? Is there consistency, or is there blatant hypocrisy? Is there genuine love, or is there pretense and sham?

What does Jesus see in the senior pastor? In the staff members? Are they comrades or competitors? Do they serve for God's glory or for human affirmation—or even worse, to make a living? Do they work when nobody's watching? Jesus knows.

He also knows every deacon. Does He see humble servants of the body of Christ or those who want to lord it over others? Do they live out their Christianity at home or just on Sundays and Wednesday nights?

He knows the choir and the orchestra. Do they sing for Jesus or to be heard by the congregation? Do they rejoice when someone else gets the solo, or are they jealous?

He knows every teacher in the church. Why do they teach? To glorify God by bringing the unsaved to Christ and discipling the believers or to enjoy having a platform from which to pontificate? Are they under pastoral authority, or do they have an independent spirit that wants to do its own thing?

Jesus knows every church member. He is aware of whether we come to church to be seen by others or to meet with Him. Why do we tithe? For a tax break? If the IRS stops this deduction at some future point (it's entirely possible, you know), will we still tithe? That's how it is already for almost all of our overseas brothers and sisters in Christ. Do we say we love missions but not seek to win anyone to Christ locally? Do we say we "love the brethren" but tear them down behind their backs? Do we surf the Internet for pornography on Saturday night and then come to church Sunday morning saying, "Praise the Lord!"?

Jesus knows all about this. He says to us, as He said to the Ephesians, "I have this against you, that you have left your first love. Therefore remember from where you have fallen, and repent and do the deeds you did at first. . . . He who has an ear, let him hear what the Spirit says to the churches" (vv. 4–5, 7).

Every one of us must decide whether we are going to be *committed* Christians or just *convenient* Christians. The believers in Acts were so committed that they were willing to die for the name of Christ, and many of them did. J. B. Phillips concluded his preface with this final paragraph:

> Of course it is easy to "write off" this little history of the Church's first beginnings as simply an account of an enthusiastic but ill regulated and unorganized adolescence, to be followed by a well disciplined maturity in which embarrassing irregularities no longer appear. But that is surely too easy an explanation altogether. We in the modern Church have unquestionably *lost* something. Whether it is due to the atrophy of the quality which the New Testament calls "faith," whether it is due to a stifling churchiness, whether it is due to our sinful complacency over the scandal of a divided Church, or whatever the cause may be, very little of the modern Church could bear comparison with the spiritual drive, the genuine fellowship, and the . . . unconquerable courage of the Young Church.[54]

No Time to Hesitate

I hope I live long enough to see another genuine invasion of the presence of God in this country's churches and individual Christians.

I yearn for it with all my being. For that to happen, we will have to get off the fence and quit hesitating. We will have to go wholeheartedly in the direction of God's heart.

That reminds me of something that happened one morning back in Alabama when I was driving my kids to school in my truck. I've always enjoyed spending time with them at that hour. We were headed down a narrow, somewhat hilly connector road that led from our neighborhood to the main highway. We were running a bit late this particular day, so I was pressing the speed just a bit.

As I came over the crest of one of those hills, a squirrel decided to try to cross the road. He got halfway out, looked up, and here came my truck barreling right toward him.

> ☞ *I hope I live long enough to see another genuine invasion of the presence of God in this country's churches and individual Christians. I yearn for it with all my being. For that to happen, we will have to get off the fence and quit hesitating.* ☜

The squirrel had what, in my part of the country, is called a "come-apart" right there in the middle of the road. *I'd better get back where I came from! Oooh, that's a long way, isn't it? Maybe I should keep going ahead. No, I'll get smashed!* He started quivering back and forth, jerking one direction, then the opposite, totally panicked.

My daughter Allison, the animal lover of the family, immediately screamed as only a grade-school girl can do. *"Daddy, don't hit the squirrel!"*

I slammed on my brakes, putting the truck into a downhill skid. I'm proud to say that I managed to stay on the road and come to a stop just three feet short of the creature. He was still there! He hadn't moved to one side or the other; he was too petrified. He sat there just looking up at me.

I know a lot of Christians and churches who are like that squirrel. They left a life of sin and lostness to head for the kingdom of God on the other side. About halfway across the dividing line, the devil sent a big Dodge Ram truck right at them. They looked up at this scary obstacle, and they got afraid. They're still sitting there, quivering.

You cannot walk in fear and in faith simultaneously. It will paralyze you. Those who have started for God but not gone fully after Him are left in a perilous situation. This is no place to live as a Christian.

It's time for all such people and churches to get out of the middle of the road. It's time to say with Paul, "I press on." It's time to fall on our knees and welcome the presence and glory of God back into the house of God, that His will may be done on earth as it is in heaven.

Notes

[1] Cartoon by Rob Portlock, *Leadership Journal*, Winter 1981, 31.

[2] Sally Morgenthaler, "Leading vs. Performance," *Worship Leader* (July–August 1997), 16, 49.

[3] Søren Kierkegaard, *Purity of Heart Is to Will One Thing*, English translation (New York: Harper & Row, 1938), 180.

[4] Ibid., 180–81.

[5] Posted on www.mattredman.com. Song lyrics © 1999 Kingsway's Thankyou Music.

[6] C. H. Spurgeon, *The Soul-Winner: How to Lead Sinners to the Saviour* (Grand Rapids, MI: Eerdmans, 1963), 106–7.

[7] C. S. Lewis, *The Problem of Pain* (San Francisco: HarperSanFrancisco, 2001), 5–6.

[8] Recounted in *What's So Amazing about Grace?* by Philip Yancey (Grand Rapids, MI: Zondervan, 1997), 264.

[9] Richard L. Bushman, *The Great Awakening: Documents on the Revival of Religion, 1740–1745* (Chapel Hill, NC: University of North Carolina Press, 1970), 4.

[10] George Whitefield, *George Whitefield's Journals* (London: The Banner of Truth Trust, 1960), 352.

[11] Ralph G. Turnbull, *A History of Preaching*, vol. 3 (Grand Rapids, MI: Baker, 1974), 67.

[12] Peter F. Gunther, ed., *Sermon Classics by Great Preachers* (Chicago: Moody, 1982), 19–20.

[13] Arnold Dallimore, *George Whitefield*, vol. 1 (Edinburgh: The Banner of Truth Trust, 1970), 427.

[14] Mark A. Noll, *A History of Christianity in the United States and Canada* (Grand Rapids, MI: Eerdmans, 1992), 91.

[15] Marvin Olasky, "Victorian Secret," *Policy Review* (Spring 1992), 30.

[16] Benjamin Rice Lacy, *Revivals in the Midst of the Years* (Hopewell, VA: Royal, 1968), 70.

[17] Chauncey A. Goodrich, "Narrative of Revivals of Religion in Yale College," *American Quarterly Register* 10 (February 1838): 295–96.

[18] Noll, *A History of Christianity in the United States and Canada*, 169.

[19] Ibid., 167.

[20] Frances Asbury, quoted by L. C. Rudolph, *Frances Asbury* (Nashville: Abingdon, 1966), 34.

[21] Ibid., 117.

[22] V. Raymond Edman, *They Found the Secret* (Grand Rapids, MI: Zondervan, 1960), 46.

[23] Charles Grandison Finney, *Lectures on Revival of Religion* (New York: Levitt, Lord, and Co., 1835).

[24] Ibid., 166.

[25] Frank Greenville Beardsley, *Religious Progress through Religious Revivals* (New York: American Tract Society, 1943), 40; quoted by Roy J. Fish, *When Heaven Touched Earth* (Azle, TX: Need of the Times Publishers, 1996), 24.

[26] Fish, *When Heaven Touched Earth*, 34.

[27] Ibid.

[28] William W. Sweet, *The Story of Religion in America* (New York: Harper and Brothers, 1930), 379.

[29] Bruce L. Shelley, "Moody," *The New International Dictionary of the Christian Church* (Grand Rapids, MI: Zondervan, 1978), 675.

[30] J. Edwin Orr, *Good News in Bad Times* (Grand Rapids, MI: Zondervan, 1953), 58.

[31] Edward E. Plowman, *The Jesus Movement in America* (New York: Pyramid, 1971), 26.

[32] Richard Ostling, Mayo Hohs, and Margaret Boeth, "The New Rebel Cry: Jesus Is Coming!" *Time* 97 (21 June 1971): 59, 62.

[33] Betty Price and Everett Hullam, "The Jesus Explosion," *Home Missions*, June/July 1971, 22.

[34] Billy Graham, "The Marks of the Jesus Movement," *Christianity Today* 16 (5 November 1971): 4–5.

[35] C. H. Spurgeon, *Lectures to My Students* (Grand Rapids, MI: Zondervan, 1954), 33.

[36] "Arise" by Paul Baloche and Don Moen, © 2003 Integrity's Hosanna Music/ASCAP.

[37] Charles Spurgeon, *Your Available Power* (New Kensington, PA: Whitaker, 1996), 13.

[38] Henry Wadsworth Longfellow, *Outre-Mer: A Pilgrimage Beyond the Sea* (1833–34).

[39] Condensed from Alice Morse Earle, *The Sabbath in Puritan New England* (New York: Scribner, 1909), a public-domain book now posted at http://www.gutenberg.org/dirs/etext05/8sabb10h.htm#15.

[40] Jonathan Edwards, "A Faithful Narrative of the Surprising Work of God in the Conversion of Many Hundred Souls in Northampton" (1737). Available at www.edwards.yale.edu/major-works/faithful-narrative or in *The Works of Jonathan Edwards*, vol. 1 (Peabody, Mass.: Hendrickson, 1998).

[41] Private letter by C. S. Lewis in 1946, eventually published as "Correspondence with an Anglican Who Dislikes Hymns," *The Presbyter*, VI, No. 2 (1948), 15–20.

[42] Cited by Don Miller in "Bible-Based Prayer Seminar," 1994.

[43] Ibid.

[44] Jim Cymbala with Dean Merrill, *Fresh Wind, Fresh Fire* (Grand Rapids, MI: Zondervan, 1997). See pages 98–102 for a dramatic story of how the prayer band's intercession protected the pastor from a point-blank assault by a mentally disturbed gunman who disrupted a Sunday service.

[45] Cited by *The New Encyclopedia of Christian Quotations* (Hampshire, UK: John Hunt Publishing, 2000), 783.

[46] *Return to Tradition: A Directive Anthology*, ed. Francis Beauchesne Thornton (Milwaukee: Bruce Publishing Co., 1948), 103ff.

[47] See the extensive article by G. Richard Fisher, "The Life and Times of Golden Girl and Globe Trotter Ruth Ward Heflin," available at http://www.pfo.org/goldgirl.htm.

[48] Renee DeLoriea, "Ruth Ward Heflin, Revivalist and Prayer Minister, Dies of Cancer at 60," *Charisma*, November 2000, 24.

[49] See www.saintmatthewschurches.com as well as its Internet critics.

[50] Gregg Garrison, "Pilgrims Visit a Visionary in a Shelby County Field," *The Birmingham News*, 2 August 2005, available at www.al.com.

[51] E. Stanley Jones, *Abundant Living* (Nashville: Abingdon, 1942), 4.

[52] I am indebted to my good friend Calvin Wittman for his assistance on this section. He also referred me to an excellent book, *The King James Version Debate: A Plea for Realism* by D. A. Carson (Baker Academic, 1978).

[53] J. B. Phillips, *The Young Church in Action* (New York: Macmillan, 1955), vii. This paraphrase later became part of Phillips's *The New Testament in Modern English*, but the Acts preface was not included in the larger work.

[54] Ibid., xvi.